Vibrate Higher

Talib Kweli

Vibrate Higher

A RAP STORY

MCD 〰 FARRAR, STRAUS AND GIROUX NEW YORK

MCD
Farrar, Straus and Giroux
120 Broadway, New York 10271

Library of Congress Cataloging-in-Publication Data
Names: Kweli, Talib, author.
Title: Vibrate higher : a rap story / Talib Kweli.
Description: First edition. | New York : Farrar, Straus and Giroux, 2021.
Identifiers: LCCN 2018044014 | ISBN 9780374283407 (hardcover)
Subjects: LCSH: Kweli, Talib. | Rap musicians—United States—Biography.
Classification: LCC ML420.K9815 A3 2019 | DDC 782.421649092 [B]—dc23
LC record available at https://lccn.loc.gov/2018044014

Designed by Abby Kagan

Our books may be purchased in bulk for promotional, educational,
or business use. Please contact your local bookseller or the Macmillan
Corporate and Premium Sales Department at 1-800-221-7945, extension
5442, or by email at MacmillanSpecialMarkets@macmillan.com.

www.mcdbooks.com • www.fsgbooks.com
Follow us on Twitter, Facebook, and Instagram at @mcdbooks

10 9 8 7 6 5 4 3 2 1

This book is dedicated to Beverly "Mama" Moorehead.

Thank you—Perry Greene, Brenda Greene, Jamal Greene, Aunt Jo Ann, Aunt Lori, Jaquie Perry, Amani Fela, Diani Eshe, Abena, Taiwo, Kehinde, Lloyd, Dennis, JuJu, Rubix, John Forté, Donna Dragotta, DJ Eque, Seth Byrd, Robyn, Hi-Tek, Yasiin Bey, Dave Chappelle, NIKO IS, Thanks Joey, Triska, Marshauna Campbell, Styles P, jessica Care moore, King Moore, Zean Mullings, Louis Campbell, Les, LG, Kendra Ross, Jean Grae, Kevin Weeks, Beef, Supernatural, Federico Lopez, Jarret Myer, Spintelect, Phil da Agony, Krondon, Mitchy Slick, Mari Velazquez, and Cory Mo.

Rest In Power, Dave New York.

Names have been changed to protect the guilty.

Contents

Vibrate Higher

Prologue

Muthafuck the wagon, come join the band
Vibrate, vibrate higher
—ANDRÉ 3000, "VIBRATE"

This is not the truth. My perception is only one-third of this story. The truth will be known when I'm gone. This is not a rags-to-riches story. This is not a story of how a little ghetto boy rises above all adversity to beat the odds and then eventually reconcile with his past. I have no interest in playing up how badass my childhood was; even if I did, there wouldn't be much to work with. Conventional wisdom about rappers is that we are rebels with a cause who constantly see red and express ourselves in coded rhymes that the establishment will never understand. The truth is that most rappers are supernerds. While we live at the top of the nerd food chain, we are, without a doubt, nerds who are good with words. We turn poetry into personality and nervous energy into swagger. Our need to be liked by every-one is why we use rhymes to try to explain what you are going thru and, ultimately, bring you closer to us. Hip-hop is the sound track for nerd-world domination.

This is not a rallying cry for real hip-hop, or a guidebook on how to be more conscious in the way you live. This is not a manifesto handed down from the tops of mountains. This is simply me, in all my glory, pain, splendor, and shame. This is about the people and the events that shaped me. These are stories about the places that raised me in equal measure with my parents. This is the revelation I have been running toward since I first put a sixteen-bar verse together. Writing this book has shown me what I've always known but was either too scared or too proud to share anywhere outside the box that is a hip-hop song.

I have many vices, and I do not trust anyone who doesn't. I am insecure about my physical appearance, and I am fiercely competitive. I can be selfish, and like many great artists I am often driven by ego. I also realize that my story is inspiring. I am superaware of my place in this world and what I bring to it. I recognize my position as a connector of like-minded people, as a griot, as proof that a life of creating substantial entertainment can very much be reality. I know I am a great lyricist not because others say it but because of the time I have spent dedicated to my craft. I know it whether you do or not.

This is not a lie. The life of visionaries who create capital from ideas that spring from their ever-evolving minds is not a life for the weak. To be your own boss is bravery. This book is my warrior's toast to us and those like us. For those who know you have to either put in or put out.

I never dreamed of being a "conscious" rapper for a living. I only wanted to be a great rapper. Before that, I wanted to be a marine biologist, then a baseball player. Standing in the outfield swatting away bugs during baseball practice, I realized music was my true calling. So many lyrics were running thru my head I could no longer focus on baseball. Hip-hop's mix of music and poetry was too seductive to ignore. Hip-hop sank its teeth into me and never let go.

I was blessed to come of age at a time when making conscious hip-hop music was trendy. You could not be great and frivolous at the same time; your skill was intertwined with your ability to uplift people and spread information. This coincided with how I was raised, and if I did not have the foundation in my home, I would have discarded conscious hip-hop when the trend was over. This trend, as fleeting as it was, created some of the most indelible hip-hop recordings to date. People's music preferences have always been stuck in the decades they came of age in, whether it was the 1960s, '70s, or '80s. For me, it was the '90s.

Musicians use the word *vibe* a lot. Intuition helps artists feel the vibes in the room and play off them. You try to catch a vibe in the studio. You vibe at a concert. The word *vibe* is tossed around so often that the actual meaning of the word seems to have died; it's become a cliché. To vibrate is the action of vibe. In a literal sense, my job is to vibrate higher, or to vibrate on a higher level of consciousness. The definition of *vibrate* is to move or continue to move rapidly to and fro. As I find myself writing this book on planes, trains, and automobiles, I realize that I vibrate for a living. This must be why the shark is my favorite animal. Ever since I was a little boy, I have been fascinated with the fact that most sharks must constantly move to survive. They never sleep (in the way we do) because they need water flowing thru their gills at all times for oxygen.

We see light because of vibrations. Colors represent the vibration of waves at different frequencies. We also hear sounds because of vibrations. When you repeat a word over and over like a mantra, it is not just the meaning of the word that tattoos itself on your consciousness; it is also the vibration that emanates from the sound of the word. I experienced this firsthand on my first tour, the Spitkicker tour, with De La Soul, Common, Pharoahe Monch, and Biz Markie, in 2000. In the De La Soul song "Stakes Is High," which samples James Brown's "Mind Power," Maceo Parker repeats the words "vibe" and "vibration." So to introduce the song, all of us on the tour would join De La onstage and tell the crowd that when we said "Vibe," we wanted them to say "Vibration." We would reply, "Stakes is high." I saw the effect our "mantra" had on the crowd. Every night we got them to vibrate higher.

Music arranges sound in a way that creates a higher vibration. We like listening to music because it allows us to see vibrations as if they were colors. Reggae artists often talk about vibration in their lyrics, and listening to reggae music is a very physical experience. The sound system, which is a crew of DJs who play reggae on their intricate set of equipment, is an attempt to increase the vibration for the listener. This sound system started in Jamaica in the 1960s and has evolved to today's sound systems that battle one another in what are known all over the world as sound clashes.

Bass instruments have a rich vibration that you feel in your midsection. This comes from the low register of the bass, and it is what makes you move your hips when it hits. The bass instruments used in the blues, jazz, rhythm and blues, and reggae have an even lower register than the electric bass preferred today. When you are aware of how the music affects the mind, body, and spirit, you realize its importance. It is a natural resource. It is as essential to us as the fossil fuels we wage war for control of. As musicians, it is imperative that we do our best. It's why Rakim said, "It's a must that I bust any mic you handing me." It's why André 3000 said, "Muthafuck the wagon, come join the band / Vibrate, vibrate higher." This word *vibrate* is repeated like a mantra, over and over, on André's record.

Around 2009 a friend of mine, Wizdom Selah, gave me a book as a gift, *The Hidden Messages in Water*, by Masaru Emoto. Emoto is a Japanese science hobbyist, author, and entrepreneur who photographs ice crystals. His experiments reveal that water exposed to positive energy such as classical music and the words *I love you* creates beautiful, well-formed crystals, and water exposed to negative energy such as the words *I hate you* and heavy-metal music creates ugly, malformed crystals. He suggests that since human beings are 70 percent water and the earth's surface is 70 percent water, and because water combines with and takes on the properties of everything it comes in contact with, we can purify ourselves by purifying the water on this planet and in our bodies. Water has a great memory. So drink more water. Check.

What was interesting to me was that the concept of vibration kept coming up. Everything in the universe creates its own vibration. Since vibrations create sound, they can be measured by water. Some feel that Emoto's book is a hoax, pseudoscience tailored for a gullible audience searching for meaning in life. Admittedly, while the results of his experiments made sense to my spiritual mind, my intellectual mind said, "Yeah, right." However, even if his claims are false, what I have learned about vibration holds true. Whether this is science or not, hundreds of thousands of people have bought this book, and I hope it has helped them to think more positively and drink more water, which would be great.

As a musician, I was fascinated by the use of music in these experiments. As I was reading the book, I had flashbacks of being onstage with De La Soul, chanting "Vibe" and "Vibration" with a crowd. André 3000's "Vibrate" ran thru my head. Although I had spent years as a "conscious" rapper, this was the moment that gave me a clearer vision of purpose. At a time in my life when I was trying to become a better person, I was sent this book that confirmed for me one of my great purposes: to use the music not just to pay my bills or to become famous, but to truly vibrate higher.

I

—*mm*—

Stakes Is High

Born on the after beat
He patted his foot before he walked
—NINA SIMONE, "HEY, BUDDY BOLDEN"

Talb. Talid. Talbit. Tomlid. Tabil. These are all things I've been called by people, adults and children alike, who have had the pleasure of reading my name aloud in front of a group of my peers. I learned early on that the average person gives up on a word if it is made up of a series of letters they have never before seen. *T-A-L-I-B*, pronounced *Tah-leeb* by my parents and *Tah-LIB* by most Muslims. I have had schoolteachers, without even attempting to pronounce my name, tell me that they could not pronounce it.

Talib is an Arabic name that means "student" or "seeker of knowledge." According to the Quran, the prophet Muhammad had an uncle named Abu-Talib, who was Muhammad's first convert to, or the first student of, Islam. Kweli is a name that exists in many African languages, but most prominently in Swahili and

Akan. It means "of truth" or "of knowledge." The literal translation of Talib Kweli is "seeker of truth and knowledge." With this name I could not grow up to be a crackhead.

When my parents chose this name out of some African name book in 1975, they could not have known the political connotations that would come to be associated with it. They could not have known that smartphones would autocorrect the spelling of my name from *Talib* to *Taliban*, or that executives at Rawkus Entertainment would ask me to consider a professional name change after the destruction of the World Trade Center on September 11, 2001. Perry and Brenda Greene only knew that their children must have strong, African names, names that had meaning and would let the world know before we opened our mouths that we had self-esteem and would not be taken for jokes in this world. Like many Black parents of the 1970s, they gave their boys unmistakably African names: Talib Kweli Greene and Jamal Kwame Greene.

During the 1960s, many aspects of the status quo were challenged. By the time Perry and Brenda were ready to have children, in the mid-1970s, Pan-Africanism, or the active celebration of and participation in African culture, had gone mainstream. Brothers and sisters proudly rocked dashikis and Afros, and *Ebony* and *Jet* magazines were taking their fashion cues from Africa. Perry and Brenda both rocked Afros, even though Perry's hairline was making a break for it. They had gone to Ghana and they celebrated Kwanzaa regularly. Their Pan-Africanism was a natural extension of the political philosophy they shared, which was Black Cultural Nationalism. As cultural consciousness began to sneak into Black American homes, Black Cultural Nationalism became the predominant philosophy of forward-thinking Black folk. As a concept, Black Cultural Nationalism began its journey as a child of the Haitian Revolution. Those Haitians influenced Africans all over the diaspora to begin thinking about independence from an overbearing and oppressive Europe.

After the American Revolutionary War, many free and literate Africans in the North of the United States were members of the same Masonic lodges as the white Americans who had gone to war with Great Britain. These white folk were greatly influenced by the ideas of the Enlightenment, which was taking place in Europe at the time, but their "enlightenment" did not seem to extend to their African brothers. African Masons like Prince Hall and Richard Allen formed separate, but equal in concept, halls for Africans and encouraged Africans to stand on their own without being dependent on European social constructs. These men, along with the Haitians and the Maroon people of Jamaica, were studied by Marcus Garvey, who in June 1919 incorporated the Black Star Line, a shipping company charged with the mission of taking Black people from the Americas back to Africa so they could build lives in the homeland of their ancestors. Marcus Garvey, with his focus on African self-reliance, remains a standard-bearer for Rastafarians, political activists, and Black Cultural Nationalists alike. He had tremendous influence on the Nation of Islam and the Black Power Movement of the 1960s. The term *Black Power* was made famous by Stokely Carmichael, aka Kwame Ture, and the concept was put into practice when Kwame Nkrumah became president of Ghana. Malcolm X, perhaps the greatest symbol of the Black Power Movement, came out of the Nation of Islam and in 1964 went on to form the Organization of African American Unity, which had more of a Pan-African focus.

Black Cultural Nationalism, and to a larger extent Pan-Africanism, informed the values in our home. Both of my parents were teaching, and although we were living in an integrated neighborhood in Park Slope, Brooklyn, at 701 President Street, my parents enrolled me and Jamal in Weusi Shule, an Afrocentric independent school in Flatbush created by a Black educator named Ayanna Johnson. Weusi Shule later moved to a larger location and changed its name to the Johnson Preparatory School; it is now more Christian based. After two years at Weusi Shule, Jamal and I left to attend Junior Academy, an African-American owned and operated independent school in Bedford-Stuyvesant. My parents chose this school to ensure that we had a nurturing learning environment and that the cultivation of pride and self-esteem were core principles of this environment.

As the son of two teachers, I developed an early love for reading and learned how to write long before I started school. To the dismay of every elementary school teacher I ever had, I held my pen in the awkward fashion of someone who taught himself how to write without listening to instructions. I loved reading about nature, and when I wasn't reading about it, I tried to be in the midst of it. Our apartment at 701 President was on the first floor, so we had access to the backyard. Jamal and I would stay back there for hours, collecting insects and making rivers in the dirt with the garden hose. We would often try to collect every different species of insect we could find and put them in a fish tank to see how they cohabited. There was a series of children's books called Childcraft that functioned like an encyclopedia for children, and I identified many of the insects in our backyard from reading those books. I loved those Childcraft books so much I would stay up and read them over and over with a flashlight under my covers after bedtime.

My interest in nature was also stoked by our proximity to Prospect Park. Prospect is Brooklyn's largest park and has a lake that attracts all sorts of wildlife one doesn't normally get to see in the city. I would go to the lake and catch frogs, salamanders, and more insects and bring them back home. I always knew how to put a fish tank to good use. As I got older, I focused less on amphibians and insects and started getting into reptiles and birds. I owned a couple of snakes, a few frogs, loads of fish, and two parakeets as pets throughout my early childhood. I got this love for animals from my father, who had a pet python that he gave up when I was born and a dog, King, who passed away of old age when I was about eight.

On many visits to Prospect Park with my father and brother, we would stop to watch Little League baseball games. My father enjoyed watching all sports and was a fan of every New York team, but baseball was his game, and the New York Yankees were his favorite. Each year from spring to fall we would watch every game together. Knowing how much my father loved the sport made my brother and me want to play it, and soon we were members of St. Francis Xavier's Little League program.

I was naturally athletic and always played well, but I didn't get really good until I went to baseball camp years later. I began to rack up baseball trophies every season, which was wonderful for my self-esteem. My parents came to every game of mine, and my father soon joined the Little League program as a coach. Playing baseball for my father's team was one of my greatest childhood experiences. It brought us closer and helped me develop character. I also established a great love for the game, and it is still my favorite sport.

My parents always placed an emphasis on family, and we spent a lot of time either visiting ours or having them over at our apartment. My father was close with his parents—my grandparents, Stanley and Javotte Greene—and with his cousins Jackie and Warren. We would go to New Rochelle or Long Island for the weekends to see these folks. My mother's family lived mostly in Brooklyn, except for her father, Lloyd, who lived in Harlem. Her mother, my grandmother, and Brenda's two sisters, Jo Ann and

Lori, all lived in Flatbush, and we would alternate spending weekends with them as well. Jo Ann's daughter, Abena, and her twin sons, Taiwo and Kehinde, were all close to Jamal and me in age, and I spent most of my childhood free time with these first cousins. My cousins were my best friends. In 1986 my mother's sister Lori gave birth to my cousin Lloyd, named after his grandfather, and he became the baby of our family crew. We would ice-skate in the winter, roller-skate in the summer, and play wiffle ball in the fall. On Friday nights, my grandmother Beverly, who we all called Mama, would have all of her grandchildren over for marathon sessions of Monopoly. We would start at 7:00 or 8:00 p.m., with *The Love Boat* or *Fantasy Island* on the TV in the background, and go until everyone fell asleep around 3:00 or 4:00 a.m. These games were friendly but deadly serious. Mama loved to gamble, and Monopoly was a way for her to get a gaming fix and spend quality time with her grandchildren at the same time.

My father and mother also had many friends, mostly other teachers, and they would come over often. My parents' apartment seemed like the place to be, and they were always hosting. As a college-radio DJ, my father had amassed an impressive vinyl collection spanning many decades and genres. He would play these records at these get-togethers. When it got late and the kids were sent to bed, the song selection would switch up. I remember hearing party records like Dillinger's "Cocaine" or Shorty Long's "Function at the Junction" seep up thru the ceiling into my bedroom while I was pretending to be asleep. Straining my ears to make out the rhythms of the songs that my parents played after I went to bed was what took me down the music rabbit hole. I was fascinated that different songs created very different moods. At this young age, my primary interests were still baseball and nature, but music was beginning to flirt with me and would soon become my truest love.

~m~

A knife, a fork, a bottle and a cork
That's the way we spell New York.
—DILLINGER, "COCAINE"

December 2005 was the first time I truly gained an understanding of the power of words. I was in the Cutting Room Studio on Broadway, working hard on what was to become my third solo album, *Eardrum*. The snow was on the ground, the hawk was biting, and South Beach was calling my name. New York City winters are gorgeous, but they are no match for Miami's perfect mix of sun, sand, and heart-pounding nightlife. JetBlue airlines, barely five years old at the time, had good deals on flights to Fort Lauderdale from JFK, so it didn't take much for me to hop on the phone and book a flight.

I was toward the end of my recording and by then the studio had become my home. My apartment became a place that I would simply visit for a few minutes to shower and change clothes. The Cutting Room Studio was right next door to Rawkus Entertainment, the famous indie record label I had just parted ways with. It felt good to be in control of my own career and life.

Eardrum needed an introduction that would announce the intention of the album but also pay tribute to the ancestors and living legends who made it possible for me to do what I love for a living. Before the legendary poet/professor Sonia Sanchez laid down the beautiful poem I would eventually use, I had considered starting the album with an iconic speech set to music. My quest for this speech brought me to Nubian Heritage, an African-American cultural hub in Brooklyn that sold mostly books but also calendars, cosmetics, and music designed to meet the needs of the African diaspora. On that day, I purchased some audio recordings of speeches on CD by Malcolm X and Stokely Carmichael, now known as Kwame Ture.

Kwame's speech, recorded in 1963, was blaring thru the studio speakers when I decided to book my trip to Miami. I went in the next room but kept it up loud so I could listen to it while I made my reservation. Kwame was on fire, talking about the meaning of and necessity for Black Power. His message is essentially at the root of most hip-hop entrepreneurship, even though it's been bastardized by my generation's lack of historical context. When you see young Black people who are able to change their circumstances and the world with something as organic and creative as poetry and music, that is true Black Power. However, when these same young people take the individualistic stance that their success is solely a result of their hustle, then that success can actually be detrimental to the community. Kwame's language was the language of 1960s street empowerment; it was common for Black speakers of the time to refer to the white man as "cracker" to take away his seemingly infinite power. It must have taken less than five minutes to make my reservation with the pleasant-sounding lady from JetBlue. I then went back to work.

A week or so later I headed to John F. Kennedy Airport to catch the flight at JetBlue's brand-spanking-new terminal. I stuck my credit card in the kiosk, and a message flashed across the screen saying that there was an issue with my reservation and I needed to see the agent. When I went to see the agent, she said there shouldn't have been an issue and went to print my ticket. As she was doing so, she looked up and noticed something behind me and her face went pale. I quickly turned around, and breathing down my neck were two men in black. One said he was from the Transportation Security Administration; the other said he was from the FBI. They asked if I would come with them;

I asked why. They said they needed to talk to me in private, so I obliged.

The two men took me into a room with no windows and began to ask me questions about my trip. The FBI guy did the talking; the TSA guy said nothing. Before I answered, I asked them again what this was about. The FBI agent explained that a speech I was listening to while I booked my reservation had given the agent on the phone a reason to be concerned. Thank you, Patriot Act. I began to think about what was more likely: some JetBlue agent freaking out because of Kwame Ture's speech, or the government listening in on my conversations. I decided it didn't matter and I needed to focus on answering the questions properly and getting out of there. They asked me where I was going and why I was headed there, then showed me a list of phone numbers that were blacked out, save my manager's and my wife's, and asked me who these people were to me. When I asked why these two numbers had been picked out, they said these were the two people I traveled with most often. They also told me they knew I was a rapper and they thought I was probably doing what I said I was doing, but their job was to double-check. After a relatively painless ten minutes of questioning, they let me go and were even nice enough to have the plane held so I wouldn't miss my flight.

That moment was telling for me. In 2005, commercial hip-hop was extremely gangsta. Backed by Dre and Eminem, 50 Cent was dominating the charts, ushering in a new, grittier form of street rap. 50 was real enough to convince mainstream America that he might actually show up at their house and shoot them. And they loved it. But while my peers were being stopped by the hip-hop police, here I was being stopped by the FBI at the airport, for listening to a speech that was forty years old. Kwame Ture's forty-year-old Black Power speeches were more threatening to the establishment than the current crop of gangsta rappers.

Kwame's words were enough to get me stopped at the airport for listening.

I didn't get into hip-hop to spread a message or to be some sort of leader. The foundation that my parents provided, mixed with the popular, pro-Black hip-hop that was out when I started listening to music, determined my lyrical content. I just wanted to be a famous rapper, like many other boys from my neighborhood. I had not experienced a struggle similar to or nearly as deep as my ancestors'. Yet still, rapping about the needs of the people came as naturally as breathing. Now, with me on the FBI's radar, it was clear that the stakes were higher.

2

Growing Up Greene

> My songs are personal music; they're not communal. I wouldn't
> want people singing along with me. It would sound funny. I'm not
> playing campfire meetings. I don't remember anyone singing
> along with Elvis, Carl Perkins, or Little Richard.
>
> —BOB DYLAN

Late one night after performing at a nightclub, I
was attempting to drift off to the lush sounds of basic cable. After
lazily flipping thru channels for a few minutes, I stopped on a movie
called *The Landlord*, starring Beau Bridges. However, it wasn't
the actor I recognized immediately, it was the scenery. The movie
was shot on what looked like the street I had grown up on in the
Park Slope section of Brooklyn. Movies had been shot in and near
my neighborhood, most notably Spike Lee's *Do the Right Thing*
and *Mo' Betta Blues*. *Crooklyn*, which took place in the 1970s,
captured on film a childhood experience I could relate to. But *The
Landlord* was different; it was actually shot in Park Slope in the
1970s, not in the 1990s, like *Crooklyn*.

In the movie, Beau Bridges plays a rich white guy from Connecticut who decides to give up his inheritance and make his own money running an apartment building in Brooklyn. Park Slope is a colorful character in the story. Its inhabitants provide a collective reality check for the story's protagonist. One character in particular kept me watching the movie until the end, even though I had intended to fall asleep shortly after turning it on. My grandfather Stanley Greene, Sr., was playing the role of a limo driver for Beau Bridges's character.

Seeing my grandfather in a movie that night was surprising but not shocking. Growing up, I had heard stories about how important and influential an actor my grandfather was, but I figured that was just the type of intrafamily bragging that every family does. I had no real point of reference up until then. Stanley Greene, Sr., had passed away when I was still a kid, so my memories of him were of how great a grandfather he was, not how great an actor he was. His career meant nothing to the eight-year-old me. Seeing him on TV that night was a eureka moment. I instantly realized I was part of something bigger than myself—a lineage. I wasn't just Talib Kweli, I was a Greene, and I wasn't the first Greene attempting to make his name a household one. By this time I had developed enough drive and ambition to become a performer, but watching my grandfather's legacy being celebrated and preserved years after he passed away give me a new drive and sharpened my inner focus.

Stanley Greene, Sr., was a rock of a man. Born in 1911 on 134th Street in Harlem, to Laura Etta and Percival Greene, Stanley decided at an early age to become an actor. He had a lot to live up to. His father, Percival, the grandson of an enslaved African named James Greene, was the first in his family to achieve a higher education. Stanley graduated from City College and became a teacher and later a principal. Teaching as a profession would eventually take over the Greenes' legacy, but Stanley had to make his own mark on the family. He acted until he was drafted into the army during World War II, when he served proudly in Burma. Upon returning home, he jumped right back into acting. His character's daughter in one of his roles was played by a beautiful young woman named Javotte Brooks. Javotte was born to Mae Brooks in 1921 in Greensboro, North Carolina. Javotte had the light complexion of Dorothy Dandridge, allowing her to pass for white, an asset for a working Black actor at that time. According to my father, the family never spoke about her father, and Javotte's sisters did not share her light complexion.

Stanley and Javotte hit it off immediately. They were both young working-class Black actors, something of a rarity in those days. They took on many stage and film roles. Stanley most notably played a preacher in the 1964 film *Nothing But a Man*, reportedly Malcolm X's favorite movie. In 1978 Stanley played Uncle Henry in the film version of *The Wiz*. As a result of this, I was cast as one of the star babies in the scene where Lena Horne sings "Believe in Yourself." Around the same time, Javotte Greene was doing TV commercials and had a recurring role on CBS's long-running soap opera *Guiding Light*. Although Stanley came under scrutiny during the McCarthy era for being sympathetic to socialist and communist causes in the 1950s, he and Javotte became fixtures on the Black acting scene, living in the same neighborhood as Ruby Dee and Ossie Davis and appearing in plays alongside such actors as Cicely Tyson, Billy Dee Williams, and Denzel Washington. They performed in independent, Black-owned theaters around New York City.

Stanley Greene, Jr., my photographer uncle, was the couple's firstborn child, arriving in 1949. My father, Perry Greene, named after his grandfather Percival, showed up in 1950. Perry spent his first ten years as a child actor, appearing onstage and in films as well, most notably as Sidney Poitier's son in the classic *Edge of the City* at five years old. In 1960 Stanley Greene, Sr., Javotte Greene, and Perry were cast in an integrated traveling production of *The Miracle Worker*. Stanley and Javotte played the servants in the Keller household, and Perry was given a significant role as the boy servant, Percy, who helped Ms. Sullivan teach Helen Keller how to read. Traveling thru the rural South on a bus with an integrated cast may not seem like much now, but in 1960 this was a huge decision.

Seeing this side of America, the rural, unpleasant underbelly, had a profound effect on my father's worldview. At eleven years old, he would experience daily some of the most stubborn racism the world ever knew. He once told me a story of the troupe's bus pulling up to a restaurant and their being told that only the white people on the bus would be served. My father had always known his father to be a strong man, not easily broken. However, in this situation, Perry could see the defeat in his father's eyes. The white actors left with the Black cast members. They all headed to a restaurant down the street, which also would not serve them for fear of local retribution, but did let them come in and cook their own food. This story did not end in violence, but that initial look of defeat on my grandfather's face shook my father to the core. From that moment on, social justice became a focus for him. These travels would cause Perry and Stanley Jr. to develop perspectives that extended far past their home block. The best education is in application, and being Black traveling thru the American South in the 1960s had to be the best applied learning of its day.

The Greenes eventually settled down in 1961, buying a house in New Rochelle, New York. Stanley Jr. entered New Rochelle High School, and Perry went to Professional Children's School in Manhattan. The drug counterculture of the 1960s that enveloped America impacted both Stanley and Perry; moreover, Perry was taking the train from New Rochelle into Manhattan. They both became Black hippies, listening to the sounds of Motown and Bob Dylan in equal measure.

Because of his work hours and the lack of professional Black actors at the time, Perry did not have many Black friends. Most of his friends were white actors who lived in New York City. During high school, he continued to act professionally, but he spent most of his time protesting America's involvement in the Vietnam War. With his friends from the city, he would march, protest, and get attacked by the police. When a high school guidance counselor informed Perry he wasn't college material, he took those words to heart and decided to move to Greenwich Village and act for a living. He got a job at a clothing store and felt that this would be his life's path, until a draft card came in the mail. The war my father had spent years protesting against was calling his name, and he had no interest in fighting what he considered to be an unjust war. Living and working in Greenwich Village meant he was virtually living on the campus of New York University, so he applied for a college deferment as fast as he could. It was August 1968, and he enrolled at NYU as an English-education major, the only program still available for such a late enrollee. He ended up in a literature class and took a seat next to a pretty young Black girl with a big Afro named Brenda Carol Moorehead.

While Perry stumbled into NYU as some sort of antiwar protest, Brenda Carol Moorehead had been preparing to go there for her entire life. Brenda was born on the Fort Monmouth, New Jersey, army base. Her favorite game as a child was playing school, and she would cast herself as the teacher. Her parents were the hardworking couple Lloyd and Beverly Moorehead, and Brenda was determined to make them proud by becoming the first one in her family to go to college. Lloyd Moorehead was born in Harlem Hospital in 1930 to Kate Benjamin from Saint Croix. He spent his teenage years running the streets of the South Bronx with his good friends MJ and Jimmy Footmon, who were born in St. Matthews, South Carolina, until Lloyd volunteered to fight in the Korean War. He served in Japan for three years, then returned to the South Bronx to hang with his old crew. Over the years, Lloyd became smitten with MJ and Jimmy's younger sister, Beverly Footmon.

Beverly had Southern charm and grace, but New York City living had given her a no-nonsense attitude that was attractive to Lloyd. She and her brothers arrived in New York as part of the Great Migration of Black Southerners, eventually settling in the South Bronx. As the youngest and the only girl, Beverly learned early how to fend for herself and be independent. Lloyd asked for Beverly's hand in marriage in the late 1940s and soon took a job teaching technical writing at the army base in Fort Monmouth. In 1950, Brenda, my mother, became their firstborn child. My mother's sisters, Jo Ann and Loretta, were born shortly after. However, the pressure of raising a new family got to Lloyd and Beverly, and they split when Brenda was nine years old. Lloyd began a new relationship, and Beverly raised her daughters as a single mother. She moved her daughters to an apartment in Flatbush, Brooklyn, and tried her hardest to instill a pure strength in them that would carry them thru these hard times.

In 1965 Brenda attended Erasmus Hall High School in Brooklyn. In her free time she loved being in the boosters, roller-skating, and especially reading. Her constant consumption of books would land her in an honors program the high school offered. While Erasmus's current population is predominantly Afro-Caribbean, in 1965 the school had few Blacks, and Brenda was the only person of color in most of her classes. Most of the Black students who attended Erasmus at the time were bused in from Bedford-Stuyvesant or Crown Heights. Observing this, along with the social climate of the 1960s, made her want to become more culturally conscious. She continued to excel in school, and in the winter of 1968 she was rewarded for her focus and dedication and accepted by New York University on a financial aid package that would pay her tuition.

On April 4 of that same year, the Reverend Dr. Martin Luther King, Jr., had been gunned down on the balcony of the Lorraine Motel in Memphis, and the country erupted. The bullet that James Earl Ray pumped into Dr. King also killed the happy, free-love spirit that stereotypically embodied the 1960s. America was becoming darker, more aggressive. The Black students who were at NYU in 1968 channeled that aggression and became active in a fight to create a Martin Luther King (MLK) scholarship at the university. Brenda became part of this struggle by being awarded this scholarship, and she began attending classes in the fall of that year. This struggle was a turning point in her life. The role of student activist fit her well and gave her more direction. She became involved in BASA, the college's Black student organization, and began to actively participate in the Black Arts Movement.

Cultural identity was a hot topic in the 1960s. The myth of the American melting pot that was fed to children in elementary school was being crushed by the images of social unrest and war that were being broadcast into homes nightly. Abandoning the language and customs of their ancestors is what people were told to do to make it in America, but doing so could prove to be a death sentence for your spirit. The search for a cultural identity would bring Perry Edward Greene and Brenda Carol Moorehead together. Perry's background in antiwar activism and Brenda's in the Black Cultural Nationalist Arts Movement at a politically and socially active time in this country brought these young people together while they were at a critical stage in the formation of their identities.

Brenda and Perry quickly fell in love, got married at Perry's parents' house in New Rochelle, and started a life together in Brooklyn. In 1974 Brenda convinced Perry to move to a larger apartment in Jamaica, Queens. On October 3, 1975, in Brooklyn Jewish Hospital, their first son, Talib Kweli Greene, was born, and on August 10, 1977, their second son, Jamal Kwame Greene, was born.

Life in Jamaica, Queens, did not suit my parents. They missed the diversity of Brooklyn, New York's largest borough, and wanted to return there to live. The young family moved back to Brooklyn in 1977 and chose Park Slope as the place to raise their family. At the start of the 1970s, Park Slope had become one of New York's most desirable neighborhoods to live in. It had come full circle from the time when a wealthy lawyer and railroad developer named Edwin Clarke Litchfield purchased large chunks of land there and sold them to the city of Brooklyn for residential development. In 1883, the Brooklyn Bridge was completed, and this led to more settlers in the area. Brownstones were built, and by 1890, according to the U.S. Census, Park Slope was the richest community in the country. The neighborhood continued to flourish until the 1950s, when wealthy Americans shifted to the suburbs and the inner cities became filled with working-class Italian and Irish families. By the 1960s, the Italians and the Irish were leaving as Black people from the South and immigrants from continents not called Europe began to call Park Slope home.

By the time Perry and Brenda moved to Park Slope, it had become a free-spirited community where many gay people, interracial couples, and others shunned by society flocked. These new residents renovated brownstones and turned them into two- or three-family homes. This led to increased gentrification, and many young couples found it an ideal neighborhood to raise a family.

The Park Slope of the film *The Landlord* was a creation of

Hollywood. Even though many of the outside scenes were filmed on location, the director, Hal Ashby, exposed his ignorance of the intricacies of Brooklyn communities. If he had really wanted to tell the story of an interloper, slums in Brownsville, Bedford-Stuyvesant, East New York, and Bushwick would have captured the ghetto realities on display in the film more accurately. Perry and Brenda had chosen Park Slope precisely because it was not like the neighborhood seen in this film. While inner-city life here was far from perfect, and we were far from rich, I recognize the hard work and inspired decision making on my parents' part that allowed me to be raised in such a special place.

This was still America, though. Even as a young child, I noticed the geographical class system that continues to exist in what we affectionately call the Slope. Park Slope is named for its connection to Prospect Park, Brooklyn's biggest public park. The neighborhood starts at the park and slopes downhill from Prospect Park West to Fourth Avenue. Directly across the street from Prospect Park on Prospect Park West are the Victorian houses that used to be collectively known as the Gold Coast. One block down on Eighth Avenue, you can find trust-fund kids for whom Manhattan is still too expensive, living among hardworking middle-class Brooklyn families. Go down to Seventh Avenue and you find Brooklyn's version of Broadway; Seventh Avenue is cluttered with bakeries, restaurants, tailors, real estate brokerages, and high-end supermarkets. These are the shops whose names you see splashed across the backs of the Little League uniforms that dominate Prospect Park every spring. After Seventh Avenue, things begin to change. You see more people of color. The apartment buildings and homes, while still nice, are not quite as well-appointed as those above Eighth Avenue. By the time you get to Sixth Avenue, you begin to see more Blacks and Latinos than whites. As you cross Fifth Avenue, the neighborhood becomes mostly Latino. By the time you get past Fourth and see the Gowanus Houses projects, in which Spike Lee's *Clockers* was filmed, you are no longer in Park Slope, even though real estate agents trying to cash in on the neighborhood's reputation often expand the borders at will. I grew up at 701 President Street, between Fifth and Sixth.

Shows on PBS from the late 1970s and early '80s such as *Electric Company*, *Vegetable Soup*, and *Sesame Street* came straight from the inner city. The sets and backdrops looked like colorful versions of where I lived, and the Park Slope of my childhood was just as racially diverse as *Sesame Street* was. But this was still the hood at the time, so there were street elements. By the mid-1980s you couldn't walk down a Brooklyn street without stepping on a couple of red or blue vial tops. The crack that came in these small containers was being smoked, and the addicts we affectionately called crackheads were in plain view, and everywhere, it seemed. As I look back, these seem like problems of poor people. But as a point of pride, my parents would refer to themselves as "middle-class." It certainly didn't feel as if we were living in poverty. I attribute that to my parents' focus on family activity. Every Sunday, my father would cook a meal that would last us until just about Tuesday. Then on Wednesday, he would make a casserole out of what was left that would last until the weekend, and then we would start the process over. My mother was focused on getting us to understand the difference between "school" or "church" clothes and "play" clothes. I remember having about three outfits, which were rotated thru the week. If my mother found a hole in our clothes, she would buy these cheap-ass iron-on patches that were never the color of the ripped item. My parents worked it out and made it happen.

Today's Park Slope is a case study in the positives and negatives of gentrification. Barclays Center, on the edge of the Slope, is already changing the face of the neighborhood—whether it's for better or for worse remains to be seen. The Park Slope Food Coop is one of the best in the country, allowing people to work for access to the freshest produce. Just make sure you don't go in there unless you are a member, or they will give you the look of death and someone in an orange vest will tell you that you must leave immediately. For every new rich person who moves into a gentrified neighborhood, there is someone poor who is forced to move out, someone who has helped to make up the core of what made the neighborhood so desirable in the first place. Park Slope has come to embody the best and the worst of Brooklyn.

3

Gifted and Talented

Radio, suckas never play me
On the mix, they just OK me
—PUBLIC ENEMY, "REBEL WITHOUT A PAUSE"

Hip-hop music and culture are woven thru the fabric of New York City. Dwelling in the Rotten Apple anytime after the 1970s almost automatically made you a part of the hip-hop generation. Down by law. In the early 1980s, subway trains were covered in bold, beautiful pieces of graffiti. B-boy crews roamed the streets like carnies, putting on impromptu shows at, quite literally, the drop of a hat. In case you made the mistake of thinking you were going to avoid hip-hop music, the true proponents of the culture walked around with big, loud, flashing radios called boom boxes, turning entire city blocks into their personal iPods.

Every year my father and his cousins Jackie and Warren would organize a family reunion at Lido Beach on Long Island. Lido Beach had these huge mushroom-shaped structures with tables under them that you could rent for the day. Mama would bring her famous biscuits, Warren would bring huge speakers, and we would listen to Warren deejay or to one of the city's two "Black" stations all day, WBLS or WRKS Kiss FM. I first heard songs like Shannon's "Let the Music Play" and Herbie Hancock's "Rockit" at these functions. Hip-hop was so far from the mainstream that even the Black stations did not play it, but the songs that were informed by hip-hop were the ones that got people up and moving. I would gravitate toward pop and R&B records with hip-hop elements in them long before I immersed myself in that culture. I remember first hearing pure hip-hop records like Whodini's "Freaks Come Out at Night" and Grandmaster Flash and the Furious Five's "The Message" at roller-skating parties in places like United Skates of America in Queens and the Empire Roller Rink in Brooklyn.

In 1985, Perry Greene was teaching at Malverne High School in Hempstead, Long Island, and Jamal and I were attending Davidson Avenue Elementary School in the same town. During those long morning commutes from Brooklyn to Long Island in my father's VW van, we would listen to the brand-new station WHTZ, or Z100. Z100 introduced New York City to a morning jock named Scott Shannon, who brought with him a concept called the "morning zoo." It wasn't about the music the jocks played, which was overtly pop. The antics of Scott Shannon and his partners, especially one named Mr. Leonard, were so zany that they amused us to no end. The sound effects, prank calls, and silly jokes that we associate with the douchiest of morning radio shows were still groundbreaking in 1985. Mr. Leonard was my favorite. In his high-pitched voice he would say the most ridiculous things. He would also make his own versions of popular songs, so instead of Falco's "Rock Me Amadeus," Z100 would play a parody version called "Rock Me Mr. Leonard." I thought this was genius.

I began taping songs on TDK and Maxell cassettes and creating my own versions of pop hits. The only one I really remember is

"There's a Hog on Your Mommy," which was my version of Donna Summer's "She Works Hard for the Money." The *Z Morning Zoo* also used sound bites from popular TV shows out of context for laughs. I began to tape shows like *The Cosby Show* and chop them up so that it would sound as if Bill Cosby were answering my interview questions. I would wait for *The Cosby Show* to come on TV and hold up a radio to the TV to record the half-hour show. I would then create questions I could find answers to in the episode, get another radio, stand between the two, and conduct an interview using select Cosby sound bites for answers. Then I would tell everyone I just interviewed Bill Cosby. This took hours. I told you most rappers were complete nerds.

Side note: I switch between the terms *rap music* and *hip-hop music* often. If you notice, I refer to the Sugarhill Gang as a rap group, while I speak of Doug E. Fresh and Slick Rick being invested in hip-hop culture. Rap music is one piece of hip-hop culture, but it is certainly the most dominant. The Sugarhill Gang took lyrics from artists invested in hip-hop culture to create a popular rap record, and these artists were not paid or credited. This is the true difference between hip-hop and rap. However, from this point on, I may use the term *rap music* when you may think I should be talking about *hip-hop*. You will know what I mean based on the context. Don't tell KRS-One on me.

While Run-DMC were stars in the hood long before they collaborated with Aerosmith, their rendition of "Walk This Way," with the accompanying video, broke the walls down between hip-hop and mainstream culture. Before Run-DMC, the only Black artists MTV had ever played were Michael Jackson and Prince. MTV certainly did not play any hip-hop. When "Walk This Way" dropped, I was captivated by the pop music that I heard in the morning on Z100. Songs like DeBarge's "Rhythm of the Night," A-ha's "Take On Me," and Dire Straits's "Money for

Nothing" became my favorites. I had a Panasonic radio that I would use to record songs from Z100. It was my goal to have a recorded copy of every song I liked. I used to love the Christmas season not just for presents and seeing family but because pop stations like Z100 would play a countdown of the biggest hits and I could tape the songs I did not have copies of.

"Walk This Way" made a pop group out of Run-DMC. So when they followed that single with the classic "You Be Illin'" in 1986, it went straight to pop radio. This time, however, Run-DMC did not drop a record that crossed over to white people listening to the Top 40. They brought the pop world over to them. A story song that presents different scenarios of some of the dumbest things people do, "You Be Illin'" was hands down a Black-sounding hip-hop record, complete with the ebonically correct title. Even though I was a child, "You Be Illin'" felt more authentic to me. It also provided me with my first hip-hop rebel moment. The English teacher in my mother hated that song when it came on and hated to hear me sing along to it. She hadn't studied this hard to become an English professor at Medgar Evers College to have her son walk around saying "you be illin'."

It would be another couple of years before I would begin to understand hip-hop as a culture. I could not escape it living in New York City, but I was definitely an outsider. I didn't break-dance, rap, or write my name in graffiti on the wall. I didn't even have a tag that I would doodle in school. The first rap song I learned all the words to was "The Super Bowl Shuffle," which was performed by the Chicago Bears while they were on their way to the 1985 season Super Bowl. My favorite verse was William "Refrigerator" Perry's:

You've seen me hit, you've seen me run,
When I kick and pass, we'll have more fun.

The next rap song I memorized was the Beastie Boys' "Fight for Your Right to Party." Run-DMC's manager, Russell Simmons, owned Def Jam Records with his partner, Rick Rubin. After they succeeded in getting Run-DMC a deal on Priority and putting out hits by T La Rock, LL Cool J, and Public Enemy on their label, they focused on the Beastie Boys, a (gasp!) white rap group. The Beastie Boys were making noise in the downtown scene as a punk group with hip-hop leanings. Russell saw dollar signs and put them on tour with Run-DMC and Public Enemy, where they would promptly either piss the audience off or make every audience member a fan. There was no in between with the Beastie Boys. Their debut, *Licensed to Ill*, dropped and quickly became one of the bestselling hip-hop albums of all time. They jumped on tour with Madonna, one of music's biggest acts at the time. They were hip-hop's first rock stars, and white. people. friggin' *loved*. them. "Fight for Your Right to Party," from the debut album, took hip-hop angst and put it to a trashy suburban rock beat. This record made it easy for the white people who listened to Z100 to say they liked rap without actually participating in hip-hop culture. This probably did not make the Beastie Boys feel good, as they had great respect for hip-hop culture. I toured the world opening for the Beastie Boys in 2004. During those three months "Fight for Your Right to Party" was not performed once. Songs on *Licensed to Ill* such as "No Sleep till Brooklyn" and "Brass Monkey" were decidedly more hip-hop than "Fight for Your Right to Party." Those singles were released earlier than "Fight for Your Right to Party," but I did not hear them until the group made me buy *Licensed to Ill*.

My father's vast record collection gave me a working knowledge of the history of popular music that extended far beyond my elementary school experience. I knew all the classics of R&B, rock, funk, jazz, and soul music pretty well, but hip-hop was developing out in the street, not in my home. As much as I loved the Run-DMC and Beastie Boys records, they had crossed over into pop territory and were hard to avoid. To participate in hip-hop in the 1980s you had to look far beyond what was being played on pop radio. When puberty crept up on me as I was entering junior high school, all the girls I liked loved hip-hop music. Chasing girls led to chasing hip-hop, and that led to my listening to and recording hours of hip-hop being played in the mix on New York City's Black radio stations, 107.5 WBLS and 98.7 KISS FM.

On weekdays WBLS and KISS FM would play the standard R&B fare that you wouldn't hear on pop Top 40 radio stations. On weeknights these stations would switch formats and play nothing but slow R&B, slow jams on programs with names such as *The Quiet Storm*. But once the weekend hit, hip-hop would dominate. Every Friday and Saturday night WBLS's DJ Marley Marl and his Juice Crew would go head-to-head against KISS FM's DJ Red Alert and his Violator crew for dominance of hip-hop radio. The competitive nature of this kind of radio programming greatly enhanced the culture, as the rappers and DJs had to creatively outdo one another to maintain the attention of the fans who listened faithfully every weekend. Without support from pop radio or MTV, which pushed mostly white pop and rock artists, the hip-hop culture was challenging itself to grow, and I was listening in real time.

My initial intention when I first began listening to and recording hip-hop mix shows was to impress girls with my knowledge of the latest rap song—nothing more, nothing less. However, the more I listened, the more I felt that these rappers were speaking directly to me. These new poets were efficiently capturing my inner-city experience and doing things with language and rhythm that were mind-blowing to the son of an English teacher and a sociology professor. I always loved writing, and according to my elementary school teachers I was good at it, but I never saw writing as something the "cool kids" did until I immersed myself in rap lyrics. Listening to Big Daddy Kane's lyrical swagger on "Ain't No Half-Steppin'," Public Enemy's Chuck D's revolutionary manifesto on "Don't Believe the Hype," and the playful back-and-forth punch lines Kid 'n Play dropped on "Do This My Way" expanded my idea of what it was possible for a writer to be. These rappers became superheroes in my mind. I would sit in front of my father's Marantz home stereo system every weekend and allow myself to be transported to a magical land where young people of color could be anything they wanted to be as long as they could control that microphone. This, to me, was liberation.

This was the extent of my hip-hop experience until about 1987, when I was accepted into Summit Junior High School for the Gifted and Talented. Gifted-and-talented programs were all the rage back then. The logic was that you take the children who appear to be at the head of the class out of regular classes and have them around only other "gifted and talented" children. But if we were the gifted and talented ones, how were the other children made to feel? Were we better than them? More worthy of proper education?

Nevertheless, the sixth grade at Summit was a success for me. I performed well in school, made many new friends, and began to develop my personality. The neighborhood I spent my child-hood in, Park Slope, was becoming gentrified, and many of the people who made the neighborhood as desirable as it was to live in were being priced out of their homes. Perry and Brenda Greene could no longer afford to live there, so we moved deeper into Brooklyn, into a three-bedroom attached brick house on Avenue K in Flatlands. My parents purchased it from an elderly white couple who were more than ready to escape the dark tide that was on its way to the neighborhood. Even though we left Park Slope because of skyrocketing rent, in many ways this new house was a step up for the family. We had a garage in the back, a backyard, a lawn, a laundry room, and a basement where my mom could set up her office. I went from sharing a bunk bed with Jamal to having my own room. I thought I was grown, so I gave Jamal the bigger room and all my toys. I displayed my baseball trophies and put up posters of a black Porsche 911, my preteen dream car. That summer, Jamal and I enrolled in the St. Thomas Aquinas Summer Camp Program at the St. Thomas Aquinas school on the corner of Flatbush and Flatlands Avenues. I had fun at this camp, but also had a couple of sobering moments.

The camp put on a talent show, and campers were encouraged to participate. I was already writing plays and poetry, but who reads a poem out loud? That sounded crazy! This was years before spoken-word poetry experienced a renaissance in Brooklyn, which was later capitalized on by Russell Simmons's *Def Poetry Jam* and films like *Love Jones*. I knew I wanted to do some sort of performance onstage, though, and I turned to the comedy of Bill Cosby. That year, as parents often do, my mother had bought a book, Bill Cosby's *Fatherhood*, for my father as a birthday present from my brother and me. One day soon after, while looking for some quality bathroom reading, I grabbed the book and read the first chapter. Cosby's anecdotes read like scenes from his TV show and reminded me of my family. Four visits to the bathroom later, I finished it. Although I was already a fan because of *The Cosby Show*, *Fatherhood* made me a bigger one. I began to inhale all things Cosby. I memorized his classic Noah bit, found a brown suit, and performed it in that hot auditorium filled with—mostly white—young kids.

I bombed. The kids didn't so much boo as look tortured, as if to say, "Why are you putting us thru this?" They talked loudly over my routine. I couldn't understand why they weren't paying attention. I was confused why they did not find this bit as brilliantly hilarious as I did. They were rude, but I kept going till the end. I swore to myself I would never lose a room like that again. To this day, whenever I take the stage, I remember that feeling.

4

mm

The Poetry of Practicality

Hip is the knowledge, hop is the movement
Hip and hop is intelligent movement
—KRS-ONE AND MARLEY MARL, "HIP-HOP LIVES"

The amount of creativity and growth that happened in hip-hop in 1988 is widely considered unparalleled in hip-hop circles. Here's a list of hip-hop albums that were released and changed my life in 1988:

1. *It Takes a Nation of Millions to Hold Us Back*—Public Enemy
2. *Long Live the Kane*—Big Daddy Kane
3. *The Great Adventures of Slick Rick*—Slick Rick
4. *By All Means Necessary*—Boogie Down Productions
5. *Follow the Leader*—Eric B. and Rakim
6. *Strictly Business*—EPMD
7. *Lyte as a Rock*—MC Lyte
8. *World's Greatest Entertainer*—Doug E. Fresh

9. *He's the DJ, I'm the Rapper*—Jazzy Jeff and the Fresh Prince

10. *A Salt with a Deadly Pepa*—Salt-N-Pepa

11. *2 Hype*—Kid 'n Play

12. *In Control, Volume 1*—Marley Marl

13. *Road to the Riches*—Kool G Rap and Polo

14. *Tougher Than Leather*—Run-DMC

15. *Goin' Off*—Biz Markie

16. *Straight out the Jungle*—Jungle Brothers

While many people are initially drawn to the beats behind great hip-hop songs, as the son of educators I was always first drawn to the lyrical content. In 1988 an explosion of lyrical rappers became successful, and for fans of hip-hop at this time, the best lyricists became gods in our minds. We've all seen some variation of a teacher in a movie attempting to use hip-hop lyrics to introduce students to the wonders of poetry, but this phenomenon was happening organically in the streets of New York in 1988. Rakim, who has done interviews about trying to use his rhymes the way John Coltrane would use a horn, was putting together verses that were far more intricate than the stuffy Eurocentric nursery rhymes that were being passed off as poetry in classrooms around the world. KRS-One, who fancied himself a teacher and a philosopher, actually had songs called "Poetry" and "My Philosophy," the latter of which redefined for me what it meant to be a king. Hip-hop has always been extremely competitive, and while taking a dig at the older, more established act Run-DMC, who called themselves the Kings of Rock, KRS poetically broke down why the title *teacher* was more desirable to him than the title *king*:

—ᴍᴍ—

Teachers teach and do the world good
Kings just rule and most are never understood
—KRS ONE, "MY PHILOSOPHY"

Hip-hop is often the poetry of practicality. The purpose of the lyrics extends far beyond impressing the listener. For many artists, these lyrics are life itself. Hip-hop started as freedom songs written by the descendants of slaves, even if that freedom was represented by fame, wealth, and material gains that remain rooted in white supremacy and patriarchy. This poetry is ugly and gorgeous all at once, and to the untrained ear hip-hop's passion can be mistaken for a desire to be negative. I counter that hip-hop at its best is an attempt to make sense of senseless conditions and a quest for power embarked on by the powerless. A voice for the voiceless, hope for the hopeless.

As a cultural movement, hip-hop was beginning to find its voice, and that voice sounded a lot like voices from the Black Liberation Movement of the 1960s. Young Black academics from the early 1990s were moving away from pursuits of upwardly mobile capitalism that defined the 1980s and were rediscovering ambassadors of Black Cultural Nationalism such as Dr. Yosef Ben-Jochannan, John Henrik Clarke, and Frances Cress Welsing. Professors like Leonard Jeffries at City University of New York were embracing the philosophies of the Louis Farrakhan–led Nation of Islam, and Dr. Molefi Asante was at Temple University, redefining what it meant to be Afrocentric. Books that championed the beauty and intelligence of Black people were becoming prized commodities in the hood, and hustlers began selling academic titles on street corners, which eventually led to many impromptu "ciphers" on street corners.

The New York rappers of the time, particularly those influenced by the Nation of Islam or its younger, more street-savvy cousin, the Five Percent Nation of Gods and Earths, were the first to take this new Black consciousness mainstream. It was no longer enough to just be nice on the mic, as MCs began to add historical and academic knowledge to their skill set. As the child of Black Cultural Nationalists this type of hip-hop spoke directly to me, and I was pulled in. The lessons I received in my household became staples of great hip-hop right when I was at my most impressionable.

This is the environment that made a group like Public Enemy one of the biggest acts on the planet of any genre. Even though Chuck D and Flavor Flav were older than most of their rap counterparts even back then, the balance of Flavor's clown-prince antics matched with Chuck D's booming delivery and fiery, pro-Black lyrics was the perfect vehicle to drive home a musical version of what people like Malcolm X had taught us. The first big conscious hip-hop song was Grandmaster Flash and the Furious Five's classic "The Message," but Public Enemy, and later Boogie Down Productions, helped to turn conscious rap into a reputable genre.

Nowadays, even though some of the biggest rappers in the game, like Kendrick Lamar, J. Cole, and Chance the Rapper, are considered children of the conscious-rap movement, the term *conscious rap* is often frowned upon in rap circles. Hip-hop was once a small fraternity requiring its participants to be down by law, but as hip-hop grew into a billion-dollar business, many in the hip-hop community began to value the dollar over the culture. For so-called hip-hop fans, as long as you were making money, any ignorance you represented was forgiven or, worse, praised. While many in my generation embraced the conscious rap label, I'd be willing to bet that many younger artists shy away from it. It can be seen as self-righteous and corny, mainly to those who grew up in an era of hip-hop that praises flashy materialism over knowledge. While it must be stated that hip-hop started out as mainly party music, by 1988 it had grown in scope to be flexible enough to also inspire those looking for more than escapism in their music. However, by not labeling themselves conscious rappers, artists like Kendrick, J. Cole, and Chance the Rapper may be able to reach more people with messages that need to be heard. I am from a generation that wore our conscious identity on our sleeves, sometimes literally. The consciousness found in younger successful artists seems more nuanced, which can be a good thing. Consciousness should always be about action over lyrics.

5

∼∽∿∼

The Word Became Flesh

Niggas with knowledge is more dangerous than niggas with guns.
—TALIB KWELI, "THE PROUD"

When I returned to Summit Junior High School in the fall of 1988, my hip-hop education was going strong. I had spent the summer listening to WBLS and KISS FM, studying hip-hop albums, and watching hip-hop videos. I wore the clothes I saw my favorite rappers wear. I understood the rudiments of the culture, but I still had lessons to learn. Hip-hop was still street music at this point. My street education had not begun until the Summit program moved from the top floor of an elementary school to the top floor of a junior high school in Fort Greene—blocks away from the high schools Brooklyn Tech and Bishop Loughlin. Going to school in the Intermediate School 113 building meant dealing with insecure high school bullies who would lurk outside and prey on younger students. They didn't want much, your lunch money or your bus pass, sometimes your sneakers or your winter coat. I had to learn how to hold my own in a fight, and after one fight too many, my parents removed me from Summit and put me in my neighborhood zone school, Roy H. Mann Junior High School.

When my parents moved us from Park Slope to the alphabet avenues of Flatlands in 1987, we were the third or fourth Black family in the neighborhood. By 1989, one white couple was left on the block. I witnessed white flight firsthand. However, it wasn't African-Americans who were moving in, it was Caribbean-Americans and Caribbean immigrants who were changing the face of the neighborhood. In the short time we had lived there, Avenue K went from Irish and Italian to Jamaican, Bajan, Haitian, Trinidadian, and Dominican. Roy H. Mann JHS, which was in neighboring Bergen Beach, Brooklyn, had an interesting mix of Italian and Irish kids with kids from all over the Caribbean. I had spent the last two years hanging out in Fort Greene, Clinton Hill, and Bed-Stuy, and had never taken the time to get to know the kids from my current neighborhood. Now I was forced to.

Around this time my parents were going thru their first breakup. For the past few years, every once in a while the music of the argument was what I heard at night instead of "Function at the Junction." I never thought much of it because it wasn't consistent. I subconsciously rationalized it by thinking that people who live together are going to argue every once in a while. There was no way for my mind to grasp that my parents, after fifteen years of marriage and two children, would want to break up. As I began to occupy my mind with the trivial pursuits of puberty, I did not notice that my parents were hardly in the house at the same time unless they were sleeping. We were also eating together as a family less and less. In October 1988, Perry and Brenda sat Jamal and me down and explained that while they still loved us, they were having marital problems and were going to attempt a separation. This took me by surprise. I remember being upset, but I also remember appreciating the way that they focused on telling us as a team and letting us know that they still loved us. I had a feeling, even at my young age, that as long as they were trying to make themselves happy, they would figure out what was best for them. I trusted my parents' love. My younger brother, Jamal, did not receive this in the same way I did. He was ten years old and my parents were his whole world. This world was being shattered before his eyes. I remember hearing him cry thru the night.

Jamal was upset every day for a month after my parents dropped the bad news. He was so upset, my parents couldn't take it anymore and eventually got back together. As impressive as my parents are to me, this is one of their greater moments. Now that I am an adult with my own relationship issues, I have great admiration for their having put their differences aside for the sake of their children. If two people are not meant to be, it is often suggested that they split as soon as possible, especially when children are involved, so that the children don't get caught in any drama. I see clearly now that my parents needed time apart. But they worked it out in that moment to make sure Jamal was okay. They split up again two years later. But this time Jamal took it way better. Those two years could not have been easy for them. But they pulled it off. I don't remember hearing any arguing at night during those two years.

I might no longer have heard the arguing because my focus was elsewhere. I tried to dive headfirst into the social scene of Roy H. Mann JHS, but being a Black American-born kid at this school full of the children of Caribbean immigrants and Irish or Italian families on their way out of the neighborhood was like being on another planet. I made new friends—a Haitian kid named Cyriac St. Vil and Adrian Noel, who used to rap under the name Pure Skills and was the first person I ever met who called himself a rapper.

But the Caribbean culture was different from African-American culture. The slang, the dress codes, the cultural references were all hard for me to keep up with, and most of these kids had been going to school together since elementary. These kids were wearing Travel Fox shoes, Sergio Tacchini tracksuits, and colorful Kangol hats. I was shopping at the Gap. They ate cow-foot soup, curry goat, and beef patties. I ate Chef Boyardee and pizza. I did not fit in. The struggle to fit in became overbearing, and I made a decision that would forever alter my academic life. I decided to cut school.

I'd heard about kids cutting, but I had never thought to attempt it until this warm spring day. Normally if I did not want to go to school back then, I would pretend that I was sick, but that only worked half of the time, and I had already done that twice that winter. I needed a strategy. Every day my mother would go to the basement and work in her office until about 10:00 a.m., then head to Medgar Evers College for work. I came up with a juvenile plan of hiding in the backyard quietly under the porch until my mother left. I had to be extremely quiet and still because my mother's basement-office window faced that space under the porch. I sat motionless just to the left of the window listening to her type and make phone calls for three hours, as I usually left for school at 7:00 a.m. After she left, I went back inside and spent the day eating cold cereal and watching reruns of *I Dream of Jeannie* and *I Love Lucy*. I was in heaven. I thought, Why hadn't I been doing this more often?

My entire life I had been rewarded for academic achievement. Parents and teachers loved me and would make me an example for the class to follow. Teachers would ask other kids why they couldn't be more like me. At a certain point, let's call it puberty, the accolades I received from parents and teachers began to mean less and less to me. I was more interested in the opinions of my peers. They meant the world to me. My world was flipping on its head. The kids who cut school and did not hand in homework seemed way cooler than the teacher's pets in junior high school. I started not caring about what parents and teachers thought and began to actively solicit the approval of other junior high school kids who, like me, didn't know anything about the world.

New York City is chock-full of schools for different vocations. Eighth graders are encouraged to figure out which high school they would like to attend based on interest, not location. The only reason to go to a zone high school in New York City is if you have not quite figured out where your interest lies or if you can't afford the commute to a different neighborhood. These are both valid reasons. In the fall of 1988, I took a test that, if passed, would enable me to go to one of New York City's specialized schools, the most popular being Stuyvesant High School, Bronx High School of Science, and Brooklyn Technical High School, in that order. The test is called the Specialized High School Admissions Test (SHSAT), and the cut-off score for admission to each school varies every year. The year that I took it, you needed a 430 to get into Brooklyn Technical High School, aka Brooklyn Tech. I got a 432. Along with my new friends Cyriac and Adrian, I was going to Brooklyn Tech in the fall.

When the summer of 1989 hit, I was mostly hanging out with Cyriac. He seemed to be a sensitive soul like me, we had younger brothers the same age, and we both felt like outcasts. Me because I was African-American, and him because he was Haitian. In ancient times before the Fugees, Haitians were greatly discriminated against in Caribbean circles. Cyriac and I would stay up and talk about girls and music. He was a good friend to me back then. Even though he was the low man on the totem pole in the neighborhood because he was Haitian, he had been around long enough to be down. He would look out for me and help me to understand how the neighborhood worked. I still had my fish and my turtle, and Cyriac would come stare at that aquarium for hours. Later in life he opened up a pet shop in Flatlands that focused on fish.

That summer also found me hanging out with dudes like my man Saeed and George and Pierre Bain, who were Haitian as well. But unlike Cyriac, whose complexion was Africa Black, George and Pierre were light skinned, which gave you status in the 1980s. In fact, ever since the eighties, light-skinned brothers have been trying to make a comeback. Everybody knows this; you saw *Coming to America*. George and Pierre were liked by all, and they showed me a lot of love. Saeed used to like to fight, earning him the nickname Set It, and he and I would argue and then make up often. This was my crew that summer. We would spend our days riding around Sheepshead Bay and Marine Park on our bikes, getting chased by or chasing the white kids. At night as the sun went down, we would stand around on the corner of Avenue J and E. Forty-Eighth Street protecting our little corner and talking shit. In one of those shit-talking sessions, we decided that we needed to organize to protect ourselves. The Decepticon gang was growing in numbers, and they were beefing with dudes from the Vanderveer projects who called themselves VIP, or Vanderveer International Posse. Also, white boys from Marine Park and Sheepshead Bay were calling themselves the Kings Highway Boys. If we wanted to ride our bikes to those neighborhoods or go to parties in Vanderveer or Flatbush, we had to posse up. Adrian came up with what is probably the corniest gang name ever, the

Outlaws of Destruction, aka OOD. We weren't outlaws, and we didn't destroy anything, but the name sounded cool to a bunch of thirteen-year-olds.

I caught the rapping bug from spending time with Adrian. I had already penned poems, short stories, and plays, but writing raps was a way to impress my peers, which had become my top priority. I had no interest in performing as a rapper, but hearing what Adrian and others were coming up with, I knew I could write at least as good or better. I started writing rhymes for Adrian, trying to give him concepts and ideas. I am not sure if this offended him, and I don't remember if he ever used any of this stuff, but he was always gracious about it. In retrospect, I probably came off as pretty pretentious. When I finally worked up the nerve to spit my own rhymes, I took up the name Mad Skills, and Adrian and I became the Skills Crew. If the actual Mad Skillz, aka Skillz from Virginia, is reading this, I don't know why I never mentioned this before. Apparently great minds think alike.

I don't remember the first rhyme I wrote because it was in Adrian's voice, not my own. I remember that the subject matter revolved around writing rhymes and getting girls. The first thing most rappers rap about is rapping, which may seem redundant but is actually very much in line with hip-hop culture. The first rappers ever rapped about the DJ at the party. I was growing up in an era where the rapper was seen as more of a star than the DJ. I quickly grew out of wanting to emulate Adrian and dropped the Mad Skills moniker after a couple of months, opting for the name Genesis instead. Calling myself Genesis gave me inspiration for the first rap song I ever wrote: "Word Is Flesh." It came straight from the book of Genesis.

*In the beginning was the Word, and the Word was with God,
and the Word was God.*

—JOHN 1:1

And the Word became flesh and dwelt among us.

—JOHN 1:14

A friend of mine and a great MC named Jay Electronica once told me that we as MCs were "iller than Shakespeare." I tend to agree. Poetry connects us to our spirit and allows us to connect with and relate to others, but poetry set to a drum connects us to the African origins of music. The first hip-hop lyrics I wrote were to the beats of songs I taped off the radio back in 1988, and it took me another couple of years to find the inner rhythm that allowed me to write without listening to a beat. I didn't know any producers in junior high school, and I damn sure didn't have any studio access, so I would fill notebook after notebook with rhymes that had no home. This is how I developed such a wordy, loquacious rap style. By the time I got ahold of some beats, I would often struggle to fit all the words into bars, and it often sounded like it.

Adrian and I would write rhymes in the morning and have them memorized by the afternoon to spit for everybody. I was writing new rhymes every day, studying other rappers, and honing my craft. These junior high school years are when I truly discovered who I was. The posters of Porsches and baseball players were taken down and replaced with pictures from *Rap Masters*, *Right On!*, and *Word Up* magazines. I no longer followed childhood pursuits. Chasing tail made me fall into this abyss of hip-hop, and now I was drowning in it. When September came around,

I would be attending Brooklyn Technical High School, which boasted a student body of over five thousand. I decided that the Talib Kweli Greene who arrived there would not be the sensitive, shy geek who was beloved by teachers and parents. I was subconsciously fashioning a new persona, one that it would take a nervous breakdown to shed. Ladies and gentlemen, TK enters stage left.

6

~~~

The Cipher

I could take a phrase that's rarely heard
Flip it, now it's a daily word.
—ERIC B. & RAKIM, "FOLLOW THE LEADER"

I have always tried to maintain a certain standard of MCing, even when the trends changed and lyrical content evolved for better or for worse. When I began to listen to hip-hop, you had to have a certain type of knowledge to be considered one of the best. Back then rappers like Big Daddy Kane, Rakim, and KRS-One of Boogie Down Productions dominated the top of my favorites list. Great lyrical MCs who weren't necessarily rapping about Black Power, such as Kool G Rap, LL Cool J, and Slick Rick, were the exception to this rule. Conscious rap was the trend, and like all trends it quickly played itself out. For every KRS or Rakim there were countless wack MCs who claimed to be conscious. Just throw on a dashiki, some African beads, rap about the struggle, and voilà—you thought you were a dope rapper. Soon, this New York–based trend became out of step with the hip-hop the rest of the country wanted to hear, and there was backlash against these conscious-rap poseurs. The fiercest came in the form of N.W.A, Niggaz Wit Attitudes. As a Los Angeles–based hip-hop group, their musical choices were different from those of their East Coast peers, and their lyrics were influenced by a gangbanging street culture that New York wasn't then privy to. N.W.A was raw, unapologetic, and misogynistic, but by no means was it empty music. Songs like "Fuck Tha Police" and "Dope Man" contain some of the most blistering social commentary hip-hop had ever heard, and by the end of 1990, Ice Cube, N.W.A's chief lyricist, had joined the list of my favorite MCs.

Ice Cube had a falling-out with the members of N.W.A after the release of their debut album, *Straight Outta Compton*, a gangsta-rap record that went number one on *Billboard* with no radio single and earned the group a warning letter from the FBI. By May 1990, Cube was rolling out his debut solo album, *AmeriKKKa's Most Wanted*, which was fueled by the same gangsta angst as *Straight Outta Compton* but lyrically was more laser focused and personal. Ice Cube also had the foresight of linking up with Eric Sadler and Hank Shocklee, a Long Island, New York–based production team called the Bomb Squad, who were responsible for the sound of the conscious hip-hop supergroup Public Enemy. The Bomb Squad's production style was similar to the sonic collages that N.W.A producer Dr. Dre was sculpting, and Ice Cube felt right at home on their tracks. If Public Enemy's Chuck D was hip-hop's fiery voice of the struggle, Ice Cube came off as his gangsta-ass West Coast cousin down for the cause and ready to put in work. When the four police officers who were caught on tape beating up Rodney King were acquitted of all charges in 1992, Los Angeles erupted with race riots that made the things that Ice Cube rapped about on *AmeriKKKa's Most Wanted* look like prophetic statements.

Tupac Shakur, born in New York but raised in Marin County,

California, quickly picked up the torch from Ice Cube and became the embodiment of that delicate balance that exists between the streets and the struggle. When his debut album *2Pacalypse Now* dropped in 1991, he was best known as one of Humpty Hump's background dancers in the video for "The Humpty Dance." No one expected the depth and brilliance that Tupac displayed on his debut; songs like "Trapped," "Young Black Male," and "Soulja's Story" made me feel as if Tupac were talking directly to me. With songs like "If My Homie Calls" and "Brenda's Got a Baby," Tupac made incredible songs that were inspired by folks I saw on the block daily. As the son of Afeni Shakur, a Black Panther who was arrested as part of the New York Panther 21, Tupac laced his lyrics with revolutionary references that he experienced firsthand rather than with abstract ideas he got from some book. He successfully married the movement to the streets and went on to release a mountain of material before his untimely demise at twenty-five. On top of being a great MC, he solidified his respect as an actor with roles in hood classics like *Juice* and *Poetic Justice*, and by shooting two off-duty cops during a heated exchange in Atlanta and ultimately beating the case, he became a folk superhero. This was all before he went to jail on rape charges and was released to put out his biggest hits with Death Row Records. To this day, Tupac's music and life are synonymous with the best and the worst of our culture. His story most accurately depicts what it is to be hip-hop.

The first rapper to be heralded as the next great thing before he even dropped an album was Nasty Nas, from the Queensbridge housing projects. In 1991 Nas came thru on Main Source's "Live at the BBQ" and stood out among the greatest Queens MCs of his day with rhymes about murdering police, kidnapping the president's wife, and "hanging niggas like the Ku Klux Klan." It was lyrically precise shock-and-awe rap; he bodied that record. Nas's reputation on the mic was so crazy, by the time he began to work on his 1994 debut, *Illmatic*, the best producers in the business were lined up to work with him. Produced by Pete Rock, DJ Premier, L.E.S., Q-Tip, and Large Professor, *Illmatic* quickly became the standard-bearer for great hip-hop and is heralded as one of the greatest albums of any musical genre. Like Tupac, Nas weaved narrative that was raw, unflinching, and uplifting at the same time. His father is the jazz musician Olu Dara, and Nas incorporated jazz rhythms and sensibilities into his gangsta street tales. Nas rapped about what he saw in the projects from the perspective of the smart, observant kid sitting in the window taking it all in. As his career progressed, his perspective evolved from observer to reluctant participant. The poet inside him wrestled with the celebrity he was becoming, and he has explored this thru rhyme with such precision that he remains a favorite of many hip-hop fans over twenty years later.

Top five dead or alive is a term that's thrown around in hip-hop as some sort of measurement for who is the best, but it is flawed because the criteria to be considered the best change so frequently. One must master so many skill sets to be considered a top-tier MC, and so many factors change the landscape that the top five constantly fluctuates. It's too hard of a question to answer. Up until Nas, you still had to have some knowledge flowing thru your music to even be in the conversation. When Biggie Smalls came out, he changed all of that.

To be clear, what Biggie did on the mic was genius. His genius wasn't about what he had to say to the community but about what the community was saying to us. Biggie was a feeling—raw emotional portrayals of not being satisfied with your lot in life. If Tupac and Nas were speaking directly to us, Biggie was speaking for us, and what he had to say was often not pretty. Influenced by his mentor, the Uptown Records founder Andre Harrell, and the success of West Coast superstars Dr. Dre and Snoop Dogg, the hip-hop mogul Sean "Puffy" Combs was out to find a hard-core East Coast rapper who would sound natural over samples of the soul and R&B music that we grew up with. Biggie Smalls, whose professional name was switched to the Notorious B.I.G. after he lost a lawsuit to a lesser-known rapper called Biggy Smallz, was making a name for himself in the New York underground with Puff by his side all thru the early 1990s, and when his debut, *Ready to Die*, dropped in 1994, he was easily the most popular rapper in the city. The success of *Ready to Die* made Biggie the biggest rapper in the world for years to come, rivaled in popularity only by Tupac Shakur. Like Tupac, Biggie was gunned down at the height of his success. Tupac was twenty-five, Biggie was twenty-four. I often wonder how much brighter their lives would've been able to shine had they not been snuffed out so quickly.

Biggie's death left a void in New York City hip-hop. He often referred to himself as Frank White, a character played by Christopher Walken in Abel Ferrara's film *King of New York*. After Biggie passed, New York needed a new king, and MCs competed fiercely for the throne. Bad Boy Records, the label owned by Puffy and that Biggie was signed to, had a lock on the streets and the clubs nationwide, and it looked as if one of the rappers associated with Bad Boy would be the next king. New York has always been respected as the birthplace of hip-hop, but by the mid-1990s the city was experiencing a sort of renaissance in its hip-hop culture. Whoever would take Biggie's place as king of New York would be the king of hip-hop.

Biggie was the first MC to be considered the best without having any "positive" rhymes on his album. The only exception would be "Juicy." While songs like "Everyday Struggle" and "Suicidal Thoughts" spoke in depth about the effects that living in poverty has on the mind, the overall tone of *Ready to Die* was somber, dark, and more concerned with individual gain than the community as a whole. Post-Biggie, many young, aspiring MCs felt that to be the best you had to be bussing your gun and selling drugs in your rhymes. This was the era of tough-guy rap. Bad Boy artists like Mase and the Lox were the new favorites in New York City, and Puff, who after several name changes was now going by P. Diddy, had thrown his hat into the MC arena and began marketing himself as the curator of Biggie's legacy. Big Pun was heating up, representing lyricism heavy for the Latinos and for hip-hop's birthplace, the Bronx. Lox associate DMX seemingly came out of nowhere and set the city on fire with his aggressive, larceny-laced rhymes punctuated by dog barks, and Mase associate Cam'ron was reinventing himself as the leader of a new Harlem crew called the Diplomats, but it was the "skinny nigga on the boat" who would soon dominate hip-hop more than any MC before him. Jay-Z, an intricate MC from Marcy Projects who was first seen on a boat with his mentor Jaz in a video for a novelty hit called "Hawaiian Sophie," had a Brooklyn connection with Biggie. They were both Bed-Stuy dudes who got put on by members of fellow Brooklyn MC Big Daddy Kane's crew. On the strength of his debut album, *Reasonable Doubt*, and the business moves he made with his company, Roc-A-Fella Records, Jay-Z became the street favorite and the self-proclaimed heir to Biggie's throne.

I was listening to *Reasonable Doubt*, released in 1996, long before the world recognized Jay-Z's complete skill set, and I remember telling people that they were missing out on what was soon to be a classic MC. The singles that Jay-Z chose, such as "Dead Presidents" and "Can't Knock the Hustle," featuring Mary J. Blige, were deceptive; they did not capture what Jay-Z did lyrically as well as album cuts like "22 Two's" and "Regrets." Many hip-hop purists wrote off early Jay-Z as materialistic, hedonistic rap at best. It would take years for Jay-Z's critical acclaim to catch up with his commercial success. Not until he dropped *The Blueprint* in 2001 did many true-school hip-hoppers begin to give him his props as a lyricist. Produced largely by Kanye West and Just Blaze, *The Blueprint* married Jay-Z's swagger and braggadocio with an underground sonic aesthetic that had been missing from commercial hip-hop for quite some time. Just Blaze and Kanye were chopping up sped-up loops of old soul records, which gave the album a warm, nostalgic feel. Because the voices on these loops would be sped up, this production style began to be referred to as chipmunk soul. It reminded the purists of the heydays of sampling, 1987 to 1992.

As tough-guy rap began to capture the attention of the hip-hop masses, I was still drawn more to what Native Tongues MCs like Q-Tip from A Tribe Called Quest and Posdnuos and Trugoy from De La Soul were doing. They looked like and dressed like Black nerds, which is an aesthetic that is celebrated these days with events like the Afropunk Festival, but was still cutting-edge back then. De La Soul's video for "Me Myself and I" was almost like a documentary for me. In it, they are in a "rap class" being clowned for how they dress, while rapping about how different they feel from other rappers over a sample of Funkadelic's "Knee Deep." These MCs were the direct lyrical descendants of more Afrocentric groups such as the Jungle Brothers and Boogie Down Productions, but when that trend died out, these artists carried the torch by keeping the message in the music. Tribe and De La also continued to crank out the hits for a long time after many of their peers had fallen off.

Long Island hip-hop collective Leaders of the New School were not only brought into the game by the Native Tongues crew but were named by Chuck D, who also grew up on Long Island. The MCs of Leaders of the New School were Dinco D, Charlie Brown, and Busta Rhymes, and each brought something special to the mic, but it was clear from the beginning that Busta Rhymes was the breakout star. Busta, who identified as a Five Percenter, soon signed a solo deal with Elektra Records around the same time as Brand Nubian and KMD, two groups also featuring members of the Nation of Gods and Earths. This Elektra collective was referred to as the God Squad in industry circles, and the music they made broadened the influence of the Five Percent philosophy in hip-hop. The lead MC from KMD, Zev Love X, was also from Long Island. However, after the loss of his brother Subroc he disappeared for a spell and resurfaced as the supervillain MC MF Doom. These are the MCs I was studying when I developed my style.

One day back in 1993 I was shopping my demo tape to labels all around the city, and I found myself in the elevator of the Loud/RCA Records building with Raekwon the Chef of the Wu-Tang Clan. He handed me a cassette with a white cover and the Wu-Tang logo that said "Protect Ya Neck b/w Method Man" and asked me to give it a listen. I thanked him, played it as soon as I got home, and was overwhelmed by the number of different styles that the Wu-Tang Clan had come up with. When I saw the Wu-Tang running around with guns and swords drawn in the "Protect Ya Neck" video on Ralph McDaniels's *Video Music Box*, I was able to put the faces to the names, and that sold it for me forever. The Wu-Tang is the most impressive collection of lyricists that has ever been. Their debut album, *Enter the Wu-Tang (36 Chambers)*, is a master class in the art of hip-hop; it's gorgeous, it's epic, and it was the scariest shit out in 1993. Method Man and Ol' Dirty Bastard were the Clan's breakout stars, but by the time I heard solo projects from Raekwon, Ghostface Killah, and the GZA, I realized that the Wu were on a mission to bring lyrical content to the forefront in a real way.

In the early 1990s, the shadows of Ice Cube, Dr. Dre, and Snoop Dogg loomed large over California, and it was challenging for the more "conscious" West Coast MCs to get noticed.

Groups like Freestyle Fellowship and Souls of Mischief had to work extrahard to catch the ears of hip-hop fans nationwide, and this work was evident in their music. The year 1993 saw the release of both Freestyle Fellowship's *Innercity Griots* and Souls of Mischief's *93 'til Infinity*, two albums that made me reevaluate what I was doing lyrically and helped me to improve my style. In 1994, Chicago's Common, who was still going by Common Sense, dropped his masterpiece of a sophomore album, *Resurrection*, and immediately became my favorite MC. In 1995, Philadelphia's own the Roots also dropped a sophomore album, *Do You Want More?!!!??!*, which featured MCs Malik B and Black Thought absolutely ripping every track to shreds. While Malik B stayed away from live shows and ultimately left the group for personal reasons, the criminally underrated Black Thought began to grow by leaps and bounds. With a style reminiscent of Kool G Rap and Big Daddy Kane, Black Thought became famous for lyrically annihilating anyone he appeared on a track with. Black Thought and I share a birthday, October 3, and so I've always felt a connection to him. On the day we did our first song together, "Rolling with Heat," from the Roots' 2002 album *Phrenology*, he told me that he didn't care about what anyone other than other MCs thought about his rhymes. This has been his gift and his curse, because it seems as if it's only other MCs who truly recognize his gifts. As lead MC for a powerhouse collective like the Roots, he has not been marketed to the masses as the superb MC he is. For my money, Black Thought is my favorite. He is the best working MC in the business and has been for quite some time.

The 1990s saw hip-hop extending beyond the borders of New York City and experiencing a new wave of creative energy, and found acts like Common and the Roots retooling and coming back with sophomore albums that were superior to their debuts. In 1996 the Fugees, from East Orange, New Jersey, but representing

Haiti, redefined the idea of musical self-improvement with their second album, *The Score*. Made up of Haitian-American MCs Wyclef Jean and Pras and East Orange's own Lauryn Hill, the Fugees used a couple of remixes from the producer Salaam Remi and supercharged live shows to make people forget about the frigid reception their debut album, *Blunted on Reality*, received. When they dropped *The Score*, largely produced by Wyclef Jean, Lauryn Hill emerged as one of the best MCs to touch a mic. As an accomplished actor and a talented singer, she was a triple threat. The Fugees blew up because of Lauryn's beautifully sung rendition of Roberta Flack's "Killing Me Softly," but it was clear that Ms. Hill was nice with the rhymes. Influenced by the dope female MCs who paved the way for her, like Queen Latifah and MC Lyte, Lauryn Hill was one of the first female MCs to not just be as good as the boys but to be better than them.

Growing up in New York in the late 1980s and early 1990s meant I didn't get to hear many MCs who were not from the Tri-State. Los Angeles had an entertainment industry so we got to hear West Coast hip-hop in New York, but if you were from the Midwest or down South, you had to head to the coasts to be heard. Groups like 8Ball & MJG, from Memphis, Tennessee; The Geto Boys, from Houston, Texas; UGK, from Port Arthur, Texas; and Outkast, from Atlanta, Georgia, had MCs who could rhyme with the best of the East Coast spitters but had no outlets thru which to get their music heard. To this day, many consider Scarface from the Geto Boys the best storyteller in hip-hop. UGK's Bun B, a friend, a mentor, and one of the best MCs I've ever heard, wasn't noticed nationally until Jay-Z tapped him and his partner Pimp C to rap on a single called "Big Pimpin'" from 1999's *Vol. 3 . . . Life and Times of S. Carter*. Both Big Boi and André 3000 from Outkast are phenomenal MCs who can rap circles around most, but André tapped into something inside himself that allowed him to leave the world of hip-hop and go astral traveling in his rhymes. Among MCs André's name is held in high regard. When the discussion of top five comes up, André 3000 is hardly mentioned; not because he doesn't belong but because he is so good that he's almost a ringer. It's considered a given that André is the best, so he doesn't get to compete. Many people see Suge Knight dissing Bad Boy Records as the most classic moment of the 1995 Source Awards, but for many Southern hip-hop fans the most classic moment was when, shortly after Outkast shocked the East Coast–centric hip-hop industry by winning an award for best group, a young, passionate André 3000 grabbed the mic and defiantly shouted, "The South got something to say!"

While Diddy was taking over New York City's nightclubs, I was working at Nkiru Books in Brooklyn, throwing poetry readings called Foundations that also attracted the borough's best MCs. I was rapping at Lyricist Lounge events and participating in open mics all over the city. The scope of MCs who held my attention began to sway more underground around 1996. The more I focused on becoming a musician, the more I focused on the purity of the art form. On my lunch breaks I would go visit the freestyle titan Supernatural, who lived in Park Slope, a few blocks from Nkiru Books. We would order roti from this sweet lady named Ms. Carmella who had a restaurant on Fifth Avenue, smoke blunts, freestyle, and watch a little Japanese anime. Then I would head back to work, high as shit. Supernatural taught me a lot about MCing and was a mentor to me in many ways, and I applied much of it to the freestyle spirit of those sessions at Nkiru. The group dead prez, consisting of stic.man and M1, both high-caliber MCs, were consistent guests of Foundations as well.

Jean Grae is an MC I've known since I was fifteen years old, before either of us knew exactly what we would end up being for real. To me, she is an artist who defines the spirit of New York City.

Whatever it is you do, if you are serious about your craft, you will have to visit New York City. You have to walk these streets! That's how I feel. That's how I feel about Jean Grae when it comes to lyricism; if you are serious about the art of lyricism, you have to study what Jean is doing. Jean Grae is the purest MC I've ever heard, male or female. Her songs are wonderfully crafted, and she throws every ounce of herself into her art.

While Jean was navigating the industry completely independently, I was signing to Rawkus Entertainment, which would later become a subsidiary on a major label. Yasiin Bey, aka Mos Def, became my partner in rhyme and one of my favorite MCs. Eminem was on the battle scene, getting ready to sign with Dr. Dre's Aftermath. Soon after, Eminem skyrocketed to stardom and became widely hailed as possibly the greatest lyricist ever. One of Eminem's favorites was Pharoahe Monch. Pharoahe, originally a member of the group Organized Konfusion and a stellar MC of mind-blowing proportions, reemerged as a solo artist, signed to Rawkus, and dropped a monster of an album called *Internal Affairs*, which contained one of the all-time greatest hip-hop songs ever recorded, "Simon Says." For me, Pharoahe Monch is the gold standard of great MCing.

In the years I've been rapping professionally, many MCs have come and gone, but few have stood the test of time required to be hailed as one of the greats. Those few, however, remain impressive. Jadakiss from the Lox has been hailed as one of the top five, but his fellow group members Sheek Louch and Styles P are cut from that same cloth. Southern rappers like Lil Wayne and T.I. stepped up to the plate, declaring themselves "great" and "king" respectively, then went on to effectively prove their claims. True to form, the superhero lyricist Eminem put together his own Avengers and called them Slaughterhouse. Slaughterhouse consisted of Joe Budden, Joell Ortiz, KXNG Crooked, and Em's

Detroit partner in rhyme Royce da 5'9". Dudes such as Chance the Rapper and Jay Electronica keep making conscious hip-hop popular for younger fans, while artists like Future and Migos dominate the clubs and the airwaves with what has come to be called trap rap. As polarizing as Drake is as an artist, only a fool would deny his superb lyrical skill, hip-hop credentials, or impact on the culture. Like Eminem, Jay-Z, and Kanye West before him, Drake is such a great MC that he elevated himself to the level of pop star. Not as mainstream as Drake but equally respected are MCs like Kendrick Lamar and J. Cole. Cole, who plays Big Daddy Kane to Kendrick's Rakim, waxes poetically about relationships with women and his place in the music business, while Kendrick takes a more abstract route while discussing the Black condition thru a first-person narrative in his music.

Some hip-hop fans can't see past the hip-hop that was out when they were in high school or college, because that's when they were defining themselves. Music that is attached to the memories you made as you were figuring out who you are will always sound better to your ears than anything that comes after that time; this is our nature. These hip-hop purists will tell you music is getting worse and that younger artists are incapable of making golden-era-quality hip-hop. This is a lie. From NIKO IS to Rapsody, young artists are making hip-hop right now that's every bit as good as the hip-hop of yesteryear. Sure, it may often sound different from classic boom-bap hip-hop, but it should. These young people are influenced by an entirely different paradigm and set of experiences than my generation was. If you aren't the same age as them or didn't grow up with the same circumstances as they did, you don't have enough information to offer a solid critique of their creative output. The older generation should always embrace the art the younger generation has to offer; that's how we grow and maintain our canon.

7

～mm～

Village People

> Each friend represents a world in us, a world not born
> until they arrive, and it is only by this meeting
> that a new world is born.
>
> —ANAÏS NIN

When I entered Brooklyn Tech in the fall of 1989, I had just started to develop my own sense of fashion. Previously, I let my mother take me shopping, and I would simply approve the colors. Now, with hip-hop becoming the dominant factor in my life, I wanted to dress the part. I spent all my school-clothes money in Greenwich Village, and I got a hi-top fade that lived somewhere between Kid's and Play's. In November I had a peace symbol cut into my fade, and by Christmas my style had evolved into a series of hair steps that leaned off the top of my head as if they were drunk. As I got more into hip-hop, I became drawn to the Native Tongues, a loose collection of artists that included Jungle Brothers, De La Soul, A Tribe Called Quest, Queen Latifah, and Monie Love. These artists were taking their fashion cues from the

Afrocentric movement and the downtown house-music culture of the time. They wore loud colors, cowrie shells, and Dave from De La, Q-Tip from A Tribe Called Quest, and both Afrika and Mike Gee from the Jungle Brothers had begun rocking twists or baby dreads, as they were called.

Greenwich Village, known by most New Yorkers as simply the Village, is a magical place to me. Its reputation for being a hub of bohemian counterculture notwithstanding, it's where my parents first met as students at New York University, whose campus is also in the Village. First settled by freed Africans in 1630, by the 1950s Greenwich Village was the meeting point for the Beat Generation poets, and in the 1960s it was the stomping ground for some of the most brilliant artists to ever walk the planet, such as Bob Dylan and Jimi Hendrix. Because of hot spots from Cafe Wha? to the Blue Note, many musicians spent years in the Village honing their craft and often returned to prove it. The comedy clubs of Greenwich Village are where the world's best comedians go to live or die, and as the home of the Stonewall Inn, the Village is the site of one of the most important moments in LGBT history, the Stonewall Riots.

As inspirational as the Village can be in its entirety, no single location represents the soul of the neighborhood more than Washington Square Park. Located in the center of the Village and boasting the triumphant Washington Square Arch, the park is said to be built on top of a pauper's grave. These dead were the people who made up the fabric of New York City—the poets, the gangsters, and the overly criminalized—and their spirits are clearly felt by all who spend time in Washington Square Park. The more time I spent in the park, the less the Village was about shopping for me. The dry fountain in the park's center would often be filled with magicians, painters, hustlers, and musicians, all making a living on the street. They seemed to me to be the freest people in the best city in the world. Washington Square Park was where I would develop my rhymes until they reached a competitive level. Hip-hop fit in quite nicely with the culture of the park.

Freshman year at Brooklyn Tech I started to take my lyrical ability seriously. The year I spent memorizing newly written lyrics paid off in Brooklyn Tech's lunchroom, where fierce lyrical battles were taking place. I had a stockpile of written material, and I could recite new rhymes daily. Because of the large student body of five thousand, Brooklyn Tech had to separate lunchtime in the cafeteria into four shifts over four periods. The rap battles going on in the cafeteria were way more interesting to me at fourteen than class was. When one lunch period ended, we would simply move to a different section and continue rhyming for the next four periods. The lunch tables were our percussion; one person would handle the beat, and we would go.

〰〰〰

Yeah, I cut class, I got a D
Cause History meant nothing to me.
—MIKE GEE, JUNGLE BROTHERS,
"ACKNOWLEDGE YOUR OWN HISTORY"

My rap style was still developing, but I was heavily influenced by the Black consciousness that prevailed in hip-hop culture. These themes found their way into my little raps and gave them content, which ultimately made me a better rapper. I was already clever enough to come up with witty braggadocio in rhyme form, but when I started rhyming about things that were going on in the community, people began to notice me. My punch lines began to hit harder, and the constant lunchroom battling made me better stylistically. Within a month of my first year, I was known as the freshman who could rap as well as any senior. But there was one other.

Justin Cozier was from the heart of Bed-Stuy, and his rap name was Prophetical Prince. He was too small for people to believe he was in high school, and he wore thick glasses that covered his face. On the surface he looked like a nerd, but he had this magical baritone, and he could rhyme for days. His content was as strong as mine, and he had a degree of confidence that I had yet to develop. He and I went head-to-head in the lunchroom as the two nicest freshmen. I can't recall if one of us was declared a winner, but we formed a friendship that day.

What helped Justin and me become even closer was his friendship with another Bed-Stuy dude, Sidda Phillip. Sidda and Justin came from the same block and were inseparable. They were both thin and wore those thick glasses. Many people thought they were brothers. One day soon after my battle with Justin, Sidda came up to me and informed me that he was my cousin. His father was Duwad Phillip, who was editor in chief of the *Daily Challenge*, a local paper that addressed the needs of the African-American community. Before Duwad married Sidda's mother, he was in a relationship with my mother's sister Jo Ann and was my cousin Abena's father. Even though we weren't technically blood, from then on Sidda and I told everyone we were cousins. Soon, Justin, Sidda, and I formed our own rap group. As huge fans of the clothing store the Gap, we named ourselves G.A.P. I was the *G* for Genesis, Sidda took on the name DJ Assault to become the *A*, and Justin as the Prophetical Prince was the *P*. We set about taking our lunchroom act to the next level, which meant recording our songs. Every day after school we would go to either Justin's house or my house with arms full of hip-hop records and tapes that we would create instrumentals from. Back then there was no internet to download instrumentals from, so we created our own using the pause-tape method.

The pause-tape method was a primitive analog way of looping music without vocals until we had enough of an instrumental for a song. We would find a song with four bars of music without any vocals, record those four bars onto a cassette, press pause, and repeat. It would normally take almost an hour to create a three-minute-long instrumental. We were essentially employing the same method that early DJs like Kool Herc used when they created breakbeats, but we weren't sophisticated enough to know that yet. Once we had the musical bed, we would position ourselves between two stereos. One stereo would play our cobbled-together instrumentals, and the other would record us rapping to them. There was no mic; we would just rap into the air. This meant doing entire songs in one take, which seemed perfectly normal then. My memories of those early G.A.P songs are vague, but I do remember having one called "Them Young Boys Ain't Nothing," where the hook was lifted from a line in LL Cool J's "Big Ole Butt." We used to walk around as if a record deal were right around the corner.

Once we had a few songs, Justin played them for his uncle Martin Moore, a DJ who hosted a late-Friday-night hip-hop radio show right in the Village on New York University's station, WNYU 89.1. Eventually Martin Moore would let us come up to the show to select records and rap on the air. Promotional stickers and the tags of some of my favorite artists cluttered the walls, and the room, with all the vinyl in it, felt like heaven to me. We visited that show for about two months.

Going to the Village every day created distance between me and my neighborhood crew, Adrian, Cyriac, George, Pierre, and Saeed. These guys had grown up in Flatlands and Flatbush, and it was all they knew. I spent time in many different neighborhoods, and, as a result, standing on Avenue J and E. Forty-Eighth Street all day and night was no longer cutting it for me. It seemed to me that as we got older, hanging on that corner became less and less of an innocent pursuit. While I still spent a lot of time with Cyriac and Adrian because they were commuting with me to Brooklyn Tech, I started to see the rest of the crew less and less. Outlaws of Destruction was never any match or competition for the bigger gangs, and Saeed eventually got down with the Decepticons. He got shot that year but survived. Pierre, however, was not so lucky and was shot and killed on that corner, God rest his soul.

On the other side of the neighborhood, across Kings Highway, were two dudes who used to go to the Village regularly. I would see them around the way, then see them in the Village as well. Their names were Ryan Chung and Norris Mullings. They were both a couple of years older than my crew; we knew them, but we thought they were a bit off. Ryan had a cut called the Nefertiti, which was a sloped flattop with a patch of blond running down the front. He used to wear nothing but Guess and Ralph Lauren Polo, which he would curiously try to match with argyle socks and sometimes a Woody Woodpecker hat. Norris rocked orange dreadlocks and often wore all black with some black Doc Marten boots. They were both dancers, and they knew all the new dances before I would see them on TV. They knew more about fashion and music than anyone in the neighborhood, which is why they were always headed to the Village. It wasn't long before I started spending more time with them than with the Avenue J crew. Ryan, who later began to call himself Rubix, and Norris, who took the name JuJu, would eventually become my two best friends.

In the eighth grade I cut school about three times and never got caught. In the ninth grade, I took truancy to new heights. At first, it was cutting the middle of the day to stay in the lunchroom with Justin and Sidda, rapping. I still went to my morning and later-afternoon classes. In the late fall, though, I started to completely lose interest in high school. It wasn't just the desire to rap all the time, it was the challenge those teachers had to motivate individual students when five thousand of us were roaming the halls. There was also the added stress of going to high school in Fort Greene in 1989. You couldn't get on the train without having a run-in with either the Decepticons, who seemed to terrorize people as a rite of passage, or the Lo-Lifes, kids from Brownsville and East New York who were stealing clothes from department stores in the city as well as anyone who dared wear Ralph Lauren Polo around them. Their weapons of choice were hammers and box cutters, which earned the name buck fifties from the amount of stitches it would take to sew your face back together after having it sliced by one. The hardware store was a dangerous place in the hood. That year I had to fight in the street to keep my Polo goose down. That $400 coat, which I convinced my mother to get for me for $100 at an outlet in Pennsylvania, created so many problems for me in Brooklyn I stopped wearing Polo for a while.

Every day I would show up at Brooklyn Tech for homeroom at 8:30 a.m. to check in. Then I would head with the rest of the truants to McDonald's on Fulton Street and Flatbush Avenue and stay there until the lunch period. It was important to not get caught in the building while you were cutting. Once you were out of the building, the school security couldn't touch you. We were always faster than them. We would come back for lunch to rap, then once lunch was over, we would pick someone's house for a hooky party. Because both my parents worked late into the night and I was a latchkey kid, my house was often the spot. My hooky parties became legendary. Ten to twenty of us would be on the 2 train headed to my house, loud and rowdy in the middle of the day. We were chased by truant officers every once in a while, but we were never caught. When I arrived at my house, a yellow note from Brooklyn Tech was usually in the mail, meant to inform my parents that I was missing school. That was the extent of the school's efforts at curbing our truancy.

One of the worst feelings in the world anyone can experience is seeing their mother cry. An even worse feeling than that is to be the source of your mother's tears. I made my mom cry more than once during that year, and those are only the times she cried in front of me. My mother had completely dedicated her life to education. She saw it as the first priority, especially for young Black men in America. She felt that my current path was a death sentence, that she was losing her son, and she did not know what to do. Halfway thru the school year my father, who was antiviolence and had never laid a hand on me, let me know that he was at the end of his rope. He told me that since I was too big to spank, if he found out I cut one more time, he would take me in the garage and fight me. To hear my father say this was jarring. I cut back on the hooky parties at home, but that just meant going to hooky parties in Bed-Stuy, Fort Greene, and sometimes as far away as Queens or the Bronx. Sometimes we would go into other high schools in the city such as George Westinghouse, Martin Luther King, or our favorite, LaGuardia, to try to meet girls. Other times we would ride to Coney Island or Far Rockaway beach. We didn't necessarily go for the fun of the destination. Both Coney Island and Far Rockaway were notoriously dangerous neighborhoods, and as I look back, it feels as if we went to prove to ourselves that we weren't scared. By constantly ditching school and creating our own rules, we thought we were on our way to adulthood, when in truth we were on our way to becoming statistics.

During this year I got to know the subway system like the back of my hand. Living in a city with a public transportation system as great as New York's allowed me to think and travel far beyond my inner-city boundaries. If you lived far enough from school, the school would give you a paper subway pass each month to ride for free, but we didn't need that. As far as we were concerned, the subway was free. The turnstiles were so decrepit that you could pull them back a bit and squeeze thru without putting your token in. If you didn't feel like going thru that trouble, you could simply hop over the turnstile or walk thru the exit gate. The token-booth clerks were powerless. If they left the booth to chase you, many more people would hop the turnstile. All they could do was yell, "Pay your fare!"—which we found hilarious. We treated the subway system like our personal playground, banging on the seats and rhyming, not caring about the other passengers. We were rowdy, but we weren't malicious. At least, we didn't intend to be.

As the school year was coming to a close, so was my focus on academics. I was now completely immersed in participating in and creating hip-hop. The only reason I showed up to school at all was to rhyme in the lunchroom. Justin and I, along with Sidda, were cutting school daily, going to high schools all over the city looking for other rappers to battle. After school and on weekends I was hanging out in the Village with Rubix and JuJu, rhyming in Washington Square Park. My parents were now threatening to send me away to boarding school. My father never made good on his threat to fight me, so I was ignoring my parents. That is, until May 1990, when the dean of students at Brooklyn Technical High School asked me not to come back. I remember my mother being devastated, and my father being disappointed. They were on the verge of separating for good that summer, so my delinquency probably could not have come at a worse time. My fourteen-year-old values confused them. I was putting my peers and myself first, and they knew they had raised me better than that.

8

God Lives Thru

You cannot believe in God until you believe in yourself.

—SWAMI VIVEKANANDA

The greatest gift my parents gave me, besides life, was the ability to see beneath the surface. They taught me to not accept things for what they were but to find out what they could be. Perry and Brenda Greene achieved this by giving my brother, Jamal, and me strong African names, and having African cultural influences all thru the house. They took us to the library and to museums every weekend they possibly could. They encouraged a respect for culture and an active, constant search for knowledge. This came back to bite them in the ass when I got to high school and began to question the idea of specialized schools. When I cut class in Roy H. Mann Junior High School, it was because I was sick of being the teacher's pet. Being a nerd didn't earn me any friends, and I did not realize at that young age that nerds grow up to run the world. When I added that to not getting along with some of the other students, lying to stay home became attractive.

When I cut my Brooklyn Tech classes, the root of it was the confusion of being at a school that was supposedly preparing me for a career in science and engineering, when hip-hop music was increasingly becoming my first love.

Even in truancy, my parents' love of education and culture stuck with me. Some days that we skipped school we went to the Museum of Natural History, one of my favorite places in the city. Justin, Sidda, and I left school to see the Reverend Al Sharpton speak in front of City Hall. Sonny Carson, a legendary Black activist from Fort Greene, Brooklyn, had a son named Lumumba Carson, who was a founder of the group X-Clan. X-Clan was the hip-hop part of a larger organization that Lumumba, professionally known as Professor X, was a part of, called Blackwatch. Blackwatch had strong roots in the Brooklyn high schools, and the lead rapper from X-Clan, Brother J, was a favorite of Justin's and mine. When Blackwatch did things like organize a march to City Hall to protest the racially motivated murder of a Black man in Bensonhurst named Yusef Hawkins, we cut school to go to that as well. I missed five out of nine months of school my freshman year. But that year I also read *Nigger* by Dick Gregory, *Soul on Ice* by Eldridge Cleaver, and *Pimp* by Iceberg Slim. These books were not given to me in school. I was educating myself.

When I was fourteen, I became an atheist. I don't remember the exact circumstance that made me say out loud that I do not believe in God, but I do remember the series of events that got me there. Like that of most Black families in America, the faith of the Greenes was rooted in the Christian Baptist tradition. However, we did not go to church every Sunday. My mother developed a pattern over the years that I would guess was a result of Christian guilt. Every Christmas, she would begin to talk about how we needed to spend more time in church. By January, she would begin to take my brother, Jamal, and me to Salem Missionary Baptist Church on E. Twenty-First in Flatbush, Brooklyn, which was presided over by the Reverend Thomas J. Boyd, a pastor my mother had grown up with and the man who married my parents. By Easter, we were going every Sunday, and to Sunday school as well. About a month after Easter the church spirit began to leave my mother. Sundays did not seem to provide enough time for worship and weekend activities. By the beginning of the summer, we would not be in church on Sundays, but my mom would still drop us off at Sunday school whenever she could, or she would make us listen to some church program on the radio so she could feel as if she got at least some churchifying in. I don't remember my father coming with us to church unless it was a special occasion. When I asked him about it years later, he explained that while he considered himself a Christian, the energy of the church just wasn't for him.

The energy of the church? I don't think I was able to articulate it as a child, but I think I felt the same way my father did. I didn't like the energy, and I didn't like the answers I was getting to the questions I asked. I first began my dissent in Sunday school. The stories they told us from the Bible seemed no different from stories about Santa Claus and the Easter Bunny, which by nine years old I knew to be fiction. One of the fundamental tenets of dogmatic Christianity is that the Bible is God's word, and God is infallible, therefore the Bible is infallible. But that was not good enough for my precocious mind. I needed the stories to make sense, and the only answer I got was that if it was in the Bible, it must be true.

By the time I was twelve, I was sure how I felt about the church. I did not want to go, and I told my parents this. I was too old for Sunday school, and I did not like having to dress up for church. In Baptist churches, people dress as if they are going to meet Jesus and they ain't coming back. The perfumes and colognes were in full effect. The hairdos, the hats, the dresses, the suits were all on display. It seemed to me, even at a young age, that these people were dressing up to impress each other, not for God. A child hears whispers, and I heard people talk about one another's outfits and personal business. Another Baptist tradition is a full day of church on Sunday. We would get there by 9:00 a.m. and not leave until 4:00 or 5:00 p.m. I didn't understand why we needed to dress up and be uncomfortable for so long. The God they were asking me to believe in couldn't have intended this.

"If God is all seeing and all knowing, then he's seen me naked. So why do we have to dress up to go to church?" I remember asking my mom this at nine years old. She replied, "We dress up to show respect to the church and to God. We show up in our best clothes to show that we honor God." My reply? "I thought God don't want us to care about material items, though."

These were my selfish thoughts. My selfless side was focused on the problems in the world. I had watched the Space Shuttle *Challenger* explode on live TV. New York City was the crime capital of the country in the mid-1980s. The Cold War was at its climax, and the news was talking every night about the end of the world by nuclear fallout. I didn't understand how a loving God could allow these things to happen. I started to think that maybe this "God," with his crazy stories and rituals, was the most active figment of our imagination.

As a Christian, my mom began to worry about where my thoughts on religion were headed. As an academic, she knew that she could not control my beliefs, she could only provide me with options. She set out to provide me with the only options she knew, and she took me to visit other Christian churches of different denominations. The only one I remember was the Catholic church, because it felt like church lite to me. Although the rituals were more solemn and involved, it seemed as if the Catholic church required less of its followers' collective attention span. We would go to mass, listen and watch quietly for forty-five minutes, and leave, church quota filled. No long, drawn-out singing (although I later came to have great appreciation for gospel music), no testifying, no three-hour sermons, and you could wear what you wanted! I was Catholic for about two months.

As I approached puberty, my attention was taken away from God and given to girls and my peers. I began to come into my own as a person and establish my own belief system, and naturally my thoughts became more selfish. The stories in the Bible began to make less sense to my analytical mind. A literal interpretation of the Bible was all anyone provided for me, and I was not familiar with the concept of allegory. The idea of creation being started by a big bang, while only a theory, was a lot more plausible to me at fourteen than the literal interpretations of the Bible I was expected to believe. Religion was battling science for my heart and mind, and science was winning. I did not know the difference between religion and spirituality. As far as I knew, they were one and the same.

Malcolm X brought me back to God. At thirteen years old, el-Hajj Malik el-Shabazz, also known as Malcolm X, became the greatest influence over me, other than my parents and my city. Most things a child takes interest in are started from influences in the home. As African-Americans who came of age during the late 1960s, Perry and Brenda Greene continued to support a pro-Black, culturally nationalistic lifestyle. We celebrated Kwanzaa with the same passion that we celebrated Christmas. African and African-American art was throughout the house, and Black history was considered to be world history. In our house, February was just another month. I learned about such people as Matthew Henson, Charles Drew, Ida B. Wells, Sojourner Truth, and Nat Turner all year round.

Hip-hop was having a huge effect on me during puberty, and the hip-hop of that time was very pro-Black. The references that hip-hop was making to leaders from our past, such as Malcolm X, combined with what I learned about Malcolm at home, and the news that Spike Lee was directing a feature about Malcolm's life starring Denzel Washington, created a perfect revolutionary storm in my head. In what was a genius marketing move, Spike Lee was selling *X* hats out of his 40 Acres and a Mule shop long before the movie was finished. This shop was located exactly across the street from my high school, Brooklyn Tech. After Spike moved out of the retail business, that location would become the first Carol's Daughter, long before Oprah discovered Brooklyn's home-grown multicultural beauty company. This was obviously a special corner of Fort Greene.

Along with 8 Ball jackets, Guess jumpers, and Hi-Tec boots, the *X* baseball hat was fashionable in 1989. Black kids were going to school with kente-cloth book bags and T-shirts that read IT'S A BLACK THING, YOU WOULDN'T UNDERSTAND. Black pride was experiencing its first American renaissance. Determined to not be seen as a bandwagon rider, I devoured *The Autobiography of Malcolm X* long before the movie came out. The first thing that struck me was the rawness of the first half. I was reading Donald Goines and Iceberg Slim novels, so I wasn't shocked by Malcolm's behavior, but to know that this was a real person who was now seen as a great leader was impressive. When Malcolm goes from being a selfish hustler to realizing the vast disparity between whites and Blacks in America, it is convincing because he does not seem to have any agenda but the truth.

Years later when I worked at Nkiru Books, we would sell a cassette of Malcolm X's speeches called *Make It Plain*. That was the perfect title, because the way Malcolm made things plain made them hard to argue with. I had never read anything that talked about racism so plainly and made so much sense on the matter until I read his autobiography. After reading about Malcolm's ultimate spiritual conversion toward the end of the book, I concluded that if Malcolm was right about everything else, he must be right about God. I did not decide to follow Islam, but I decided that God must be real for a man like Malcolm to exist.

The more real God became for me, the more I began to have conversations with my peers about what God was. When I was a teenager growing up in Brooklyn, the people who seemed to me to be best equipped at discussing the concept of God were members of the Five Percent Nation of Gods and Earths. Started in Harlem in 1964 by Clarence Smith, also known as Clarence 13X, the Five Percent Nation of Gods and Earths was an offshoot of the Nation of Islam. A former student of Malcolm X's, Clarence 13X believed that if the white man was the devil, as the Nation of Islam had taught him, then the Black man must surely be God. He called Black women who accepted this belief Earths. Clarence 13X became known as Allah the Father to his followers, and he taught them that Black people were the makers, the owners, and the cream of planet Earth. He developed systems of communication called the Supreme Mathematics. Clarence 13X's followers became known as Five Percenters, and they would often declare that there is no mystery God in the sky. They pointed out that the world's image of God is a white man, and that contrary to this belief, the Black man becomes God when he attains knowledge of himself. This idea was attractive to young Black people who were under the boot of systemic oppression.

To become a Five Percenter you had to study and memorize the 120 lessons, which back then you could only get by knowing a Five Percenter personally. Part of the 120 lessons was that the Five Percenters are the poor righteous teachers who know that the living God is the son of man, that 85 percent of the population is mentally enslaved and does not know who God is, and that 10 percent of the population are the rich, the devils who teach lies about God to the poor. According to the Supreme Mathematics that Five Percenters also had to memorize, each number from 0 to 9 represented an ideal. The series of numbers used to define a date would tell you the Mathematics for that day. The number 1 represented knowledge, and the number 2 represented wisdom, so when a Five Percenter was asked on January 12 what the day's Mathematics was, the right and exact answer would be knowledge wisdom. Five Percenters took powerful names like Justice Allah and Knowledge Born, while referring to one another as God or Godbody. They would often form ciphers in which they would build and destroy. This is Five Percenter speak for standing in a circle and testing one another's understanding of the true nature of God.

My introduction to the Five Percent philosophy came thru many people, but most notably John Forté of Refugee Camp All-Stars fame, a Brooklyn MC who was a year older than me. In addition to producing my first demo tape and teaching me how to structure a song, John also introduced me to his mentors, Five Percent cats named Alyasha and Shabar Allah. Alyasha, a light-skinned mixed dude, was a fashion designer who helped Russell Simmons start the Phat Farm clothing label, and Shabar was a dark-skinned dude who ran the streets of Brownsville with gangsters and hustlers. They were on opposite ends of the Godbody spectrum, but getting to know them gave me a complete picture of the diversity of thought Five Percent philosophy had to offer. I was impressed with how these cats spoke. They had seemingly infinite wells of knowledge and could speak with a confident air of authority on any subject. The language of the Five Percent was almost mystical in nature, and learning it made me feel that I was part of a secret club that only allowed in the best and the brightest. Shabar, who was also an early influence on the Wu-Tang Clan, had a saying that found its way into a Method Man lyric—"I don't call you son cuz you mine, I call you sun cuz you shine." I found this to be brilliant.

As I got older, identifying as a Five Percenter began to have less appeal to me. The stories of big-headed scientists and grafted white devils that originated from the Nation of Islam started to seem hokey, and some of the math just didn't add up. Besides seeing basic logical flaws in some of the original lessons I was receiving, I began to see many so-called Godbody dudes act less than Godly, and this shook my faith in the teachings. I understood the historical purpose of some of the mythology that laid the foundation for both the Nation of Islam and the Five Percent Nation, and why it was necessary. Much like pastors who use biblical allegories, early leaders of these movements needed parables of Black achievements that would stimulate the minds of poor Black people who had been taught all of their lives that their Blackness was a sin. In the information age, these parables began to lose luster. With that said, I still know many members of the Five Percent Nation who leave the mythology in the past and focus on what I believe is the true core of the Five Percent philosophy: information leads to knowledge, knowledge leads to wisdom, wisdom leads to understanding, and once you have all of that, you start demanding justice. When applied properly, this lesson becomes a diving board that gives you access to a pool of self-determination.

Science and spirituality are both the search for the unknown. They are strange bedfellows but bedfellows nonetheless. While science requires empirical evidence, spirituality requires faith. Something exists before and after us, running thru and connecting all of us. There is a natural balance. Scientists bravely test our limits and build our world; science makes us the best we can be. But science, admittedly, does not have all of the answers. Science does not answer the mysteries of creation, or where consciousness and self-awareness come from, or how and why we make art. These mysteries connect all living things, and all living things should be shown compassion and kindness. Call it what you want. Call it God, Jesus, Yahweh, Allah, Buddha. Call it Ralph like the head of lettuce Rerun had on that one episode of *What's Happening!!* Or don't call it anything at all, be atheist, be agnostic, I don't care. Compassion is the key. As long as you remain kind and compassionate at all times, who you worship or what rituals you do or don't participate in don't matter. Abraham Lincoln said many great things, but one of the greatest was:

When I do good, I feel good.
When I do bad, I feel bad.
That's my religion.

9

The Nigga Ya Love to Hate

> I never learned hate at home, or shame.
> I had to go to school for that.
> —DICK GREGORY

My freshman year of high school was an intense rite of passage. I was thrown out into the cold to face the wolves and I came back healthy, but mentally weary. I was happy when summer arrived, and I looked forward to riding my bike, going to basement parties, and hanging out at Kings Plaza mall with my crew. My parents had different plans. They informed me that I was going to go away to boarding school. I couldn't believe what I was hearing. It had always been the city and my parents that raised me together.

Perry and Brenda weren't trying to hear any of that. They packed lunches, threw me in the car, and headed to New England. The first school we ended up at was Choate, in Wallingford, Connecticut. The only thing I remember was it seemed super-white, super-uptight, and super-cliquey. I protested loudly. The next school my parents took me to visit was a military academy. This was a shrewd move on their part. Their next move was equally inspired. My parents drove me to Cheshire Academy, in Cheshire, Connecticut, just outside New Haven.

Cheshire Academy sold itself as an international school, and out of its 120 students, about one-third were indeed from other countries. Everyone we met on that visit was extremely pleasant and outgoing, teachers and students alike. However, after seeing that military academy, I was prepared to go anywhere but there. Cheshire accepted me as a student on two conditions. First, I had to attend summer school in Cheshire to learn how the school worked. Second, I was to repeat the ninth grade to make up for the months of classes I'd cut. So here I was, son of two educators, former honor-roll, straight-A student, being left back. It was humiliating, but at least I would be around a brand-new set of kids, most of whom would have no idea that I'd already gone to ninth grade.

That summer, my parents and I packed into my father's Volkswagen Jetta and drove two hours up I-95 to Cheshire, Connecticut. We arrived on a campus that looked bare. During the school year there were about 120 students, but during the summer only about 50. I was given a room in a dormitory named after someone named Van Der Pool, and it was called VDP for short. Students who had been there over the last year would often sing the hook to the Boogie Down Productions song "Stop the Violence," replacing BDP with VDP:

> One two three! The crew is called VDP!
> And if you wanna go to the tip top!
> Stop the violence in hip-hop! Why ohhh!

My roommate in VDP was a Japanese student named Koji Shitoto. Koji loved hip-hop music and culture. The idea that not only suburban white kids but Japanese kids, from the other side of the world, loved a music that was still local was mind-blowing. It forever altered the way I saw hip-hop's potential as a culture. Koji didn't love hip-hop from a distance. He sought to actively participate, especially thru dance. He mastered the West Coast–based, electric boogaloo style of B-boying made famous by Fred Berry, aka Rerun, from the TV show *What's Happening!!* Koji never missed an opportunity to talk to me about new hip-hop, and he danced all day long.

Out of the fifty or so summer-school kids that year, the majority were students from Asia like Koji. They came early to get a better mastery of English before the official school year. That summer I was educated on the differences between Japanese, Chinese, Vietnamese, and Korean cultures, all of which were represented at Cheshire Academy. There were some kids from European countries like Spain and Holland, but most of the foreign student body was from the Far East. The academy used this as a selling point, but not everyone in town, who we called townies, was as enthused about the academy's foreign presence.

James Van Der Beek, who would later star as Dawson on the hit TV show *Dawson's Creek*, is from Cheshire. He performed exceptionally well in public school, so much so that he became one of the only townies to be invited to attend the academy, and we became friends. Some of the other townies weren't as friendly as James, and they made their negative feelings about the academy kids known by being generally unpleasant or trying to bully us on sight. While we walked back and forth to the local 7-Eleven, they would yell at us as they drove past us in their vehicles. If we yelled back, things would escalate and the townies would throw stuff at us. On one occasion, one of the townies threw a battery at us. When I retaliated by throwing the soda I was drinking at their car, the car stopped, the window rolled down, and the barrel of a gun came out of it. My friends and I began to run toward the school while being chased by gunshots.

In September of 1993, I started my new life at Cheshire Academy. Even though a few of the townies tried their best to make me feel unwelcome, I was excited to face the unknown. I knew I would miss my friends, but I was already making new friends, like Koji. My parents also made a deal with me that worked out well when I was in Brooklyn for the weekends. As long as I kept my grades up, I would be treated like an adult when I came home. I had no curfew as long as I told them where I would be, and I moved from my room into the basement. My mother, who was still working on her Ph.D., transformed my old room into her office.

Everything seemed to be starting to fall back into place. Hip-hop was now not only my favorite music, it was my cultural identity, and I depended on it to keep me in touch with New York City. I couldn't hang out in the Village as much as I wanted to, and the days of recording with G.A.P seemed to be in the distant past. I had a void in my life, so I devoured everything that had to do with hip-hop. I bought every record I could afford, and I taped every radio and video show that supported the music. I tore thru all the magazines—*Rap Masters, Word Up, Right On!, Black Beat, Source,* and *Rap Pages*—reading every article. I ripped out the pictures and covered my walls from floor to ceiling with pictures of hip-hop artists. I had pictures of Biz Markie and Cool V with 40 Below Timberlands on, Ice Cube's St. Ides ad, and De La Soul holding up a handwritten sign that said YOU ARE PISSING US OFF WITH YOUR PICTURES, while pretending to be peeing. My room was like a modern hip-hop museum. People would come from other dorms to check it out. School tour guides would stop by and use my room as an example of Cheshire Academy's diversity. My dreads would cause the other students to ask me if they could touch my hair, and my name was hard for them to pronounce. I began calling myself TK, short for Talib Kweli. After seeing pictures of De La Soul's Posdnuos with glasses, I started rocking a pair of specs to emulate one of my heroes. I developed a brand-new image for a brand-new situation.

For the first couple of months at Cheshire Academy I struggled academically. I was not used to studying by myself, and I was horrible at self-motivation. The time at Cheshire was carefully regimented. There was not much room for distraction, but I managed to distract myself anyway. Every morning we would have to be up for a mandatory breakfast at 7:30. By 8:30 we were in homeroom, then in class by 9:00. There was a lunch break, more classes until 3:00, then we had some sort of mandatory after-school activity such as drama club or a sport. After this activity was mandatory dinner, then free time for about an hour. From 8:00 to 10:00 p.m. was mandatory study hall, with lights out by 10:30. I wasn't used to this type of discipline. The stress of the schoolwork got to me early. This was before the days of Wi-Fi and smartphones everywhere, so I would communicate with my family thru letters and the one pay phone in VDP that everyone in the dorm used. One night that October, I broke down and called my father, who had just become the dean of continuing education at NYU. I begged him to let me come home. I was overwhelmed by the regimen, was behind on the schoolwork, and felt utterly alone. When he calmly explained that he couldn't do that, I started to cry. He stayed on the phone with me for a while, giving me a pep talk about manning up and finishing what I started. He reminded me that my actions had led me to Cheshire, and now I had to take responsibility for those actions. This conversation was a turning point in my education. Little did I know I would be having the same conversation with my son two months into his first year at a boarding school, twenty years later.

Halfway thru my first year in Cheshire, I was starting to acclimate to the ways of the academy. As I made friends, I began to excel academically, and I joined every extracurricular activity I could. I was the Brooklyn version of Max Fischer from Wes Anderson's film *Rushmore*, spending time in drama club, with the yearbook staff, assisting the soccer and lacrosse teams, making the honor roll, joining the Blue Key Society, giving campus tours as the token Negro, and being everyone's Black friend. On Martin Luther King, Jr.'s birthday, which in 1991 was still not observed as a holiday at Cheshire Academy, I staged a sit-in. By explaining to almost every student individually that I'd found a way for us to have a day off from schoolwork, I convinced the entire student body to stay seated when the bell rang for class after breakfast that morning. We spent the day in that cafeteria learning about the history of civil rights. In drama club, I became a popular performer from playing the fisherman in a production of *The Fisherman and His Wife*, and when I played baseball for Cheshire Academy that spring, I became the surprise clutch player that our team needed. I was determined to prove my worth to myself and to the school, and I was finally behaving in a way that would make my family proud again.

～✍～

Kicking shit called street knowledge
Why more niggas in the pen than in college?

—ICE CUBE, "THE NIGGA YA LOVE TO HATE"

The first concert I ever saw was Ice Cube. I found out he was going to perform in New Haven, Connecticut, with Del the Funky Homosapien and WC and the Maad Circle, at a small rock-and-roll club called Toad's Place. As the former lead rapper of

N.W.A, Ice Cube had had a recent and public financial feud between him, the group, its founder Eazy-E, and their manager, Jerry Heller. Justin Cozier, my old partner from G.A.P, was a huge fan of N.W.A, and Ice Cube in particular, before this feud began. I couldn't get into the West Coast "gangsterism" they were selling. I wasn't sophisticated enough to recognize the artistic merit of Eazy-E, MC Ren, Dr. Dre, Ice Cube, and Yella, the men who made up what according to the FBI was the most dangerous music group in America at the time. Justin would always tell me back in Brooklyn Tech that I needed to get into N.W.A, but when Ice Cube left to record his debut album, *AmeriKKKa's Most Wanted*, many East Coast hip-hop fans, including Justin and me, fully embraced Ice Cube's movement. I had to see this show.

I took a public bus from Cheshire to New Haven, which was about a half-hour ride. What I remember most about passing thru the different cities of Meriden, Wallingford, and Hamden before finally arriving in New Haven is how pristine they seemed. New Haven was the first place I saw any of Connecticut's hood elements. From the bus window I began to see crackheads, dealers, hustlers of all sorts. It felt like a tiny version of New York City. After a couple of blocks, the urbanization subsided and I began to see more cafés than liquor stores. Smack-dab in the middle of New Haven is the campus of Yale University. Toad's Place was a restaurant built on Yale's campus in 1975 that became a music venue in 1976. Artists such as the Rolling Stones, Billy Joel, and John Lee Hooker played there, and Bob Dylan performed his longest concert ever, five hours, at Toad's in January 1990. This place reeked of rock-and-roll history.

Because Toad's Place had a fence to separate the legal drinkers from the underage concertgoers, they could put on shows for all ages. These shows traditionally started early, and I was the first one there at 7:00 p.m. when the doors opened. I found a spot directly in front of the stage, which was much smaller than I imagined, and waited for the show to begin.

The Ice Cube concert was spectacular to me. First, the West Coast hip-hop legend WC opened with his group, the Maad Circle, which boasted an unknown rapper named Coolio who would soon achieve international fame. I wasn't familiar with their songs, but I enjoyed watching their West Coast mannerisms, which were still a complete mystery to me. Next up was Del the Funky Homosapien, a rapper who was being marketed by Elektra Records as Ice Cube's weird, rapping cousin. Del had a song out that I liked called "Mista Dobalina," and even though he was from Oakland and running with a Los Angeles–based gangsta-rap crew, I related to Del's brand of hip-hop music and subject matter. These openers properly whet my appetite for Ice Cube. After Del performed, someone came and put three fake headstones on the stage, one reading R.I.P N.W.A, one reading R.I.P JERRY HELLER, and the last reading R.I.P EAZY-E. No one could know back then that Eazy-E would pass away due to complications from AIDS four years later. All that could be known was that Ice Cube was angry with his former group, and he wasted no time in letting his fans in on it. He came out and stalked that stage like a panther, getting the audience emotionally charged while performing songs from *AmeriKKKa's Most Wanted* and his *Kill at Will* EP. He rocked ferocious versions of "The Nigga Ya Love to Hate," "Jackin for Beats," and "Gangsta's Fairytale." He made the audience laugh while performing "Once Upon a Time in the Projects" and closed the show by bringing WC and Del back on for an encore. The concert was better than I had imagined it could be. It was inspirational for me to see a Black man with a microphone saying anything he wanted. Some of it was derogatory, some of it was political, but all of it was free. In that moment, Ice Cube seemed to possess superhuman powers. I knew I had to get back to New York City and start my career as soon as possible.

Every weekend I could, I would leave Connecticut for Brooklyn, drop bags off, and head to the Village. Hanging out in Greenwich Village allowed me to become part of a loose-knit fraternity of MCs who would come there from all different boroughs. Washington Square Park in particular was the hub for artistic expression of all sorts, and rhyming was no exception. We freestyled combatively, often calling out MCs for kicking written rhymes. These battles became so intensely entertaining that they would draw huge crowds, made up of both people who loved hip-hop and passersby who had no clue. Legends of that period include 8-Off the Assassin, who is now professionally known as Agallah; Supernatural; and Mos Def, who is now professionally known by his chosen name, Yasiin Bey.

Yasiin was one of my favorites to watch because he never looked the part. While we were wearing Polo, Tommy Hilfiger, and Timberland boots, Yasiin would show up in gabardine suits. He already had a record deal with his crew from Bed-Stuy named Urban Thermo Dynamics, and their videos were being played on *Video Music Box.* He was also doing bit parts on short-lived TV shows like *You Take the Kids* with Nell Carter and *Here and Now* with Malcolm-Jamal Warner. However, none of this professional success stopped Yasiin, born Dante Terrell Smith in Brooklyn, from being right there at the center of those Washington Square Park rhyme ciphers.

Even back then, Yasiin's rhymes were more engaging than his carefully put-together outfits or burgeoning acting résumé. His laid-back style was simple yet incredibly informed. He modeled his pattern after Double Trouble, his audacity after Chuck D, and his powers of observation after Slick Rick. Once he layered his thick Brooklyn accent on top of this mix of influences, it made what he was doing seem effortlessly natural. If that wasn't enough to make Yasiin stand out from the crop of Washington Square MCs, he also possessed a uniquely organic singing voice that he would add to his flow. The first time I heard him rhyme was with Urban Thermo Dynamics, which consisted of him, a female rapper named Ces, and his younger brother DCQ, who he credits with first inspiring him to start rhyming. While Ces went harder than any other female rapper I'd seen up until then, and DCQ had a break-out-star-quality flow, it was Mos Def whose verses I found myself rapping along with.

IO

~~~

The Salad Days

There's, I think, how we like to think of ourselves,
and there's how we're perceived. More often than not, those two
are on opposite ends of the room. But, sometimes
they dance closely together.

—JOHN FORTÉ

While I was toiling away at Cheshire Academy during the school year, my neighborhood friends JuJu and Rubix were going to school in Brooklyn during the day and establishing themselves as great dancers on the club scene at night. Hip-hop dance then was a mix of old-school B-boy moves, martial arts, and the African and Latin influences that were permeating the house music scene. The best dancers at the clubs were not asking girls to dance; they were still forming ciphers and battling it out.

During the weekends, I would accompany JuJu and Rubix, who were both two years older than me, to these nightclubs. Because I had no dancing skills whatsoever, I became the coat holder. If a record like "J. Beez Comin' Through" by the Jungle

Brothers, "Hot Music" by Soho, or "Give It Up or Turnit a Loose" by James Brown came on, JuJu and Rubix would turn to me and say "Hold my coat" as they jumped into the dance cipher.

Being so immersed in the dance scene, JuJu and Rubix earned the respect of party promoters all over the city, and they parlayed this respect into getting us into the hottest hip-hop clubs for free. The most memorable club experience for me from this time was seeing KRS-One record pieces of his live album at a club called the Building. Despite my age, JuJu and Rubix got me in, and I was introduced to a world where celebrities mixed and mingled with the common folk. That night I met and took pictures with Jamalski, Ali Shaheed Muhammad from A Tribe Called Quest, and Nikki D. When I ran into the comedian Tommy Davidson outside the bathroom, I asked him to do his famous Sugar Ray Leonard impersonation from the TV show *In Living Color*, and he obliged. If meeting these celebrities was the night's appetizer, then the main course was watching KRS-One rock that club. The Building had no stage, only a balcony where KRS's brother Kenny Parker was deejaying from. At around midnight, with no formal introduction, KRS grabbed the mic and started rocking along with his brother, right from that balcony. Up until then the concerts I had seen were all on stages, with a lot of buildup before the main act. KRS was rocking this club the old-school way. As I was jumping up and down in the air along with JuJu and Rubix as KRS performed classics like "South Bronx" and "The Bridge Is Over," I remember thinking that this was the spirit of hip-hop. It amazed me that this man could hang over a balcony with nothing but a DJ and a microphone and rock a nightclub until it felt like a concert venue.

That summer all I wanted to do was go to Washington Square Park during the day and nightclubs at night to rhyme. My mother helped me get a summer job as a counselor at the Medgar Evers

College summer camp program, and I spent all of the money I made buying hip-hop singles on vinyl so I could record over the instrumental tracks. Every day JuJu and Rubix would meet me at Medgar Evers College after work and we would head to the Village. This was still pre-Giuliani New York, and artists of all types made Washington Square Park their home away from home. Amid the comedians, painters, jugglers, and musicians, we were staging epic rhyme ciphers that competed for crowds with these other artists. Rubix and I would join Yasiin Bey, Supernatural, Jean Grae, and others in public rhyme sessions while JuJu would provide the beatbox. It was always amusing to watch JuJu stop beatboxing abruptly after doing it for an hour straight, then exclaim, "My lips are tired, someone else has to beatbox!"

One of the people who had a huge impact on my rhyme style was John Forté, the same guy who had introduced me to so much about the Five Percent Nation. When Rubix introduced me to Forté, as he was calling himself then, the first thing I noticed about him was his style of dress: he was wearing Zodiac shoes and jeans with huge holes. His dreadlocks peeked out of a French-style tam. This meticulous bohemian look was deliberately put together to look as if he didn't care. I was trying to achieve that look, and he pulled it off with seemingly little effort. John Forté's fashion sense, charming attitude, and rhyming abilities made him a welcome asset to our crew. Soon he was introducing Rubix, JuJu, and me to a whole new world of music-industry events. Even though John and I were about the same age, he seemed to be way more serious about hip-hop, and he was certainly further along in his artistry. He knew every club bouncer and DJ in the city and had made enough of a name for himself to be a regular at the hottest hip-hop events. As if all of this weren't enough to tighten our friendship, John also attended boarding school, at the prestigious Phillips Exeter Academy in New Hampshire.

In September 1992 I was a senior, starting my final year at Cheshire Academy. I had established myself as one of the school's most popular students, which wasn't hard for a kid from Brooklyn to do in a school of 120 students. I came back in September more confident than when I had left and focused on getting into college. The only school that seemed to fit me was New York University. NYU was where my parents met, and it was where my father currently worked, which meant I might catch a break on the tuition. NYU was also located right in the middle of Greenwich Village, my favorite place to be. When Cheshire Academy suggested that I apply to at least eight schools so that I would have enough backups, I ignored that advice and only applied to NYU. I thought that if I focused all my energy on one school instead of eight, I could will my acceptance into existence.

Even though hip-hop was engulfing my life, theater was giving me strength in the academic world. I highlighted these strengths and applied to NYU's Tisch School of the Arts, hoping to get into their experimental-theater program. I wrote an essay in my application that the university liked, and I was invited to New York for an audition. I nailed that audition and was accepted into Tisch. This was happy news for my family, especially my mother, who'd thought she was losing me a few years before.

11

Friends with Rappers

I am America. I am the part you won't recognize. But get used to me.
Black, confident, cocky; my name, not yours; my religion,
not yours; my goals, my own; get used to me.

—MUHAMMAD ALI

I graduated from Cheshire Academy in June 1993.
Even though my parents were in the middle of a separation, they
came together to support me, and I will never forget how elated
my mother was. The worst thing in the world I could be to my
mother was a high school dropout, and she'd believed that was the
direction I'd been heading in a few short years back. Now I was
graduating with honors from a prestigious boarding school and
heading to my parents' alma mater, the place where they met, New
York University. Ever the rebel, I stuck a STOP APARTHEID NOW
sticker to the top of my graduation cap, making one last political
statement before I left Cheshire Academy. I did not attend my
prom or my senior trip; I was more eager to get back to what I
considered the real world, Washington Square Park.

Upon arriving in Brooklyn, I went to what was now my mother's house, dropped off my bags, and headed right back out to the Village. I was beginning to hit my stride as a lyricist, and my name was beginning to be recognized in hip-hop circles around the city. JuJu, Rubix, John Forté—who was also going to NYU, to the Stern School of Business, and who was my official roommate in the dorms—and I began our summer innocently, mostly by hanging out at an incense stand that John's friend Jason set up in front of Tower Records on West Third and Broadway every day. While Jason would hawk incense and oils, we would mostly chase girls up and down Broadway, always ending up back at that incense stand. Once we had enough of that, we would head to Washington Square Park and freestyle until the clubs opened. Inside the clubs, JuJu and Rubix would dance all night, while John and I would find rhyme ciphers in the club and rap loudly over tracks with vocals blaring out of massive speakers. There were weekly parties that we never missed, such as Soul Kitchen at SOB's on Mondays, where you could hear soul classics while eating fried chicken and drinking 40s, or Sticky Mikes on Thursdays, which was a party that played nothing but dance-hall reggae. But none of these parties generated excitement like a party Funkmaster Flex was going to be deejaying at.

Funkmaster Flex got his start in the Bronx during the early days of hip-hop as a young DJ following his heroes to all the hip-hop clubs to watch them spin. By 1992, along with Pete Rock, he was the go-to DJ on New York City's WBLS when Marley Marl was unavailable. Marley Marl and Red Alert were beginning to age, and Funkmaster Flex and Pete Rock were the new kids on the scene, with more knowledge about hip-hop's current trends. Funkmaster Flex used his time on WBLS to promote parties he was deejaying at and soon became the most sought-after hip-hop DJ in the city. However, while hip-hop was popular in the clubs and on urban stations, it was not played on pop stations like Z100 and Hot 97 at all. Z100 was strictly Top 40, while Hot 97 leaned heavily on freestyle music, a dance/pop musical hybrid that appealed to New York's Latinx community. Funkmaster Flex made his name so hot in the clubs that soon Hot 97 was paying him to play hip-hop records for two hours on Friday and Saturday nights on their station. This move brought tens of thousands of new listeners to Hot 97 every weekend and created an even larger profile for Funkmaster Flex. His manager at the time, Jessica Rosenblum, helped to parlay Funkmaster Flex's popularity into an unprecedented reign over New York City's hip-hop club scene. Jessica ran Stress Entertainment, and with Funkmaster Flex as her star DJ, she began to bring all of the city's hottest hip-hop DJs into her fold.

John Forté was already a staple on the club scene, but when Jessica found out how well he could rhyme, she signed him as Stress Entertainment's first rapper. She paid for studio time for him to record at D&D Studios, the most hip-hop-friendly recording studio in the city. John recorded a lot of songs, but none of them appealed to Jessica's more commercial sensibilities. One day she decided to have him record with Funkmaster Flex, who had secured a record deal with Nervous Records for his mixtapes. Flex had a friend from the Bronx named 9 Double M who had a song called "6 Million Ways to Die" that they were about to release as a single. For the B-side, John recorded the song "The Boom Spot." I helped write the hook, and I also performed background vocals on it. Working on that record in D&D that night made me feel as if my time to shine couldn't be that far off.

Soon after becoming one of New York City's hottest party promoters, Jessica linked up with a Howard University student famous for throwing elaborate events named Sean Puffy Combs. Jessica had the relationships with the venues, and Puffy, who would eventually come to be known as Diddy, had the swagger and the crowds. JuJu, Rubix, and I wanted to be in the "industry," so we would often visit John at Jessica's Chelsea apartment, which doubled as the Stress Entertainment office. John would hang out there soaking up game from Jessica, and all types of artists would come thru constantly. DJs like Enuff, Big Kap, and Mad Wayne were trying to snap up whatever gigs Funkmaster Flex could not do, so they were always around. The DJs Jessica managed soon started calling themselves the Flip Squad, and Funkmaster Flex got a few of them guest spots on Hot 97 as well. Because of Funkmaster Flex's influence, Hot 97 switched from its freestyle format to an all-hip-hop format. While they were not the first all-hip-hop FM station—that honor goes to KDAY from Los Angeles—they were certainly the biggest, and the first in hip-hop's birthplace. Hot 97 captured the pulse of New York's hip-hop community, and its format became the gold standard for hip-hop radio for years to come.

Stress Entertainment expanded at a rapid rate, and Jessica needed foot soldiers to promote her growing list of weekly parties. From Tramps on Twenty-First Street to the Supper Club on Forty-Seventh, Jessica had the city's hip-hop nightlife scene on fire. Every time she looked up from her desk, she would see JuJu, Rubix, and me milling about, hanging out with John Forté. Jessica put us to work handing out flyers for parties. The internet age was still a ways off, and she very much depended on our canvassing the city to get the word out. We were assigned different neighborhoods to hit, mostly in Manhattan, and we did not come back until all of the flyers were gone. We were not paid much, but we got access to all of the hottest hip-hop parties in the city. This was almost better than cash to us. We could put whoever we wanted on the guest list, so we would spend our days meeting girls on the street, inviting them to the parties, and then impressing them with our celebrity acquaintances. Biggie was also a fixture at these parties. He would often have Tupac Shakur with him, and they would always be the life of the party.

When the semester started, I had much less time to hang out with rappers. My schedule at NYU was demanding, and I had to be there from 9:00 a.m. to 4:00 p.m. every day during the week. At NYU's Tisch School of the Arts, the theater programs are broken down by schools of thought. Some schools were dedicated to learning the acting methods of people like Lee Strasberg and Stella Adler, or you could take experimental theater, which employed a more new-age approach to acting. I enrolled in experimental theater. In this program you learn to remove all baggage, habits, and conditioned behavior to become truly free to inhabit your character onstage. We would achieve this by practicing yoga-like breathing techniques and improvising and developing backstories for the characters we would play. Much of what I learned in this theater program I later applied to the character I developed for myself to rap onstage. I quickly saw the parallels between the sense memory we created for theater and the names and personalities rappers fashion for themselves. Rapping was essentially acting, except rappers are writing their own scripts, doing their own blocking, and creating characters that draw heavily from personal life experiences.

Meanwhile, working for Stress Entertainment gave me access to popular nightclubs and helped me forge relationships with music industry types, but I wasn't making enough money to support my lifestyle. Determined to get a job close to school, I walked all over the Village until I arrived at Shakespeare & Co. Booksellers on Broadway. Shakespeare & Co. was located directly across the street from the Tisch School of the Arts building where I was studying experimental theater, which made it the ideal location for me to work. They hired me that December, starting me at the bag-check counter and then eventually moving me to the sales floor after they realized I knew a lot about books.

By January 1994 John Forté was no longer a student at New York University. He dropped out to pursue music full-time and added music production to his repertoire. I was trying to fit music into my schedule, but it was becoming more and more challenging to do so. My day started at 7:00 a.m., when I woke up to be at my theater class by nine. When I left school at four, I headed straight to Shakespeare & Co., where I worked every night until ten. After finding enough time to quickly eat and change, I headed to one of Jessica's parties to hand out flyers for the next one. I would be at these parties until two or three in the morning, then have to get up and repeat this cycle. For two or three months, I barely got any sleep, and my creative flame seemed to be dying out. I knew I couldn't do everything at once, and that something needed to be sacrificed. What I didn't know was that I was already sacrificing my college education. As my schedule got more intense, I started making it to theater class on time less often. Some days, I didn't go at all, bringing me back to the same mentality I had when I was fourteen years old at Brooklyn Tech. The only difference now was that my parents were paying such a large sum for me to attend NYU. I felt guilty when I slacked on my schoolwork, but not guilty enough to stop cutting. When one of my fellow students in ex-perimental theater, a Dominican kid named Yorlin Madera, left NYU that winter to move to Hollywood to find work, I thought it was a ballsy move. When I saw him in commercials and soap operas only a couple of months later, I felt that he had made the right choice. Watching Yorlin and John Forté achieve success so quickly without finishing college gave me the incentive to seri-ously consider dropping out to focus on my passion. By the time spring arrived, I had stopped attending classes altogether.

Even though I was no longer going to my NYU classes, I was still receiving my hip-hop education. I began hanging with a young lady named Pam Wilder, who was good friends with the rapper MC Lyte and ran Lyte's burgeoning management company, Duke Da Moon Management. Pam, who was a student of Five Percenter philosophy and rapped under the name Makeba Mooncycle, was a beautiful dreadlocked sister who got her start in the business running around with X-Clan back in the day. She seemingly knew everybody in the industry, had access to studio time, and was a fan of what I did lyrically. With the help of a producer named Self, who had a studio in Crown Heights, Makeba and I recorded many songs together, but she also positioned herself as my manager and began to get me small, local shows. I was never paid for these shows, but I was more than happy to have the opportunity just to rap for people. Makeba Mooncycle was the first person outside my immediate crew to see my vision and go out of her way to try to help this vision come to fruition. It was 1994, and Nas had just released *Illmatic*. By all accounts that album changed the perspective of what a classic album could be, not just hip-hop but of any genre. Nas's lyrics were astonishingly brilliant, and the production was like a beautiful puzzle put together by the most cutting-edge hip-hop producers of the day. *Illmatic* made every rapper step their entire musical game up. It was no longer okay for me just to be rapping over whatever beat I could find—I had to develop a sound. I had to find my sound.

Before I met Self, I didn't have a sound of my own. One can go only so far by rapping over other rappers' instrumentals. I came from a community of impressive MCs, but other than the early songs I had made with John Forté, I had no songs to offer. Self seemed to be the only dude around with a fully functioning studio, in his mom's Crown Heights basement, so many local MCs would converge there, and this provided a great challenge for me. This motley crew consisted of, but was not limited to, artists like Problem, a fifteen-year-old rapper who was Self's younger brother, Maestro Fresh Wes, who had achieved moderate success in Canada, and a female MC named Queen Pen, who would go on to make great records with Teddy Riley. Shabar Allah, who I had met thru John Forté years before, and his brother Allah Sun had a group called Population Clique. They also worked with Self and rounded out his crew of MCs. Because Self offered his studio to us for free, we all had to be on his schedule. A family man with a day job, Self would schedule an hour or two whenever he could to work with all of us broke, around-the-way MCs who were clamoring for free studio time.

While Self was helping me to develop actual songs and create a sound, my lyrics were being influenced by the MCs around me more than ever. Queen Pen, who normally rapped about street life, had recently been beat up by the police while she was attending an anti-police-brutality rally. She was pregnant at the time, and I went to visit her in the hospital daily during this trying time. When Queen Pen returned to the studio, she rapped with renewed fire and passion about the abuse she had just gone thru, and this inspired me to make my lyrics less about rapping and more about what my people were going thru.

Being connected to the Wu-Tang before the Wu blew up made Shabar Allah and Allah Sun hood famous, and I could see their influence in that crew. Ol' Dirty Bastard and the GZA were from Brooklyn, and RZA had a lot of family in the neighborhoods of Brownsville, East New York, and Bed-Stuy, so a crew of Brooklyn-born Wu-Tang affiliates is who I was running with. There was Universal Soldiers, Sunz of Man, and Killah Priest, who was also a member of Sunz of Man but was making a name for himself as a solo MC after a stellar appearance on a song called "B.I.B.L.E." on GZA's solo debut album, *Liquid Swords*. The camaraderie, the Five Percenter philosophy, and the overall street knowledge I picked up from these dudes would greatly enhance me as a person and an artist.

Always the connector, John Forté took advantage of his academic connections to achieve success in the music business early. By the spring of 1994, a year after we graduated from high school, John was the A&R director at a brand-new independent label called Rawkus Entertainment, and he asked Population Clique, Sunz of Man, and me to meet him at Makeba's apartment so that we could audition for record deals. I was equally intrigued and amused by this proposition. Jarret Myer and Brian Brater, the founders of Rawkus, had enough money to put out records, and somehow John had convinced them to take a chance on all of his homies from Brooklyn. It was classic John Forté.

Makeba shared an apartment on St. John's Place in Crown Heights with Prodigal Sunn from Sunz of Man, but it might as well have been a group home because so many of us used to stay there. Just about everyone who came thru was a Five Percenter, and build-and-destroy sessions would break out at the drop of a hat. We would argue over the influence of the Illuminati, which food products contained traces of pork, and, of course, who the best MC was. On the day that John showed up with Jarret and Brian, ten to fifteen battle-tested MCs must've been in that one-bedroom apartment, ready to rhyme their way out of the hood. Jarret and Brian were quiet, unassuming white dudes, and they seemed genuinely amused by the passion exhibited by each MC as we took turns spitting in a competitively unhinged cipher. We weren't dissing one another, but we were definitely battling for bar supremacy. As blunt after blunt and 40-ounce after 40-ounce were passed around the room, the energy got more and more intense as each MC seemed to outdo the last.

Jarret and Brian were both bass players who loved music

and had a rich friend in James Murdoch, son of the News Corporation head honcho and real-life version of Lord Business from *The LEGO Movie*, Rupert Murdoch. This meant that Rawkus seemed to have no limit on what they could spend, which allowed them many false starts before they figured out their lane. Jarret was easygoing, the good cop, always relaxed and always with a word of encouragement. Brian was the bad cop, the hyper record-industry guy, as passionate about money as he was about music and always down to party. In 1994 they were experimenting with drum-and-bass, punk rock, and rap/reggae-fusion records, throwing all types of shit at the wall to see what stuck. Hip-hop excited Jarret and Brian the most, but they didn't have an in into the hip-hop community until meeting John Forté. Two months after that meeting at Makeba's crib, Jarret and Brian signed Population Clique to Rawkus Entertainment. John asked me if I was interested in a deal, but I wanted to see how they did with Shabar and Allah Sun before I committed. Label recognition was a big deal to me back then, and I had not heard of Rawkus.

It would be three years before the Rawkus guys would come back into my life. The opportunity to sign with them was placed before me in 1994, but something in me told me not to take advantage of it. I thought it was because they were an upstart as opposed to an established label. Now I know it was because I was scared. In the back of my mind I knew that neither my skills nor my brand was developed enough to compete with what Population Clique was bringing to the table. They carried themselves as if they were already on, while I was still trying to find my voice. I knew that I needed more life experience before I would be ready to present my art to the world. Back then, I didn't have the language to articulate this feeling. But my spirit knew.

12

The Best Is Yet to Come

Growing old is mandatory. Growing up is optional.

—CHILI DAVIS

Since I was no longer attending classes at New York University, my dormitory-style apartment at Third North had devolved into a hangout spot for my friends and me. JuJu and Rubix would often spend nights sleeping on the couches or floors, wherever they could find a space. One of my roommates, Damon—who I had met at Tisch and who had become a Five Percenter and changed his name to Divine—invited a childhood friend from Cincinnati, Cornell Gibson, to stay with us for a week. Cornell, who changed his name to Omari almost immediately after setting foot in New York City, was enamored with New York's hip-hop lifestyle. Growing up in Cincinnati, Omari often felt that life there was too slow and dreamed about moving to the city where his favorite hip-hop artists came from. His heroes were rap acts like Gang Starr, Jeru the Damaja, and the Brooklyn collective known as the Boot Camp Clik. He would often quote KRS-One from the hip-hop documentary *Rhyme & Reason*, saying, "Until you stand on a corner in the South Bronx, you are not hip-hop," and taking the subway to the South Bronx is one of the first things he did when he arrived. He loved to buy weed from the bodegas on the street corners that the Black Moon rapper Buckshot described in his verses, and Omari was absolutely giddy when we started bringing him to the hip-hop events around the city that we had access to. When the week Omari was supposed to stay was up, he was so deeply in love with New York City that he decided not to go back to Cincinnati. Now five of us were living in a dorm room that was designed for two, and the summer was quickly approaching.

We decided to look for jobs so that we could afford a place in Brooklyn. Omari scored first, finding work handing out flyers to promote parties for Danny Castro and Anthony Marshall, the founders of a monthly hip-hop event called the Lyricist Lounge. Omari's passion for hip-hop and willingness to do what it took to be around it at all times impressed Danny and Anthony, and they saw his energy as an asset to what they were doing. I, too, was determined to find a job that would align with my interests. I decided that I would only be comfortable working at a bookstore or a record store. Starting in Times Square, I walked downtown dropping résumés off at every book and record shop I could think of. A week later I started at Grand Army Plaza in Park Slope and repeated this process. After about a half hour I arrived at Nkiru Books on Flatbush and St. Marks Avenue, Brooklyn's first Black-owned bookstore. Nkiru Books was founded by a young woman named Leothy Miller Owens. Noticing the lack of quality books available for Black children in Brooklyn, she rented a ground-floor space at 76 St. Marks Avenue in the heart of Park Slope and filled it with books most Black parents had never heard of or were never able to find. She called her store Nkiru, an Ibo word that loosely translates to "the best is yet to come." When the multicultural-education movement of the late 1980s hit Brooklyn, Nkiru Books was in a prime position to capitalize on it, quickly becoming a one-stop shop for all multicultural literary needs.

Helping Leothy out was her good friend Cynthia Johnson, otherwise known as CJ. CJ was well-known in Brooklyn's Black community and used her relationships to bring in clientele that Leothy did not have access to. One of CJ's ideas was to focus on in-store book readings and signings, and she started off with a newly famous author named Terry McMillan who lived on St. Marks, half a block from Nkiru Books. Because of the success of the McMillan in-store and the many that followed, Nkiru became known as a must-visit location for Black writers. When Leothy passed away, untimely, at age forty, her mother, Mrs. Adelaide Miller, came in and furthered her daughter's legacy by keeping the store alive. Mrs. Miller was a throwback, an old-school teacher who refused to use computers because she didn't trust them. She hired her sister Marilyn to be the bookkeeper, and they worked hard to continue Leothy's vision. Mrs. Miller and Marilyn would stay in the back of the store while CJ ran the floor. CJ hired her friend Paulette Mapp and a young man named Aaron Simms. The day when I walked into Nkiru looking for a job, CJ was behind the counter and I impressed her with my knowledge of books. I was hired on the spot. CJ told me that they could use a younger energy at the store, and I was put to work immediately, mopping and sweeping, receiving book orders and shelving them, and on occasion working the cash register.

While Aaron was only a couple of years older than me, my love for hip-hop culture brought Nkiru into a younger frame of mind. Aaron was more into jazz and dressed more like an adult than I did. He reminded me of Denzel Washington's character Bleek Gilliam from Spike Lee's *Mo' Better Blues*, the way he was always hanging out at jazz clubs and meeting new women. While Aaron didn't know much about the books on the shelves, he was a superior conversationalist, often keeping female customers who just wandered in off the street entertained for an hour or more. These customers would always buy from Aaron because they liked him so much. CJ and Paulette were both my parents' age, but CJ had long, flowing dreadlocks, a Pan-African outlook, and a fondness for Afrocentric clothing that made her look younger than her years. CJ was animated, knowledgeable about the books, and passionate about Leothy's vision. Paulette was a feminist and could tell you everything you ever wanted to know about writers such as bell hooks and Toni Morrison. I rounded out this motley crew when CJ hired me.

Now that I had a new job, it was time to find an apartment. After weeks of looking I found a five-bedroom duplex with a yard for $1,500 on Classon and Gates Avenues in the heart of Bedford-Stuyvesant. I secured the apartment in my name and we assembled a cast of five roommates: me, Omari, Divine, a budding producer named Lunatic, and a dude named Blue, who also worked for the Lyricist Lounge. Omari and I were the first to move in. We were surprised to find a dog hobbling back and forth in the backyard. Unsure what to do with it, Omari and I decided to go find the local weed spot. We figured we would smoke until a solution popped in our heads. We put our money together, which amounted to $5, and headed to a bodega a couple of blocks down that we thought had to be a weed spot from the way it looked. It was dark inside, and all of the food on the shelves was outdated. When I asked for a nickel bag, the dude behind the bulletproof glass handed me a small bag of white powder. "What's this?" I said. He replied, "A nickel bag. Do you want it or not?" Coke definitely wasn't it for us, and we got out of there and headed to our old faithful spot on Franklin Avenue in Crown Heights. When we arrived back at the apartment an hour later, the sick dog in the backyard was now a dead dog in the backyard. After we smoked, we figured out that we should call the ASPCA. We told them the dog was still alive, fearing that they wouldn't come for a dead dog. They never came anyway, and when we woke up the next morning, Omari and I put on dishwashing gloves, shoved that dog into a Hefty bag, and put it on the curb in front of the crack house across the street. Welcome to the neighborhood indeed.

Soon after I moved into the apartment, it was clear that I would be the only one paying the rent. By midsummer, the apartment was occupied only by Omari and me, and I was the only one with a job. My monthly salary was not enough to cover my bills, so I cut corners by walking to work, two miles there and two miles back every day. Makeba, ever the nurturer, would often come over with food and cook for us. We were learning how to take care of each other.

One morning as I was leaving for work, Omari came thru the door with one of my favorite rappers, Myka 9, from the legendary group Freestyle Fellowship. I was greatly inspired by Freestyle Fellowship, but Myka was my favorite, and I was shocked to see him standing at the door of my Bed-Stuy apartment, not just because he was a famous rapper but because he was a famous rapper from South Central, Los Angeles. Myka explained that he was staying with his manager, Kedar Massenburg, in an apartment around the corner and was looking for a place in Brooklyn to settle down and record his debut solo album. Omari spotted him at the local bodega while on an early morning blunt run and explained to him how big of a fan I was, so Myka decided to come by and meet me. We smoked and had a classic freestyle session that I will never forget. I was late for work that day, but it was worth it.

Myka's manager, Kedar Massenburg, had recently made a name for himself as the manager of Erykah Badu, a brand-new soul singer from Dallas, Texas, who was taking the industry by storm and who had also made her home in Brooklyn. Kedar was also gearing up to roll out his latest artist, a passionate R&B singer named D'Angelo. Kedar shared an apartment with Lance "Un" Rivera, a friend of Biggie's who would go on to start the label Undertainment and get into a famous "altercation" with Jay-Z years later, and Daddy-O from the classic hip-hop group Stetsasonic. I grew up on Stetsasonic, and I relished the opportunity to chop it up with one of my childhood heroes, so I would spend time at that apartment just to soak up the vibe. Myka and I became fast friends, and I learned a lot from him in a short time.

Toward the end of the summer, Myka gave us $500 as a down payment on a couple of months' rent and moved into the apartment with Omari and me. Kedar was not happy with this decision and showed up at the front door to get the money back. I think he felt that Myka needed his own space rather than being roommates with us. Even though Kedar was adamant, I backed him off, telling him that this money situation was between him and Myka, not him and me. However, a couple of days later Myka moved out and got his own spot. Omari and I also had a bad argument over some things in the apartment, so I asked him to leave. Stuck with a $1,500 duplex and no roommates to help with the rent, I gave up the apartment and moved back into my mom's basement. If having to move back home wasn't enough to make me feel defeated, I also lost my job at Nkiru Books that September. CJ told me that she liked me as an employee, but August was a notoriously rough month on independent booksellers and they couldn't afford my salary. So now not only was I not in school but I had no job and I was back living with my mom. I felt empty, shattered, and I began questioning my life decisions. Being an adult was not seeming like fun.

My mom was gracious enough not to charge me rent, but on

one condition: that I go to school, any school. The educator in Dr. Brenda Greene could not stomach having a college-dropout son. By this time, hip-hop music had engulfed me in every sense of the word. I had no space in my brain to think about anything else. Still, I was living under Brenda Greene's roof, so to please her I took night classes where she was employed, Medgar Evers College, located in the heart of Crown Heights. The only class I could find at Medgar that dealt with music was a radio communications class, but I hated it because I knew way more about the current world of radio than my professor did.

Now my focus turned to getting a job. Deciding that I no longer had the luxury of trying to find work at only a book or record store, I set out to find any job. I spent that September walking around the city, dropping résumés off with whoever would take one. After one exhausting morning of searching, I headed to my favorite place in the city, Washington Square Park, to sit and eat lunch. A light-skinned brother with green eyes and what appeared to be an S-curl sat next to me, pulled out a bag of weed, and asked if I had an extra cigar. I did. I gave him the spare Dutch Masters that I usually had in my pocket, and we began smoking and chopping it up. Let's call him Puma. Puma, who claimed to be a stockbroker, explained that he had the cure for my financial woes and offered me a job with his company. I told him I had zero Wall Street experience, and he said it didn't matter. Puma explained that Wall Street was a hustle, and that if I had hustle, I could succeed. He gave me an address in the financial district at which to show up at 9:00 a.m. the next day and provided only one instruction: wear a tie.

When I arrived the next morning, I was ushered into a loud room full of young dudes on phones. On the surface, they appeared to be selling stocks. Puma told me that my job was to get on the phone and convince people to buy stock they might not otherwise have paid any attention to. I would be working on commission, so the more stock I sold, the more I would make. I wanted to know more about what I was convincing people to spend their money on so that I could be a better salesperson. However, when I started asking questions about the stocks I was selling, Puma got tight, quick. Annoyed, he responded, "Don't worry about all of that, just get the credit card numbers." This seemed fishy to me. I tried for about an hour, but the people I called were suspicious, making it impossible for me to make a sales pitch and sound as if I meant it. I went back to Puma and asked some more questions about what we were doing until he got annoyed enough to break it down for me. He told me these were dummy stocks, stocks that did not exist, and that the people we were calling had so much money they wouldn't notice or care. So we were stealing from people. This didn't sit right with me, and I knew that I would never be good at it, so when I got to my first lunch break, I left and never went back. The first thing I did when I got outside was take my tie off.

After my bad luck with the job search and my *Boiler Room* experience with Puma, I realized I wasn't cut out for a "job" and began to pay more attention to my "career." I knew that working all day at a job I did not like would kill me, no matter how much it paid. I went back to Nkiru Books and begged for my job again, but CJ was able to hire me only for the holiday season. I did just that, and by the beginning of December I was back at Nkiru. This time, I worked so hard that I became indispensable. I scoured the bookshelves and I devoured the books. I fell in love with authors like Octavia Butler, Paulo Coelho, Ayi Kwei Armah, and Marimba Ani. I knew where every book was located, I knew the stock by heart, and I equipped myself to sell any book we had to anybody who came thru the door.

That December I also told my mom that I was going to stop

attending classes at Medgar Evers and try night classes at New York University instead. By January 1995 I was enrolled in a music business class and a Western religions class at NYU. The music business class was as obsolete, given the current, fluid music business I was interested in, as the radio communications class at Medgar was, but the Western religion class was enthralling. At that time, I spent a lot of time trying to understand why there was so much religious hate and division in the world, and the most important takeaway I got from this class was that all religions are trying to answer the same questions. I began to see the similarities in religions rather than the differences, and this changed the way I viewed religion and spirituality as a whole. The lessons I took from reading Malcolm years earlier had been abstract, but living in the world and experiencing spirituality for myself was a different beast. My professor was a Catholic man who was married to a Jewish woman, but he spoke of Islam like an Islamic scholar. I hadn't been aware people like him existed, and taking his class allowed me to understand that it is possible to have equal respect for all religions and ways of life.

13

mm

1995

Don't just count your years, make your years count.

—GEORGE MEREDITH

Of all the years I've lived, none changed my life as drastically as 1995 did. At the start of the year, I was living in my mom's basement, working at Nkiru Books, and attending night classes at New York University, but my focus was on the music. In my downtime I would attend every hip-hop open mic I could find. I knew I was more skilled than the majority of rappers, but being so close to the business forced me to understand how difficult it was to have a healthy music career, especially as a hip-hop artist. Luckily I loved my bookstore job and could see myself working there for a long time.

In the spring of 1995 Omari, the ex-roommate who I'd fallen out with, invited me to come spend some time in Cincinnati with him. He was excited about a rap group from his hometown called MOOD, and he felt that I would appreciate the music they were making. Initially, I had reservations about letting Omari back into my life, but I loved to travel, so I took him up on his offer. I hopped on a Greyhound bus to Cincinnati for a weekend, stayed at Omari's mom's house, and was introduced to Donte, Jermaine, and Jason from MOOD. Donte and Jermaine were the MCs; Donte went by the name Sicko back then, and he was on some vicious gangsta shit with a country twang, while Jermaine rapped under the name Main Flow and had more of a smooth, hustler-type flow. Jason, aka DJ Rampage, was the group's only white member and its DJ and producer.

For a group from Cincinnati, with no access to the music industry on the coasts, MOOD were not only creatively dope but incredibly self-sufficient. These guys were all small-time hustlers, but they put all of their profits into their music. They built studios, pressed up albums, and created an industry around themselves. As fans of hip-hop, particularly East Coast–sounding hip-hop, the MOOD guys looked up to the crew of MCs I was associated with, artists like John Forté, Makeba Mooncycle, and her roommate, Prodigal Sunn. However, my crew was broke. The cost of living in New York City is way higher than the cost of living in Cincinnati. So while my crew and I were rhyming in the parks, hopping trains, and splitting dollar heroes, these Cincinnati dudes were recording industry-quality material in their own studios, whipping Jeeps, and traveling back and forth to New York whenever they felt like it.

MOOD had their own sound, but they often made music with another Cincinnati group called Vicious Lee and DJ Hi-Tek. As dope as Jason's beats were, I found myself gravitating to DJ Hi-Tek's sound. A year younger than me, baby-faced Tony Cottrell, aka DJ Hi-Tek, was the youngest of the crew, and he got the name Hi-Tek by being technically advanced for his age. Lee, aka Vicious Lee, was like a mentor to Hi-Tek. Lee was a hood rich dude who loved to rap and recognized Hi-Tek's talent at an early age. Lee made sure to provide Hi-Tek with studio equipment. A superfan of great producers, like DJ Premier, Pete Rock, and Dr. Dre, Hi-Tek spent so many years trying to emulate their sounds that he eventually came up with his own. His is a lush, cinematic sound that sacrifices none of hip-hop's gritty boom bap. In Hi-Tek's words, he just had a "swing" that other producers didn't have, and for him it was all about the swing. Hi-Tek was making the most beautiful hip-hop music I had ever heard, but because he was from Cincinnati, no one knew about it.

Vicious Lee inspired Hi-Tek to create, but he was still in the streets dealing with all the drama that comes with the street life. While Vicious Lee was getting caught up, Hi-Tek continued to supply MOOD with beats, but now he was left with a collection of beats that had no rhymes. At the same time Lee was unavailable, my friend JuJu, who was my partner in Eternal Reflection, began to show less and less interest in the music. JuJu was a DJ, so there wasn't much for him to do in the studio, and I wasn't booking many shows. Impressed by my work with Self, Hi-Tek began sending me music to write to. The closer I became with the guys from MOOD, the more time I would spend in Cincinnati recording with them. I spent so much time in the 'Nati that I ended up getting arrested there.

I was arrested twice in the winter of 1995. The first time was with JuJu in Washington Square Park while we were smoking weed after a long day of shopping my demo. When I first started hanging out in the Village, the park was where people went to smoke. A few years later, it was Giuliani time. Stoners, especially young Black ones, were considered a part of the counterculture that was ruining the city, according to our new mayor. JuJu and I were arrested on a Friday afternoon, which meant we didn't get processed until Monday morning. When we were handcuffed and put in the back of the paddy wagon, I saw two people I knew in there. Clearly I was running with a circle of winners.

I have my mouth and my lack of respect for authority to blame for my second arrest. I was recording with MOOD in Cincinnati, staying with one of their homies. Unbeknownst to me, this homie hadn't paid his rent in months and was due to be evicted. On the morning he had to leave, I helped him pack and we waited for Main Flow to come swoop us. The landlord, however, showed up while we were waiting for our ride and demanded we leave the premises immediately. I tried to reason with him, explaining that it was cold outside and we were all packed up, waiting for a ride. The landlord was having no part of that and immediately called the police. The cop who showed up was Black, so foolishly I thought that I had some sort of racial connection with him, but the moment I opened my mouth, he told me to shut the fuck up and get the fuck out of the apartment.

I was taken aback by the officer's aggressive attitude. I didn't realize he was there to serve and protect the property, not to reason with another human being. I became defensive and started questioning the officer's attitude, while he was looking for compliance. When he gave me an ultimatum—shut up and leave or get arrested—I knew he was at his breaking point, but my ego would not let him get the last word. As I walked past the officer out the door of the apartment, I said, loud enough for him to hear, "This is why people hate cops." The officer was looking for a reason to arrest somebody, and I had just handed him one. Without warning, he tackled me from behind, put his knee in my back, and pushed my face into the grass outside the apartment while he handcuffed me. During the ride to the precinct, I cursed that cop out worse than I had ever cursed anyone out. I called him all kinds of bitches and hoes for the entire trip. He turned around and said, "You from New York, huh? That's why you think you can mouth off to cops. We don't play that shit down here."

As I waited in that holding cell for Main Flow to come and bail me out, I started to assess my life. I had gone from being an acting student at one of the country's most prestigious universities to a college dropout who got arrested for bullshit twice in a matter of months. My parents were professors and my younger brother was doing so well in high school that he was about to be accepted at Harvard. What was I doing wrong? Was I on course to be yet another statistic? It didn't matter that I had both parents in my life, a great childhood, and a decent education. I was beginning to fall into traps that were set for me a long time before I was born.

One night, back in New York, JuJu took me to see Ice Cube's newest movie, *Friday*. JuJu had already seen it and loved it so much he made a habit of bringing his friends so they could share his experience. After the movie we talked about how we wished we could see California. Our impression of California was purely thru a musical lens. Such 1980s pop hits as "I Love L.A." by Randy Newman and "California Girls" by David Lee Roth made us East Coasters think that Cali was all sand, sun, and sex, but the gangsta rap of the late 1980s flipped that image on its head. The video for N.W.A's first single, "Express Yourself," the sole "positive" song made by the group in an attempt at mainstream appeal, featured some of the Venice Beach culture that was popularized by rock and pop artists, but once N.W.A got that out of their system, it was straight gangsta shit. The hip-hop videos that came out of the West Coast showed us a world we only saw in movies. Sure, there were gangs and violence in New York, but from our perspective, Californians had turned the romanticizing of the gangsta lifestyle into an art.

When CJ from Nkiru Books told me to take that summer off rather than laying me off as she had the previous August, I took it as a sign from God that I was supposed to be in California. Going back and forth to Cincinnati almost every weekend that year forced me to get familiar with bus travel, and in 1995, a one-way ticket from New York City to Los Angeles on the Greyhound was $137. Shit, I had that. JuJu was seeing a girl who lived in California, so he came with me. We left the day after we made our decision. First, we stopped at the weed spot on Franklin Avenue and Lincoln Place. The first shoot-out I'd ever seen had been right in front of this spot. I was with Omari and Santi White of *Santogold* fame, and some Jamaicans got into it and pulled out the heaters right in front of us. I still went back, though, because they had those pillows, twenty bags of weed so fluffy you could take a nap on one. JuJu and I bought as many bags as we could stuff in our pockets and got ready for our trip.

The last thing I did before I left my house for California was cut my dreadlocks off. Since the beginning of that year I had been developing a bald spot on the top of my head. Because I was barely an adult, I hoped it was just the way my locks were growing, but since my father, his brother, and their father before them were all bald men, in the back of my mind I knew my hair loss was a much more permanent reality. When I asked my father about his hair loss, he mentioned that he also began to lose his hair at eighteen. I wasn't aware that men could lose their hair so early, and my vanity took a blow. How was I supposed to pick up women as a balding eighteen-year-old? I decided to do what any vain balding man does when his hair starts to go and cut it all off.

I made a mental list of rappers who rocked baldies—artists like Common, LL Cool J, and DMX. I took comfort in knowing I wasn't the only one who experienced hair loss at such a young age.

I needed this comfort because my dreadlocks were a huge part of the personality I'd developed for myself. My locks identified me without my having to speak and allowed me access to an exclusive club, the dreadlock club. When people with locks pass each other on the street or make eye contact, they give each other a knowing nod. I kept this habit up for a few months after I cut my locks off, which would at times confuse the person I was nodding at. Now, with a fresh cut, I felt that I needed a fresh start, and California, where no one knew me, was the perfect place to debut my new look.

For three days JuJu and I hopped from bus to bus, crossing the country, seeing America in all of her majestic splendor. We found ourselves traveling thru states we never imagined we would ever see, like South Dakota, Utah, and Idaho. At every rest stop, we rolled up smelly, big blunts and found hiding spots to smoke in, so we were pretty stoned for the entire trip. Whenever we got back on the bus, the dank smell of New York City pot would emanate from our clothes throughout the entire closed space. Once one person was brave enough to ask if he could smoke with us a bunch did, and we soon had a little stoner crew in the back of the bus. We got threatened to be put off the bus more than once.

All of the romantic mental images JuJu and I had of Hollywood, California, were instantly dashed the moment we got off the bus at the Hollywood Greyhound station. For my entire life Hollywood had been sold to me as a place that epitomized glamour and glitz. What I saw instead was drifters, prostitutes, homeless people. I don't know what I expected to see at a bus station, but this was truly the boulevard of broken dreams. JuJu's girlfriend picked us up and drove us to her family's mini-mansion in Los Angeles's tony Brentwood neighborhood. She stayed a few houses down from the house where O. J. Simpson had allegedly murdered Nicole Brown Simpson, and in the summer of 1995 that house was surrounded by paparazzi and news cameras. The Simpson trial ushered in the era of the twenty-four-hour news cycle. We would be staying here, a far cry from the destitution of the bus station.

JuJu and I got into all of the mischief that hip-hop fans from Brooklyn visiting Los Angeles for the first time could possibly get into. We partied on the Sunset Strip, ate at Roscoe's House of Chicken'n Waffles, and made trips to places like the Santa Monica Pier and Venice Beach. We smoked incredible weed, got into an altercation because JuJu was wearing blue in a Blood neighborhood, and almost got arrested for jaywalking.

Seeing all of the touristy stuff was cool, but one of the primary places I wanted to visit in Los Angeles was the famed Good Life Cafe. The Good Life was a health food store located in the heart of South Central that doubled as a performance space for up-and-coming poets and MCs. Within the MC community it was famous for having been the training ground of California hip-hop groups that achieved national prominence, like Freestyle Fellowship and the Pharcyde. Anybody who had bars could bust, but there were two rules, one written and one unwritten. Because the owner of the Good Life was a little older and liked his art to be a bit more, ahem, respectable, performers were not allowed to curse. A sign said NO CURSING, and the rule was aggressively enforced. The second, unwritten, rule was that if you freestyled, it had to be from the top of your head, straight improvisation. Attempting to pass off a written rhyme as a freestyle at the Good Life was akin to snitching in the hood; the audience would call for your head. These challenges made that Good Life stage a place I had to be if I took myself seriously as an MC. Being able to say I performed there would be a badge of hip-hop honor.

My time onstage at the Good Life was underwhelming. I was young, unknown, and out of my element. I guess I did okay, because they were polite enough not to boo me, but while I was performing, I sensed that I was not bringing anything to the table that the crowd hadn't seen before. Humbled, I watched the rest of the performers from the back of the room and eventually struck up a conversation with two people, who told me they appreciated what I was trying to do up there. Their names were Tom and Corey, aka Luckyiam and Sunspot Jonz, and they were members of a Bay Area rap group called Mystik Journeymen, which was part of a larger collective of California artists known as Living Legends. Tom and Corey graciously let me know that if I was ever in the Bay Area, I could stay with them. A few days later I would take them up on this offer.

After about a month, JuJu and I ran out of money and over-stayed our welcome in Los Angeles. While he was ready to head back to Brooklyn, I was enjoying California too much and worked out a way to stay longer. I had friends from the Bay Area and knew that if I could make it there, they would look out for me. I caught a ride to San Francisco with a girl I met at a nightclub.

I wasn't able to stay with my Bay Area homies, but Luckyiam and Sunspot made good on their promise to put me up. I found my way from San Francisco to their sparse apartment in Berkeley and quickly realized I might need to stay someplace else. Besides their beds, the apartment had no furniture. The Mystik Journeymen were definitely living the life of the starving artist, and even though I knew I couldn't stay, that they were willing to share what little shelter they had with me, a stranger, endeared them to me for life. For the two days I stayed with them, we ate hella Top Ramen noodles and did an awful lot of freestyling. On the West Coast, freestyle was developing into a different beast, particularly in the Bay. Cut off from the music industry of New York, and more into lyrical hip-hop than the gangsta rap that was popular up and down the coast, Bay Area MCs like Del the Funky Homosapien, Souls of Mischief, Casual, and Saafir were elevating freestyle to new heights. As a New York MC, I loved the challenge. For far too long New York hip-hop had been dismissive of any act that did not originate in our city. These California MCs demanded to be heard and all but said they were better than the New York MCs.

Luckyiam and Sunspot took me to Leopold Records in Berkeley, famous because Del was working there even though he had a decent hip-hop career going. Del was the OG of the Hieroglyphics crew, an East Oakland collective that included Souls of Mischief and Casual and were quickly becoming my favorite group of rappers since the Native Tongues. Standing outside Leopold's selling their own CDs was a hip-hop group called the WhoRidas. This was the first time in my life I'd seen rappers selling their own music, and it absolutely fascinated me. In New York we were spoiled by the proximity of the music industry, which is why JuJu and I started and stopped with shopping our demos to labels. It never occurred to me that I could press my own CDs and sell them to people. After asking them more about their process, I befriended the WhoRidas and they invited me to come with them to their homie Saafir's crib that night.

Saafir, a great MC with a single out, was better known for his role as Caine's cousin Harold in the seminal West Coast hip-hop movie of our time, *Menace II Society*. However, I was more interested in talking to him about his battle with members of the Hieroglyphics crew, which had happened the night before. Saafir was the leader of a crew called Hobo Junction, a crew that the Who-Ridas were members of as well. Hobo Junction and Hieroglyphics were both talented groups of MCs who were battling for the same Bay Area props, and on this night, Saafir was adamant about the dominance of his crew. There were no camera phones, bloggers, or social networks back then, so the battle between Hobo and Heiro, especially for us East Coasters who had little to no chance of witnessing it, was the stuff of legend. Here I was hearing about it from the horse's mouth.

As gracious as he was passionate about being a dope rapper, Saafir also extended an invitation for me to stay at his house. These Bay Area dudes were extremely genuine, and it made me love the hip-hop community there. I stayed at Saafir's that night. The next day, the reality of my Cincinnati court case smacked me in the face. In September, I was due in court in Cincinnati, but I had no way to get there. The day before my court appearance, I called my parents to tell them I needed a plane ticket. I hadn't told them about this arrest, and when they found out why I needed the ticket, not only did they buy it for me but they also drove from New York to Cincinnati together to support me in court.

That they spent all of those hours in the car together for my benefit was significant because my parents were in the middle of a separation. They knew enough about the justice system to know I would stand a better chance of coming out on top if I had loved ones there to support me, and they wanted to give the impression that I came from a "good" two-parent home, so they bit the bullet and came for me. I vividly remember how the arresting officer walked in and avoided any kind of eye contact with me, and after a few minutes it became clear to the judge that the officer was overly aggressive and didn't have any justification for my arrest, so my case was thrown out. My parents, who had been worried, breathed audible sighs of relief, and we piled in the car for our fifteen-hour road trip back to Brooklyn. For the entire trip, my parents took turns admonishing me for my life decisions and tried to help me understand that I was better than the trouble I was getting myself into. They were clearly disappointed in me, but they were also clearly not giving up on me. Once again, my parents put their differences aside for the sake of their children.

14

The Peaceful Warrior

Raising Black children, female and male, in the mouth of a racist,
sexist, suicidal dragon is perilous and chancy. If they cannot love
and resist at the same time, they will probably not survive.

—AUDRE LORDE

Right before CJ gave me the summer off, I had the
pleasure of working the Nkiru Books tent at Brooklyn's African
Street Festival, which took place annually at Boys and Girls High
School in Bed-Stuy. I looked forward to this event, now known as
the International African Arts Festival, every year. Vendors from
all over the world descended on the track field of Boys and Girls
selling authentic African garb, jewelry, art, books, music, and
some of the best food I would eat all year. As an employee of
Nkiru, I set up our tent, sold books all day, and stayed in the tent
at night for the three nights the festival was in town, to guard the
books. It sounds like a lot of work, because it was, but I loved it. I
loved the sights, sounds, and smells of the festival, and I would
have been there a lot even if I wasn't working.

One day on my lunch break I stopped by a table where a dread-locked woman was selling incense and books on African spiritu-ality. She was beautiful, with a radiant smile, and even though she had on a dashiki and a long dress, she could not hide her curves. I had no game, so to strike up a conversation I bought a bunch of incense I didn't want. For the next two days, I stopped by her table and tried to say something clever, and on the last day of the festi-val I built up the nerve to ask her for her phone number. She didn't give it to me, but she took my number instead, so I thought that once the festival was over, I would probably never see her again. When she finally called me a few weeks later while I was in California, I was over the moon. We made plans to link up as soon as I returned to Brooklyn. Her name was Darcel Turner.

Darcel, who is three years older than me, was born in the birthplace of hip-hop, the South Bronx. Along with her brother, Donell, she was raised in Far Rockaway, Queens, until her mother passed away when she was seventeen and she and her brother re-turned to the projects in the South Bronx. When I met Darcel, she was back in Far Rockaway, living in an apartment with Do-nell. We were both broke, so we had our first date in her apart-ment. We smoked and she cooked and then we stayed up all night listening to music and getting to know each other better. After that night, I spent the next two weeks at Darcel's apartment. I was turned out.

The most interesting thing about Darcel was the juxtaposition of her two very different lives. The Darcel I met at the African Street Festival wore dashikis, read books about spirituality, and sold incense. She waited weeks to call me after initially refusing to give me her phone number. The Darcel that I had that first date with was seemingly someone else altogether. Her apartment was all red and black lights and provocative posters. She had on a sexy small top and biker pants that allowed me to clearly see what her

African ensembles only hinted at. The demure, quiet girl I'd met at the festival had transformed into a sexual siren in weeks, and I loved it. I thought I'd hit the jackpot.

What I didn't know was that Darcel was dancing in cabaret-style nightclubs. Unsure about where our relationship was going, she waited a week to tell me out of fear of judgment, but honestly, I was more interested in her after she told me. I didn't think the "spiritual" Darcel was a front; I just realized that Darcel had contradictions, like the rest of us. I couldn't imagine growing up in the projects with no father and having my mom pass away at seventeen. My parents did everything they could for me. Darcel raised herself. From the time Darcel was seventeen, she and her brother did what they had to do to take care of each other. Who was I to judge her lifestyle? Rather than judge, I accepted it as a part of her experience. Until she got pregnant.

Darcel was pregnant within two months of our first date. We were madly in love, and other than when I was working at the bookstore, we spent every waking moment together. When I broke the news to my parents, they were surprisingly supportive considering my recent brush with possible jail time, the fact that I was still living with my mom, and that I was barely making any money at my job. As a family, we made some decisions that would accommodate a new baby. Darcel quit dancing in the clubs and got a job at Medgar Evers College as an assistant to my mom. Jamal started college at Harvard University that year, so Darcel and I prepared the house for the arrival of my first child. On July 4, 1996, fifteen years to the day from when my grandfather Stanley Greene, Sr., passed away, one year to the day after I met Darcel, her water broke while she was walking around the African Street Festival, the same festival where she and I met. After eight hours of labor at Brooklyn's Downstate University

Hospital, Darcel brought my beautiful son, Amani Fela Greene, into the world.

Amani Fela was born with a head full of curly locks. *Amani* is a Swahili word for "peace," and *fela*, besides being the name of the greatest Afrobeat musician of all time, Fela Kuti, is also a Nigerian word for "warrior." My firstborn was a bouncy, happy baby who looked just like his mama, but in the right light, you could see he was my son. I had the privilege of being in the room, helping while Amani was born. It was one of the most beautiful experiences I've ever had. If you've ever been in the room when a child is born, you know that God exists. You also know that the function of human beings is to seek knowledge. The search for knowledge is life; once we stop seeking knowledge, we die. Children will learn more in their first few years than they will in the entire rest of their lives, which makes this a magical time for the child and for the person raising that child. I loved watching Amani's eyes light up when he learned something new about the world. I looked forward to teaching him about baseball and books and movies and hip-hop. I instantly understood my parents better by several degrees, and they took to grandparenting like pros.

Before you have your first child, people tell you all types of horror stories about how hard your life is about to be. They joke about how your life will be over, and they compare child rearing to prison. My experience has been quite different. I found having a child to be not only liberating but invigorating. My children are both my inspiration and my reward. Having a son made me more compassionate, patient, creative, and free than I ever felt before. When I would get home to my new young family, my heart would swell with love in a way that is indescribable.

It would be easy to say that being a father came naturally to me because in Perry Greene I had a great father as an example.

But many of my friends were having children at this age, and most of them were determined to be the best fathers they could be, even though most of them had little to no relationship with their own father. The narrative of the deadbeat baby daddy in the Black community had been around since slavery and Jim Crow, but I saw a great many young Black men succeed at being good fathers, despite the obstacles of systemic oppression setting us up to fail. Being there for your children in every way you can is a natural instinct, not something anyone deserves extra credit for. However, if anyone is deserving of credit when it comes to parenting, it's single mothers, because they more often than not are the ones who have to do the work of two parents. I know this because most of my friends who became great fathers to their children were raised in single-mother households.

Amani's birth forced me to make even harder decisions about my life and career. I was saving on rent money by living with my father, but a man with a family needs his own space. I realized that my bookstore job might not last forever, so if I was going to make a living as a musician, the time to take it seriously was now. Self helped me figure out what kind of sound I was looking for with my group, but it was Hi-Tek's tracks that truly began to bring that sound to life. Before I had Hi-Tek's tracks I was considered a decent rapper, but with his tracks behind me people began to understand my full vision. Danny Castro and Anthony Marshall of the Lyricist Lounge used to only let me rock as a guest of another MC. When I played them the music I did with Hi-Tek, they immediately booked us together as a group. JuJu had recently gotten married and was settling into family life. He no longer had the time to invest in music, so before this show I changed the name of the group to Reflection Eternal and told JuJu that he was out and Hi-Tek was in. Reflection Eternal would be my first artistic statement to the world.

It's hard to overstate how important to hip-hop culture the Lyricist Lounge was. For years, up-and-coming MCs had been honing their craft in the city streets, braving all the elements. In the Giuliani era many of the artists working in the New York City streets were criminalized by "quality of life" laws that aimed to make the city more inviting to tourists. Any large gathering, especially one that was mostly people of color, was quickly broken up by the police. The era of impromptu street battles was disappearing just as Danny Castro and Anthony Marshall stepped in to fill that void. Lyricist Lounge started in someone's apartment, but when it began to grow, Danny and Anthony developed relationships with local venues that were struggling, making the Lounge beneficial to all parties. A rough-and-tumble energy came with inviting hungry inner-city MCs off the streets and into these venues, but Danny and Anthony had a lot of respect for the culture, and in turn the culture respected them back.

The MCs who frequented the Lyricist Lounge and other parties like it were developing a new wave of what came to be called underground hip-hop. As someone who had worked with Diddy, who was at the top of the hip-hop food chain while the Lyricist Lounge was developing, I was in a unique position to see the stark differences between the crowd that was going to the Tunnel nightclub and this new movement that was just coming in from the cold. Mainstream hip-hop's almost singular focus on materialism was off-putting to kids who were still hopping turnstiles and eating dollar hoagies. We were the kids who went to the parties to dance and freestyle over what the DJs played. We weren't popping bottles behind velvet ropes; we couldn't afford to. The bartenders would frown when we would order waters instead of alcohol at the bar and not have enough to tip them. Even though hip-hop music still ruled the party, the hustlers and drug dealers who stuffed themselves into the VIP sections would look at us hip-hoppers with annoyance, as if we were in the way.

Being shut out of the fancy part of hip-hop culture made us more aggressively protective of what we considered to be the culture as a whole. Our rhymes became more precise, and our focus was to celebrate the rudiments of hip-hop, not decadence. Like the early MCs who were doing it in the parks before record deals, we guarded hip-hop with our lives and waxed poetic about preserving the B-boy culture that was so instrumental in hip-hop's formation. We frowned upon the record industry as it tried to force us to abandon vinyl for CDs, and we decried as fake anyone who rhymed about material things like money and jewelry. For people whose only experience with hip-hop was what the radio told them to listen to, being underground meant being broke, which was undesirable. For us, being underground was a badge of honor that we wore with pride.

When I finally got a chance to bless that Lyricist Lounge stage on my own, I did so with a vengeance. On this night the Lounge was at New York City's legendary club Sounds of Brazil, aka SOB's. I had been to SOB's many times before to see some of my favorite artists perform, so performing there for the first time was a huge deal for me. If the venue itself wasn't daunting enough, that this Lyricist Lounge would be hosted by one of my favorite MCs, Q-Tip from A Tribe Called Quest, made me even more nervous. It was February 1996 and I was sharing the bill with Brooklyn MC Problemz (not to be confused with Self's younger brother, a different MC) and the duo of Rah Digga and Young Zee, both from Newark. Problemz repped the borough well. Rah Digga was pregnant with Young Zee's child, so when she spit as hard as she did, it was doubly impressive. When it was my turn, Hi-Tek, who had driven his Mazda MPV from Cincinnati to

New York for this show, set up his MPC-3000, and I ripped thru three of his beats, raw, right off the drum machine. The response was instant and fantastic—the crowd loved it. As I exited the stage, I was greeted by Q-Tip, who I had never met before that night. "That was dope," he said with a wide grin. That was all I needed to hear. After that show, I knew I would be a rapper for a living.

15

Black Star Keep Shining

What is the black star?
Is it the cat with the black shades, the black car?
Is it shining from very far to where you are?

—MOS DEF, *MOS DEF & TALIB KWELI
ARE BLACK STAR*, "ASTRONOMY (8TH LIGHT)"

Danny and Anthony were impressed by my Lyricist Lounge performance and invited me to perform again at the next one. Held at Tramps in the spring of 1996, it was hosted by De La Soul. Meeting Q-Tip was great, but De La was my favorite group. I knew that if I could impress De La, I was sure to jumpstart my career. The night of the show Hi-Tek and I performed with the same passion that we had back at SOB's, but our lightning did not strike twice. I approached this gig with a lot more confidence than I had at SOB's, but I didn't connect with the audience in the same way. My name was starting to buzz a little bit, and I think I'd raised expectations by doing so well at the last Lounge. When people expect you to be dope, you have to perform with a different energy than if they weren't expecting anything. This was my lesson from this night.

Not one to let one mediocre performance stop my progress, I began showing up at every open mic I could, ready to prove myself. This included spoken-word poetry events. I found that as a rapper I had a skill set that many spoken-word artists desired. While they had way better vocabulary and content than the average rapper, they couldn't rap that well. When I would drop rap verses that contained content and vocabulary that could rival the best spoken-word artists, they were impressed and welcomed me into their community. Poets like jessica Care moore, Reg E. Gaines, and muMs the Schemer dominated this scene, and hearing them do poetry helped me push my creative limits. Hearing Saul Williams recite poetry about listening to Rakim on rocky mountaintops helped me to understand that hip-hop could not be contained by the inner city. We were bigger than that.

I wasn't the only MC making a name for himself in the spoken-word scene. Mos Def, aka Yasiin Bey, was at most of the spoken-word events I attended and, like me, would impress with his rhymes. By then Yasiin had done a bunch of TV, including a stint on Bill Cosby's *Cosby Mysteries*, toured with De La Soul and A Tribe Called Quest, and was growing into a local celebrity. Although I'd met Yasiin years before, I still didn't know him that well. We were acquaintances who had friends in common and I was a fan. Not until his wife became friendly with Darcel did we begin to spend some time together. They invited Darcel and me over for dinner one night at their Red Hook apartment, and I decided to bring them a copy of the Reflection Eternal demo, called *Groundation*, that Hi-Tek and I were working on. This would be the first of many nights Darcel, Amani, and I would spend with Yasiin and his family that year. We would talk a lot about music and spirituality, Islam in particular. Yasiin had grown up a Muslim and seemed to be rediscovering his faith as he was navigating newfound, but uncertain, fame and success.

Yasiin and I began our friendship before he was a fan of my music. I know this because one day I received an excited call from Yasiin about how much he loved Reflection Eternal. Even though I'd given him a copy of *Groundation* months before, he had not listened to it until his wife's son Elijah told him to. Apparently Elijah had been listening to it from the first night we brought it over and developed into quite a fan. Yasiin called me, quoting my lyrics, telling me how dope Hi-Tek's production was. I asked him to get on the album, and he said yes. I already knew which song he would sound good on. Earlier that year JuJu had come by my crib with a 45 by the reggae artist Tom Drunk, saying it was a perfect song to sample for a hip-hop beat. I passed the record on to Hi-Tek, who used it to create the track for what would become "Fortified Live." Khaliyl, aka Mr. Man, my homie from Da Bush Babees and a good friend of Yasiin's as well, heard the track early and flipped out over how good it was, demanding a verse. With a commitment from our mutual friend Yasiin in my pocket, I decided to make "Fortified Live" a posse cut with the three of us going back and forth.

While I was making moves with Mr. Man and Mos Def, the MOOD crew were making their own moves in the industry. In 1995, they dropped a video for a single called "Hustle on the Side," which was produced by Hi-Tek and featured Vicious Lee. This video was played on the local New York video show *Video Music Box* by VJ Ralph McDaniels, and it led to MOOD's securing a record deal with Steve Gottlieb's Blunt/TVT Records. *TVT* stood for "TV toons," and the label made money by releasing classic TV themes on vinyl, but Steve wanted to branch out into hip-hop, so he came up with one of the worst, most stereotypical names for a hip-hop label ever, Blunt Recordings, and began to sign rappers.

Before MOOD, Blunt had signed Lil Jon and the Eastside Boyz, Cash Money Click (Ja Rule's first group) and Mic Geronimo, but other than Mic Geronimo's modest regional hit "Shit's Real," nothing was popping. By 1997 the MOOD guys were holed up in Platinum Island Studios on Broadway recording their debut album, and they were fed up with their label. Blunt had given them a small advance, and the label reps had seemingly lost interest in MOOD and were becoming harder and harder to reach. Donte, Main Flow, and Jason were determined not to go back to hustling, so they buckled down and used whatever resources they could to finish the album—including Hi-Tek and me.

Hi-Tek produced more than half of MOOD's debut album, and I am a featured guest on five songs. Hi-Tek and I essentially became the fourth and fifth members of the group. The influence of my crew of Brooklyn rhymers and New York City's Five Percenter community on MOOD was evident as the group's members all underwent some form of spiritual transformation. Donte dropped the name Sicko and opted to rap under the name Donte instead. His rhymes became less about scales and beams and more about Kemetic philosophy and the Elohim. Main Flow traded in tales of drug dealing for tales of healthy living, and Jason changed his name from DJ Rampage to Jahson as his production became decidedly more reggae influenced. They all grew dreadlocks, even the white guy, Jahson, and they all began to spend hours discussing the Illuminati, the New World Order, and the spiritual implications of the upcoming year 2000.

MOOD's debut album, *Doom*, dropped that year, and as we recorded it in Platinum Island, Hi-Tek and I used the downtime to work on Reflection Eternal material. At Platinum Island Yasiin and Khaliyl recorded "Fortified Live" with us, and being there all day allowed me to catch a glimpse of the hustle that was required to fully participate in this business. Accomplished hip-hop producers like Ez Elpee, L.E.S., and Buckwild would hang around the studio, looking for rappers to play beats for and possibly sell beats to. Ken "Duro" Ifill, who would go on to work with DJ Clue, was the in-house, in-demand engineer, while a young Just Blaze would be interning in the next session. These engineers and producers spent all day and all night at the studio crafting their sounds; they had no life outside of music production. This all was expensive, because back then these sessions could cost up to a couple hundred dollars an hour depending on the engineer, song, and studio. That price did not include expensive two-inch reel tapes, DATs, and CDs we had to purchase after every session; there were no MP3s to email. If we couldn't record during one of MOOD's sessions, I would spend my bookstore salary booking sessions whenever Hi-Tek made it to New York, because I was beginning to realize that the studio was where the magic truly happened.

The first Reflection Eternal demo, *Groundation*, contained an early version of a song that ended up on *Black Star*, "K.O.S. (Determination)." Along with that one, several other songs would become the prototypes for songs that would end up on Reflection Eternal's debut album, *Train of Thought*, years later. These were the songs I played at shows, and I thought they were all good until I met with Jarret and Brian from Rawkus for the second time in two years. After falling in love with *Groundation*, Yasiin suggested I take my album to Rawkus because they had just given him some money for a single deal. By now, I was less concerned with whether a label was "famous," and getting money for rap was a lot more important to me than it was just two years prior. When I took the meeting with Rawkus, John Forté was still in A&R there, but he was spending less time at Rawkus and more time working as a producer on the Fugees album *The Score*. Forté and I had become good friends with Lauryn Hill during the release of the first

Fugees album, *Blunted on Reality,* and this led to Forté's forming a great musical relationship with Wyclef Jean.

The first couple of songs I played from *Groundation* didn't impress Jarret and Brian as much as I thought they would. Jarret and Brian were consistently polite, but I could tell that my songs did not move them the way they moved me. As I began to fast-forward thru the tape to find other songs they might like, Jarret heard a couple of seconds of "Fortified Live"—which features Mos Def and Mr. Man—and asked, "Wait, what was that?" I was instantly dismissive. As a twenty-one-year-old MC trying to make his mark, it was of utmost importance to me that the world knew that I could stand on my own two feet before I released a cut that depended on the services of two other, more well-known MCs. I knew "Fortified Live" was a great song, but I wanted people to know I could make great solo songs first. As businessmen, Jarret and Brian felt the exact opposite way. In addition to liking the production of the track more than that of the other songs I played for them, they liked the idea of introducing Reflection Eternal to the marketplace by having Mr. Man and Mos Def on our debut single. It would create synergy that would help them sell my record as well as the upcoming Mos Def album they were working on.

It took me a couple of months to decide if I trusted the Rawkus rollout plan, but eventually I did. By the winter of 1997, my first single, Reflection Eternal's "Fortified Live," with the song "2000 Seasons" on the B-side, was available in fine record stores all over the world. This was a defining moment in my household, because having a piece of vinyl with my name on it made it real for my parents. They grew up on vinyl, so in their minds, if I had a vinyl record, then this rap thing might have a chance of working out. Perry and Brenda were always cautiously supportive of my musical endeavors, but they had no way to gauge my success. Now they were starting to get excited at the possibilities that were before me. My friends were also excited. We now had a rapper, an official rapper, in the crew. Guys from the Flatbush/Flatlands area where I was living, like my man Louis, Rubix, JuJu, and his brother Zean, were with me during those years and watched me grow from the basement to the stage to the record deal. It felt as if the whole neighborhood had a song out.

The intense reaction to the production of "Fortified Live" from the hip-hop community let me know that Hi-Tek was working on the level of professional producers who had been in the game for a while. The song instantly became a staple of underground freestyle ciphers, and radio DJs loved playing it in the mix. One night, we got an unexpected but welcome compliment from Hov himself, Jay-Z. Jay was a guest on DJ Clue's mix show on Hot 97 and decided to participate in a freestyle cipher with some other MCs who were in the studio. As I listened to the cipher on the radio in real time, DJ Clue threw on the instrumental to "Fortified Live," but clearly he wasn't that impressed with what was being spit on it because right before Jay-Z started, Clue switched the beat to something else. Immediately Jay-Z said, "What was the beat you had on before? Bring that beat back!" I couldn't believe it. Jay-Z was beginning to be considered the best of the best, and he heard the same thing in Hi-Tek's beats that I did. DJ Clue put the "Fortified Live" instrumental back on, and Jay-Z lit it up with bar after bar, live on air.

Shortly before Rawkus released "Fortified Live," they released a single from Yasiin called "Universal Magnetic." "Universal Magnetic" had a song called "If You Can Huh! You Can Hear" as its B-side, and these songs were both produced by a shy young producer from Virginia named Shawn J. Period. Yasiin and Shawn's musical relationship paralleled the one I had with Hi-Tek, and Shawn J. inspired Hi-Tek in ways similar to how Yasiin Bey inspired me. Whenever Yasiin or I had shows, we would all go, and it became commonplace to see Yasiin and me rock together. We developed an onstage camaraderie that enhanced both of our shows, and the guys from Rawkus noticed. They were gearing up to put out a Mos Def album, but they were looking for ways to increase his buzz in the marketplace. Rawkus figured that if they could push a record featuring Yasiin and me before they dropped the Mos Def album, the Mos Def album would be even bigger. While Rawkus was making this plan, Yasiin and I were making our own plans to have me come out to L.A. to cut some songs while he was working on a movie. When Jarret approached us with the group idea, it felt divinely inspired. Yasiin exclaimed, "I already have a name. Black Star."

16

The Eighth Light

The white dwarf star invisible to the naked eye
We making the tide rise like when the moon overtake the sky
—TALIB KWELI, "UNDERSTAND"

A white dwarf is a star, approximately the size of a planet, that has undergone gravitational collapse and is in the final stages of evolution. The tribe of the Dogon, who settled in Mali, West Africa, and were one of the last African tribes to retain an oral tradition and not be colonized by Europeans, are believed to have been able to see white dwarf stars that were supposed to be invisible without the use of astronomical instruments. A black dwarf star is the theoretical celestial object that remains after a white dwarf has used up all of its fuel, cooled off, and is now a solid mass of carbon. I say theoretical because a black dwarf star has never been observed.

In the martial art of jujitsu is a school called Hakkoryu. The Japanese word *hakkoryu* translates to "the school of the eighth light." The color spectrum has seven bands, but ancient Japanese people believed that there was also another, a narrow and barely visible band called the Eighth Light. A proverb was associated with this band: From the faint and the weak in appearance comes surprising strength. Hakkoryu jujitsu employs this proverb in its teaching, and its practitioners use the body's natural motions rather than exhibitions of strength. These techniques are not necessarily visible to the naked eye, just like the black dwarf star. These kinds of things were on Yasiin's mind when he came up with the title for the second song on *Black Star*, "Astronomy (8th Light)." Black Star. You can't see us.

While Yasiin had his head above the clouds, the first image that popped into my brain when he said Black Star was Marcus Garvey. While Garvey's shipping line, the Black Star Line, never made it to Africa, Yasiin and I were determined to use our music to connect hip-hop with its African roots and to unapologetically celebrate our culture. We would use our album to help complete Garvey's ultimate goal, which was the uplifting of a race of people. In the fall of 1997, along with Hi-Tek; the Columbus, Ohio, producer J. Rawls; and my good friend and manager at the time, Rich Mason, I headed out to California to begin recording *Black Star* with Yasiin Bey.

While filming Daniel Pyne's 1998 indie comedy, *Where's Marlowe?*, Yasiin was staying at the Beverly Garland Hotel in Sherman Oaks. Even though it wasn't a suite, Yasiin was gracious enough to let all of us crash in his room wherever we could find the space to lie down. Kendra Ross, a friend of mine from my NYU days, informed her father, who owned a recording studio in Los Angeles, that I was in town, and he let Yasiin and me use his space to record what would be the first Black Star ideas to two-inch reel. Songs like "Definition" and "Brown Skin Lady" were created that week. After Yasiin finished working on *Where's Marlowe?*, we moved the *Black Star* sessions to Funky Slice Studios in the heart of downtown Brooklyn. Funky Slice was famous for being the studio where hip-hop classics were made, and we chose it after seeing it mentioned on the back covers of albums by rappers like Big Daddy Kane and MC Lyte.

Getting to know Yasiin Bey better during this period was not just one of the greatest things to happen to my career, but also one of the greatest things to happen to my life. I don't think I've ever met a more pure artist. Yasiin is every bit as charismatic in person as he comes across onstage, on-screen, or on records. His energy is infectious and his brilliance is unmatched by most. Yasiin moves to the beat of his own drum, which often means he may be late, but when he shows up, it's always on time, and when he doesn't show up, that means it wasn't meant to happen. More than any other artist I've met, Yasiin Bey knows his value, and he knew it long before the world knew who Mos Def was.

I can recall many times being confused by Yasiin's moves, only to see him eventually be proven right. He would often ask promoters and label owners for sums of money that I didn't think we could get, then I'd be pleasantly surprised when they would begrudgingly say yes. He made everyone around him work on his terms and took care of his people handsomely when things went right. Yasiin was fond of saying, "You know how you thank people? You pay them." This made him more than a friend, as he was heavily involved in helping me take care of my family. This made us family.

Creatively, we as Black Star worked because Yasiin had tools in his arsenal that I wanted, and I had tools in mine that he wanted. I would marvel at his ability to command a stage by treating it like his living room, and I was impressed at his ability to take high-minded concepts and break them down into relatively simple rhyme patterns and schemes. Yasiin would come up with an entire song concept the moment he heard a beat and often lay

it down within an hour of conception. I knew that he was draw-
ing from a plethora of concepts that were constantly floating thru
his head, but his connection to the music was so natural, it was
amazing to see these concepts come to life in the most beautiful
ways. Songs like "Brown Skin Lady" and "Definition" leaped out
of Yasiin the moment he heard those tracks.

My process was a bit different. I would need to take the beats
home for a few days and live with them. I needed alone time to
fully immerse myself in what the beat was trying to pull out of
me. You can hear this difference in our rhyme styles. I was a lot
more wordy and intricate in how I approached my verses on *Black
Star*. Yasiin was constantly impressed by this. He could quote
verses of mine at length that I sometimes couldn't even remember, and he would point out lyrical things I did that felt easy for
me but were harder for him to do. Yasiin is known for lighting up
a room with hilarious and heartfelt anecdotes about his favorite
people, places, and things. He is always on when people are
around, testing out ideas and concepts in the same way stand-up
comedians test out jokes on their friends, and I was often the subject of his routines. Yasiin's wholehearted embrace of my artistry
helped me gain a confidence that would allow me to take my
career to the next level. He didn't just help make me a better
performer, he helped make me a better man.

The *Black Star* album was finished in the spring of 1998. The
original recording budget of $30,000 that Rawkus provided for us
had ballooned to $75,000, but it was money well spent. *Mos Def &
Talib Kweli Are Black Star* was largely produced by Hi-Tek, but it
also featured stellar production from future underground hip-hop
legends like J. Rawls, Ge-ology, and Shawn J. Period. Track 2, "Astronomy (8th Light)," was produced by the Beatminerz from Black
Moon fame and featured the jazz legend Weldon Irvine on the
piano. Track 11, "Respiration," featured an incredible verse by

Chicago's own Common, and the final track, "Twice Inna Life-time," was "Fortified Live" reworked as a posse cut featuring up-and-coming MCs named Wordsworth, Punchline, and Jane Doe.

"Thieves in the Night," the second-to-last song on *Black Star*, produced by 88-Keys, may best encapsulate the creative influences that brought Yasiin and me together. The song's title and hook were lifted from the last paragraph of Toni Morrison's seminal work of fiction *The Bluest Eye*. That was one of the first books I had read that helped me to realize what great literature was, and I recommended it to many customers while working at Nkiru Books. *Black Star* is littered with book references, but this song is our most direct connection to the canon of great literature. We created this song in the basement of the Long Island home of 88-Keys's Cameroonian parents. Initially, Yasiin wasn't a fan of the track, a simple, jazzy piano loop over sparse drums, but after hearing my verse, he changed his tune.

Yasiin and I got to know each other thru his many visits to Nkiru Books, and my knowledge of books was what initially drew him to me. Having access to so many books has always given me a lyrical advantage, and this is well illustrated on "Thieves in the Night." The last paragraph of *The Bluest Eye* was one of the most well-written critiques of society I had ever read. It rattled in my brain for years, and by fashioning hip-hop lyrics out of it, I elevated the social commentary in my music. My verse on "Thieves in the Night" is essentially an attempt to explain that last paragraph in lyrical terms. When people point out the potency of my lyrics, I always have to pay it forward to great writers like Toni Morrison who influenced me. My ancestors and my OGs are giants, and by standing on their shoulders I can see the mountaintops clearly.

Even though Yasiin and I were fully invested in our Black Star partnership, from the beginning we saw it as a springboard for our other endeavors. We saw Black Star as more of a collaborative one-off than a group project. The plan was to use *Black Star* to whet the audience's appetites for what was to come next, Yasiin's *Black on Both Sides* and Reflection Eternal's *Train of Thought*. We saw ourselves as partners in rhyme who would collaborate here and there, but also as bluesmen with separate visions for how to bring music into the world. The response to *Black Star*, however, was so phenomenal that we have been linked to its legacy in ways we never imagined while recording it. *Black Star* filled a void in the music industry and reconnected to hip-hop many people who had given up on it.

Today, Black Star is often mentioned alongside giants such as Run-DMC, Outkast, and A Tribe Called Quest. Even though many of the solo albums Yasiin and I have put out have outsold *Black Star*, the album continues to resonate more with our original fan base. It has given us a cultural currency that outweighs any amount of money we've made throughout our respective careers. Because of this, our fans always ask us about the possibility of a second Black Star album. To that end, we've had many false starts, but we also realized that great music happens organically, and we've never wanted to force it. Black Star was, and is, a vibe. A vibe cannot be re-created; it can only be appreciated for what it is. The Black Star vibe started out on street corners and small stages around New York City, and when we perform together nowadays, which is often, we pay homage to that vibe rather than attempt to re-create it. We are always moving forward, never backward. Will there ever be another Black Star album? Time will tell. When Yasiin and I get together, it is as brothers first; the music is secondary.

One of the smartest things that Rawkus did with rolling out *Black Star* was to get us shows overseas early, months before we dropped the album. The first time I visited Europe was for Black Star shows in London and Paris. I flew to Heathrow in the fall of 1997 with Yasiin; his manager, Shaka; and Hi-Tek. The moment we landed, we were arrested on suspicion of transporting narcotics. Because customs agents are legally allowed to profile, the only four young Black men on that international flight were stopped by security and intensely interrogated for hours. The British customs agents wanted to know what four Black men from America with little money in their pockets planned to do in the United Kingdom. Rawkus had failed to provide us with an itinerary, telling us that all the information we needed would be provided by the person picking us up, but when we could not tell the customs agents where we were staying, it made them even more suspicious than they already were. Convinced that we must be hiding drugs somewhere, after thoroughly inspecting our luggage and finding nothing, they handcuffed us and drove us to a nearby hospital to have our stomachs x-rayed.

Sitting on a cold gurney in a hospital gown, handcuffed with my ass out waiting to have my stomach x-rayed, was not the European welcome I had expected. It was fascinating that, based solely on the color of our skin, despite all evidence to the contrary, these customs agents had convinced themselves beyond a shadow of a doubt that we were drug mules. When the X-rays all came back showing none of us were trying to sneak anything into the United Kingdom, the customs agents seemed genuinely perplexed. After about eight total hours of being treated like international drug smugglers, we were let go. On the drive back to Heathrow from the hospital, I asked one of the agents if they were even going to offer an apology for inconveniencing us for so long. I will never forget his response: "Apologize? For what? I was doing my job."

Yasiin would later immortalize our Heathrow experience in his song "Mr. Nigga" from his debut solo album, *Black on Both Sides*. The affair was a wake-up call to me and showed me exactly how Black men were viewed internationally. It didn't matter that we were on our way to being famous or that Yasiin was dressed respectably in slacks and a suit jacket, as he is known to do. Those customs agents decided on sight what kind of people we were, and they had the authority to treat us accordingly.

On September 29, 1998, Rawkus Entertainment released my debut album, *Mos Def & Talib Kweli Are Black Star*. On this same day, several other hip-hop albums were released by groups that I grew up listening to, such as Brand Nubian's *Foundation*, A Tribe Called Quest's *Love Movement*, and Outkast's *Aquemini*. I was two years into a burgeoning career, but competing for record sales with my heroes made me feel as if I had made it. *Black Star* was hailed as a new classic almost immediately, and from this day forward, my life and musical legacy would be forever linked to Mos Def. Together we began to make a lot of money in the music business, more than our parents had ever seen in a year. To stay true to the dedication to hip-hop culture that got us to where we were, the first thing we did with our rap money was purchase Nkiru Books from its owner, Mrs. Adelaide Miller.

To protectors of white supremacy, one of the most terrifying forces on the planet is an intelligent Black person. To many, "educated" equates to "rich" and "white," so when people learn that my parents are professors, they try to hold it against me, as if I am not proud that my parents worked hard to provide their children with the best educational opportunities available. While I certainly don't enjoy the privilege of having "white" skin in a society that values white people over people of color, being born a professor's son has granted me vast amounts of educational privilege that I do not take for granted. Educational privilege has a close association with class privilege, but that doesn't mean that all educated people are rich. Plenty of professors with a Ph.D. are one missed check away from abject poverty, especially in a city with a cost of living as high as New York City's.

Call it a bias that results from my academic privilege, but I have found it hard to trust people who do not keep books in their home. I realize that poor people have a far harder time gaining access to books, but I spent my teenage years surrounded by poor people who never let poverty stop them from educating themselves. The mission was to gain knowledge by any means necessary, because only thru knowledge of self could we achieve liberation. This is not a value judgment of people—just an observation. Not all pertinent knowledge is found in books, but in my experience those who strive for literacy have a far better chance of making it out of any undesirable situation. Surrounding myself with readers and getting a job first at Shakespeare & Co. and then at Nkiru Books was a matter of tactical survival as much as it was a way of getting paid.

By 1998, bookstores were considered dying businesses, and consumers' lack of interest in owning books was felt most harshly by independent Black booksellers. Big chains like Barnes & Noble were using government loans to pay their bills, which allowed them to price out the independent stores. The chains were also co-opting book signings, the last reason many consumers had to visit their local bookseller. Prominent authors began skipping visits to the independent stores, opting to do book signings at chain stores, which had a bigger reach. On top of this, online hubs for books like Amazon.com were becoming behemoths, and Nkiru Books was in no position to compete. As more and more of Nkiru's core base began to find books for cheaper elsewhere, Mrs. Miller began to worry about if the store could survive.

Black Star was first introduced as a duo at one of the many open mic events I threw at Nkiru Books that were designed to bring customers into the store. For this reason, Nkiru held a special place in Yasiin's heart as well as mine, so when he found out that the store was in financial trouble, he suggested that we use some of our Black Star show money to purchase the store and try to turn it around.

When I first approached Mrs. Miller with this proposition, she was skeptical; Nkiru Books was her daughter Leothy's vision, and the only reason Mrs. Miller came out of retirement to run it was because of Leothy's untimely death. But Mrs. Miller was also tired of the stress that came with paying that rent every month, so she eventually agreed to sell Nkiru Books to Yasiin and me.

While we certainly had more capital to play with than Mrs. Miller, Yasiin and I didn't know any more about running a bookstore than she did. Throwing money at a problem never solves the problem unless you know exactly where and how to invest that money, and our efforts to save Nkiru may have come too late. We would lose the location for Nkiru Books, 76 St. Marks Avenue, within three years of purchasing the business, but not from lack of trying. Even before the arrival of Barclays Center, that area of Brooklyn was gentrifying rapidly, and our landlord was raising the rent almost monthly in an attempt to push Nkiru out to make room for more profitable tenants. Nkiru Books moved to a location deeper in Brooklyn on Washington Avenue for a couple of years before we were forced to close its doors for good.

Nowadays Nkiru Books lives on as an online store at my website, Kweliclub.com. I try to maintain the spirit of Leothy Miller Owens's original vision by curating the store myself. We still focus on children's books and carry many multicultural titles not easily found at the more mainstream bookstores. Black Star keeps on trucking as well. Even though we only released one album together, Black Star has lived on just as it started, as a live experience. Yasiin and I were held up as the poster children for the underground hip-hop movement that gave commercial rap the middle finger. While Diddy and Jay-Z were ruling nightclubs around the world with tales of champagne, cars, and women, Black Star brought lyricism and consciousness back to the forefront of the conversation.

17

~~~

The Joy

It is our duty to fight for our freedom. It is our duty to win.
We must love and support each other. We have
nothing to lose but our chains.

—ASSATA SHAKUR

The month before *Black Star* was released, I took Darcel and Amani on a family vacation to Jamaica. We stayed at a small beach hotel in Negril, and even though I could barely afford the trip, we thoroughly enjoyed ourselves. Amani was two years old, and this was his first time seeing the ocean in its vastness. Darcel and I spent our days on the beach with Amani, and at night we drank rum punch and danced to a little boom box I'd brought with me. I loved my young family, but little did I know it was about to grow. When we returned to Brooklyn from Jamaica, Darcel was pregnant.

Even though times were hard, hard enough to consider other options, Darcel and I knew that this new child would be nothing but a blessing. My career was just beginning, and if I could afford to take my family on vacation, I certainly had the means to care for another child. The first thing I had to do was become my own man and move out of 4709 Avenue K once and for all. My parents had graciously let us stay there without charging rent and were helpful in caring for Amani, but living rent-free in someone else's house with two children was unacceptable to me, even if it was my parents' house. After a couple of months of saving I had enough to rent a two-bedroom duplex in Park Slope at 42 St. Marks Avenue, approximately half a block from 76 St. Marks Avenue, where Nkiru Books was.

I loved being back in Park Slope, the neighborhood I was raised in. Starting a new family here felt right to me, as if I had come full circle. Being so close to Nkiru Books was great as well. It would take me thirty seconds to walk to work, and now that Yasiin and I owned the store, I had to be way more hands-on. The summer months were always tough on the book business, and the time of Nkiru's transition of ownership from Mrs. Miller to Yasiin and me was especially bleak. By August 1998 CJ had left for a higher-paying job, and Aaron left because the store was too inconsistent with his salary. After Yasiin and I took over, Paulette stayed on, and I hired my good friend Rubix, who had just moved back to New York after spending a couple of years trying to make a life in Atlanta, Georgia.

That same year, 1999, Yasiin and I were booked to tour as Black Star on the Coca-Cola sponsored IYDKYDG tour (pronounced *idik-gidik*). This tour must have been the product of some sort of high-concept corporate mind-fuck marketing session, because it didn't make any sense. IYDKYDG stood for If You Don't Know You Don't Go, and no one must've known, because nobody went. Alongside the Black Eyed Peas (the first version, sans Fergie) and the legendary hip-hop icon Biz Markie, we were paid a lot of money to show up in cities to perform in empty rooms.

I guess Coca-Cola was running a promotion where consumers would find a code for tickets to these shows on the sides of cans and bottles of soda; I never understood it. I don't think they did either.

The money for these shows was good, but as practitioners of the art form, Yasiin and I felt like corporate shills. For the true artist, performing for an empty room is unfulfilling, regardless of what you are being paid. Whenever we pulled up to a new city, I would head to the local mall with will.i.am, Apl, and Taboo from the Black Eyed Peas to hand out free passes for the shows, but this was 1999, and the majority of mall shoppers had never heard of Black Star or the Black Eyed Peas.

About halfway thru the tour, on June 10, 1999, while getting ready to perform in Washington, D.C., I received a call from Darcel right before I took the stage. Her water had broken, and she was about to have her baby. This was frustrating news to me because the decision to tour while Darcel was in the final month of pregnancy had already weighed heavily on me. I decided to tour because the money was good, but knowing how important it had been for me to be in the room for Amani's birth, I hated the possibility of not being in the room for the birth of my second child. Thankfully, Darcel and I had opted to not deal with hospitals and traditional Western practices for our second child. Our experience with Amani's birth at Downstate Hospital had been negative. The doctors kept trying to force drugs and epidurals on Darcel, and because of the stereotypical myth of the deadbeat Black father, I was often not made to feel welcome at the hospital. The second time around, we hired a doula, who developed a pregnancy plan specifically suited to Darcel's personality and our family needs. There was no need to rush Darcel to a hospital; she was set up to birth our child right there at 42 St. Marks Avenue.

Back in D.C., after telling Yasiin the news, I still had to

perform to get paid. We must have done ten minutes of our set before I whispered to Yasiin onstage that I had to leave, and he was like, "Go! I will hold you down!" I left the stage, ran out the front door of the venue, hailed a taxi, and asked the driver to take me to Brooklyn as fast as he could. After he looked back at me incredulously for a few beats, I asked, "Are you gonna take me or not? 'Cause if not, I need to find someone who will." The taxi driver told me it would be $400 to $500 for the trip, so I pulled out all the money I had in my pocket and handed it to him. Four hours later, we were pulling up to 42 St. Marks Avenue.

When I walked in the apartment, I was greeted by the glow of soft red lights, the music of Alice Coltrane, and the faint smell of nag champa incense. The doula approached me and asked if I wanted to meet my daughter. She led me to the bedroom, where Darcel was in bed, cuddling with our new child. Born weighing ten pounds, Diani Eshe Greene is what we named this beautiful baby girl. Diani was the name of a beach in South Africa that I read about somewhere, and we liked that it rhymed with Amani. *Eshe* is a word in many African dialects that is loosely translated as "amen." Diani was absolutely stunning. She had a full head of hair, she was long, and she was lighter skinned than both Darcel and I. Diani was closer in complexion to my grandmother Javotte than to anyone else in my family.

Diani's birth helped to put many things back into perspective for me. With my career on the verge of becoming successful, many temptations lay ahead of me. Focusing on Darcel, Amani, and now Diani was what brought me home at night. Having a wonderful partner to raise a son and a daughter with, I understood that God had blessed me with as close to a perfect family as I could have hoped for. I was determined not to mess that up, no matter what traps this music business would set for me. Almost immediately after Diani's birth, I took our family on another vacation, this time to the Dominican Republic. Within two months of arriving on earth, Diani was already an international traveler.

Hip-hop was turning me into quite the little international traveler myself. Since the release of *Black Star*, I had been to several countries and all over America on tour. Because of the conscious content of *Black Star*, Yasiin and I were embraced by activist groups and asked to perform at many of their events. We routinely performed at events held by Refuse & Resist!, an organization that supported political prisoners, and we were invited to open for the Beastie Boys at their concert at the Meadowlands Arena in 1999 to bring attention to the case of the famed political prisoner Mumia Abu-Jamal. Even though we received a lot of hate and criticism for supporting people like Mumia, who was falsely accused of murdering a police officer and is still in prison for life right now, we knew we had no choice but to stand for the people who gave their lives for us. We could not just be conscious MCs; this consciousness had to permeate all of our actions.

One of the first groups Yasiin and I associated with closely was the Malcolm X Grassroots Movement, or MXGM, a community-based group that organized around combating systems of white supremacy and around supporting political prisoners. MXGM has many chapters, but Yasiin and I were approached by the leaders of the New York chapter, Lumumba and Monifa Bandele. Although I thought I had a pretty firm understanding of how systemic oppression affected the community, the political education I received from Lumumba and Monifa gave me a language to better describe it and a plan to combat it. Besides the annual Black August concerts I performed at that MXGM threw to raise much-needed funds for political prisoners, they started community food and clothing drives, implemented neighborhood cop-watch programs, and sponsored various forums on political education.

When MXGM asked Yasiin and me to perform at a Black

August concert in Havana, Cuba, in the summer of 1999, I knew I had to go. Black August started in the prisons of California in the late 1970s as a way to honor freedom fighters whose actions during the month of August contributed to education and liberation, people like George Jackson, Jonathan Jackson, and Khatari Gaulden. MXGM members built on the concept of Black August and added fund-raising concerts to the mix. In August 1999 I began my journey to Cuba with Yasiin; Hi-Tek; the homie Rich Mason; Lumumba; Monifa; M-1 of dead prez; the current mayor of Newark, New Jersey, Ras Baraka; and several others.

Because of the embargo the United States had had in place against Cuba since 1962, we could not fly from the States to Cuba. We had to stop in the Bahamas, then take prop planes to Havana. Upon arriving in Havana, we were let in without having our passports stamped and driven straight to the hotel. The first thing one notices in Cuba is the vintage automobiles; the embargo effectively stopped new cars from being sold in Cuba, which made the whole city look like a postcard from the 1960s. The second thing one notices in Cuba is the proliferation of prostitution. One of the most negative effects the embargo had on the Cuban economy was making prostitution one of the only things people could depend on for income, and it was blatantly everywhere. We would be there for about two weeks, which would give us enough time not only to visit Havana's cultural and historic institutions but also to explore Havana's seedy underbelly.

A few days into our trip, a group of us were offered a chance to meet the legendary freedom fighter Assata Shakur. During the 1970s Assata was a member of the Black Panther Party and the Black Liberation Army. In 1973, she was involved in a shoot-out on the New Jersey Turnpike that resulted in her being shot and accused of killing a police officer named Werner Foerster, among several other crimes. Assata always maintained her innocence, and despite providing medical evidence that she was shot while she had her hands up, making it impossible for her to have shot anyone, she was convicted of the killing of Officer Foerster, while being acquitted of every other charge. Jailed for this crime in 1977, Assata escaped from prison in 1979 and lived as a fugitive in the United States until 1984. Then, along with fellow BLA activist and fugitive Nehanda Abiodun, she made her way to Cuba, where they both received political asylum from Fidel Castro's government. Assata Shakur's involvement with the Panthers and the BLA, her refusal to comply with police orders, her injuries and incarceration at the hands of a racist state, coupled with her jail time, escape, and eventual political asylum, have made her a hero to freedom fighters and political prisoners worldwide. I had read her autobiography, *Assata*, more than once and sold many copies of it at Nkiru Books. I could not believe hip-hop was providing me with an opportunity to meet someone who had gone thru so much for our culture.

Not until 2005 would the United States declare Assata Shakur a domestic terrorist, but in 1999 one still had to take many precautions to meet her in Cuba. On the day of the meet, we were given a time and a place. A van pulled up and we were blindfolded as we entered it. After about a half-hour drive, we arrived at a home where Assata greeted us and sat with us for lunch. I did more listening than talking, as I was overwhelmed by what seemed to be a larger-than-life figure. Assata was vibrant, full of life, passionate, and extremely gracious. She spoke about missing America, especially her family, but she also spoke about how welcoming the Cuban people had been to her. She spoke of having had to make peace with the idea that she would never be able to leave Cuba. Even though she wasn't that familiar with my music, she was excited to learn that young people who listened to hip-hop found inspiration in her story. She expressed a deep love for the hip-hop community and impressed upon us the need for us to never forget the sacrifices of those who struggled before us.

Meeting Assata put a battery in my back. It renewed my vigor and made me want to be a better example for my people in general, especially now that I had a daughter to raise. It was on us to raise the next generation of Assatas, and hip-hop music provided me a unique platform with which to do so. On the day of the Black August concert, I was determined to bring my A game and show the people of Cuba how much hip-hop had their back. During the time I spent in Havana, I learned that Cuban hip-hop fans appreciated conscious lyricism far more than the materialistic drivel that was being imported around the world from the States. Even though Cuba was one of the world's poorest countries, the people I met loved their country, they loved Fidel Castro, and they were drawn to art that pushed against the status quo. In fact, the Cuban government demanded that we send them copies of our lyrics before they allowed us to participate in the Cuban hip-hop festival that MXGM was helping to organize along with Nehanda Abiodun around Black August. The government wanted to make sure that our lyrics were not anti-Castro or too materialistic.

As hard as Yasiin and I tried to impress the Cuban crowd of hip-hop lovers with our witty couplets delivered in our native English, our efforts were met with indifference. Havana already had a thriving hip-hop scene that boasted its own superstars. Cut off from the world, Cuban hip-hop artists developed their own hip-hop community, and they definitely did not see us Americans as having a monopoly on dope hip-hop. The crowd tolerated the Black Star set, but they were far more excited to see local Cuban hip-hop acts like Obsesión and Grupo Uno. The one thing that did impress the crowd during our set was Hi-Tek scratching on the turntables. Another negative effect of the embargo was a severe lack of electronic equipment, including DJ equipment.

Aspiring Cuban DJs and producers would imitate the sound of cutting and scratching by forcing two live wires to touch, but while many of them could rhyme well, they had never seen a DJ actually scratching on turntables. Hi-Tek's cuts and scratches received the hugest reception of anything we did on that stage.

Being recognized for artistic expression is seductive. It is easy to believe in and get caught up in the hype that surrounds you. In America, Yasiin and I had become hip-hop media darlings, but performing in Cuba showed me how small my world was. I knew that hip-hop was global, but having celebrity privilege was a new experience for me. Growing up in America as a Black man was hard, but I had infinitely more resources at my disposal than these Cubans did. When I returned to the States, I knew I had to put those resources to good use.

18

~m~

The Bizness

To all, rise and shine, give God the glory
I already gave a percent of mine to Bert and Corey
—POSDNUOS (OF DE LA SOUL), "HE COMES"

It was 1999 and I was now officially a rapper for a living. Like the razor blade on the company's logo, Rawkus Entertainment was slicing thru the record industry at breakneck speed. In the years since I'd met Jarret Myer and Brian Brater during that cipher at Makeba's crib, Rawkus had expanded its operation from about five people to a fully staffed label with several different departments. After finding initial success by partnering with underground hip-hop acts like Sir Menelik, Shabaam Sahdeeq, and Company Flow, Rawkus began to dominate the underground market by releasing twelve-inch singles with any artists who could make a name for themselves in the scene. By focusing primarily on the twelve-inch vinyl single, Rawkus found a dedicated fan base in DJs around the world who were bemoaning that the major record labels were only producing CDs. By the time

Yasiin and I began recording *Black Star*, Rawkus Entertainment had dropped so many hot hip-hop singles that fans were supporting artists for simply being associated with Rawkus. Seeing that Rawkus razor-blade logo on a twelve-inch single was a virtual guarantee that it would be fresh.

El-P, then the leader of the Rawkus-affiliated group Company Flow and today one-half of the standout group Run the Jewels, pioneered an "independent as fuck" mantra that Rawkus essentially co-opted and ran with. Using the money provided to them by James Murdoch, Rawkus competed for shelf and advertising space with all the major labels but sold themselves as an indie underdog. This endeared them to the movement of underground hip-hop fans and artists that felt shut out of mainstream hip-hop. In our community Rawkus Entertainment had become the vanguard, the only label that was "keeping it real." However, when Funkmaster Flex began to support the *Black Star* single "Definition" on Hot 97, Rawkus changed its direction. Being seen as "independent as fuck" was cool as long as you couldn't get on mainstream radio. Once the owners of Rawkus had a taste of a mainstream hit, they wanted more.

As fans of the culture, Jarret and Brian used their newfound success to sign respected hip-hop artists they grew up listening to, like Kool G Rap, Pharoahe Monch, and Smif-N-Wessun, aka the Cocoa Brovaz. They even put out a posthumous album by the celebrated Harlem lyricist Big L, who had been murdered the year before the album, *The Big Picture*, dropped. Big L's untimely death helped to make his album go gold, and this in turn further cemented Rawkus's reputation as the go-to label for authentic, underground hip-hop. While Jarret and Brian certainly respected this new batch of Rawkus signees, they began to invest more time in trying to tailor the singles they released to fit a radio format, rather than let the artists deliver that pure underground sound that made them famous in the first place. The Rawkus office at 676

Broadway in Greenwich Village went from being a place where underground rappers would converge to play their new music surrounded by a cloud of thick blunt smoke, to a more sleek, corporate environment where we would argue about whether a single was radio-friendly enough. This change made Yasiin want to exit the label, and right after they dropped his debut solo album, *Black on Both Sides*, Yasiin left Rawkus Entertainment for MCA Records.

When *Black Star* came out, more opportunities opened up for Yasiin and me, but Yasiin's career took off a bit faster than mine. Mos Def was the first official rock star to emerge from underground, independent hip-hop. While that was happening, I revisited the Reflection Eternal conversation with Rawkus, and we decided that my next album would be with Hi-Tek. The official name of the group would be Talib Kweli and Hi-Tek Are Reflection Eternal, and the album would be called *Train of Thought*. Now that Rawkus artists were becoming household names, Jarret and Brian wanted to have more control over their releases. They felt a bit burned by Yasiin's leaving the label and did not want me to be able to leave Rawkus as easily after they'd invested so much in us artists, so the contract for the Reflection Eternal album was a lot more involved. I knew I needed a manager and a lawyer to help me navigate this business. The homie Rich Mason had been playing the role of my manager for a few years, but I was calling all the shots, and neither Rich nor I knew how to read contracts written in complicated legalese.

While recording *Black Star*, I had showed up at a Common show at Tramps to try to convince him to spit a guest verse. I didn't know Common, but he was my favorite, and I was determined to get him to deliver the rough track. After being curved a couple of times by Common's manager, Derek Dudley, I waited outside Common's tour bus while he did press. He was filming an episode of BET's *Rap City* with the host, Joe Clair, and in that episode you can see me in the background waiting while Common is being interviewed. After the interview wrapped, Common was ushered back on the tour bus before I could get to him. I waited a few more minutes and got ready to leave; then a familiar-looking dark-skinned brother came off the bus and said, "Kweli, wassup, what are you doing out here?" Even though the dude looked familiar, I couldn't recall his name, but he certainly knew me, so I responded, "Just waiting for Common to talk to him about this song." This dude then invited me on the bus, and I chopped it up with Common about what would eventually become his verse on the *Black Star* song "Respiration." The dude was Corey Smyth, and this was the start of our working relationship.

Born in Harlem in 1973 to a schoolteacher mother, just like me, Corey Smyth was a dancer and party promoter during the early 1990s. He toured with Brand Nubian's Grand Puba as a dancer and ended up starting Rowdy Records with the Atlanta producer Dallas Austin while attending Morehouse College. After rotating back to New York City and finding a rare baseball card, Corey sold it for around $20,000 and used the profits to rent an office and start an artist management company called Blacksmith Management. One of his first groups was the Bay Area's Zion I, and for a stint he managed Yasiin Bey, but Corey's real coup was becoming De La Soul's manager around 1998. De La was an iconic hip-hop group with a platinum album under their belt, so managing De La gave a young Corey Smyth instant credibility in the business.

Noticing that I was operating without management, Corey took a managerial interest in me, sending work my way. Offers for shows and features that De La Soul turned down or were too busy for often made sense for me. Corey never asked for a dime; he was just looking out for me as a fan of my work. I appreciated him for this, and I discussed the possibility of asking him to manage Reflection Eternal. But Hi-Tek was developing a closer relationship with Shaka, Q-Tip's friend who was now managing Yasiin. Hi-Tek was more of a street dude like Shaka, whereas Corey and I were both the sons of educators, so Hi-Tek's and my styles would clash a little. Hi-Tek thought that Shaka would be the better manager for the group. Even though he wasn't fully convinced, Hi-Tek ended up following my lead and Corey Smyth became the manager for Reflection Eternal. No contract was signed between us because Corey did not believe in management contracts. He preferred a handshake agreement. We agreed that for the work Corey did, Blacksmith Management would receive 20 percent of everything the group made.

The first thing Corey did as manager was work to get more favorable terms added to the Reflection Eternal agreement with Rawkus and get the initial recording advance raised significantly. Once the contract was signed, I focused all of my energy on recording *Train of Thought*. I was respected as a lyricist but still living in Yasiin's shadow, and many believed that I wasn't talented enough to lyrically carry an entire album by myself. My sole focus was proving those people wrong and making people understand the beauty of Hi-Tek's production. While recording, I stayed in Cincinnati for months, first at the Quality Inn in Covington, Kentucky, until that got too expensive, then with friends in the area.

The more time I spent in Cincinnati, the more strain I put on my relationship with Darcel. I missed her and the kids, but I was singularly focused on my mission to become one of the world's most respected MCs. Darcel and I began to argue a lot, and what once seemed like a perfect union began to show cracks. Since I was in Cincinnati so much, I could escape and not deal with the arguments whenever I chose. I started to take advantage of my ability to escape so much that I got comfortable in that space. I met women in Cincinnati and started new relationships. On Thanksgiving of 1999, I decided to stay in Cincinnati and work rather than fly home to be with my family. I was twenty-four years old with a burgeoning hip-hop career, and I was feeling myself so much that I didn't think I needed that emotional connection I'd made with my family every Thanksgiving since I was born. Boy, was I wrong. That night, eating dry turkey by myself in the Covington Quality Inn restaurant, was one of the loneliest nights of my life.

While I was trying to keep my personal life from falling apart, Hi-Tek seemed to be in an incredibly productive zone, cranking out beats that would become the foundations for songs like "Good Mourning," "Some Kind of Wonderful," and "Memories Live." Dudes that would be in the studio with Hi-Tek like Big Del and Piakhan were added to give the album some Cincinnati flavor. Yasiin hopped on the energetic "This Means You." After finishing the recording in Cincinnati, we hunkered down at Mirror Image Studios in New York City with the famed hip-hop engineer Troy Hightower for epically long mix sessions. By the fall of 1999, I knew that *Train of Thought* was on its way to being a piece of work that Hi-Tek and I could both be proud of, but we were still missing some things. We didn't know what exactly, but we headed to Electric Lady Studios on Eighth Street in Greenwich Village to find it.

That fall, Electric Lady, built in the late 1960s by Jimi Hendrix, was the place to be for cutting-edge hip-hop musicians. In Studio A, in the basement, you would find the Roots drummer Questlove, pianist James Poyser, and bassist Pino Palladino working with D'Angelo on his career-defining album, *Voodoo*. On the second floor, in Studio B, J Dilla from Slum Village was co-executive-producing Common's fourth album, *Like Water for Chocolate*. Studio C, on the top floor, belonged to Hi-Tek and me, and we were there daily trying to put the finishing touches on *Train of Thought*. When I needed inspiration, I would walk the streets of the Village, my old stomping grounds, where I'd honed my skills as an MC. I would often run into friends and celebrities, many of whom were invited to come to the studio and kick it. Often 88-Keys came thru, and he brought the girls who didn't know how to pronounce my name at the start of "The Blast." Gil Scott-Heron stopped by while he was working on a song with Yasiin and me called "Little Brother" for the *Hurricane* movie sound track. Lennox Lewis, who was the heavyweight champion of the world, came thru. Anyone who came to the session was asked to get on the microphone and state their name, followed by a drop for the Reflection Eternal album. One guest in particular took the album-drop concept to new heights: his name was Dave Chappelle.

Dave Chappelle and I became good friends while I was recording the Reflection Eternal album, but our story begins a bit earlier than that. While I was working at the bookstore in 1995, I was dating a girl who had just broken up with Dave. I knew this because their relationship was pretty involved, and Dave was always kind of around the whole time I was with this girl. All I knew about Dave was his character Reggie from the *Nutty Professor* movie. After a couple of months, this girl broke up with me and began to date another actor/comedian who was more famous than I was. I had yet to step my game up, apparently.

Around 1998, I attended a De La Soul show in Yellow Springs, Ohio, Dave's hometown, that Dave was at. Dave, a huge hip-hop fan, had since released the movie *Half Baked*, which was one of my favorites of all time. After bugging him out by letting him know that we dated the same girl, I geeked out while he told me stories from the *Half Baked* set, then we rocked out to De La Soul together. So when I saw Dave and his future wife, Elaine, walking down Eighth Street one afternoon while I was recording *Train of Thought*, we had an instant connection and I invited him to come hang out with us at Electric Lady. Dave came by later that evening, then came to every single remaining Reflection Eternal session until we finished the album. When he was asked to do his drop, he didn't do one as Dave Chappelle but instead decided to do it as Nelson Mandela, Bill Clinton, and Rick James. We kept the Mandela and Rick James ones, even though Dave sounded a lot more like Bootsy Collins than Rick James. It would be years before his Rick James impersonation would evolve after hearing Charlie Murphy's "True Hollywood Stories." Dave's Mandela impersonation, however, was spot-on. To this day, people still ask me how Hi-Tek and I got Nelson Mandela to do a drop for our album.

19

Reflections of Our Ancestors

If you can talk, you can sing; if you can walk, you can dance.
—ZIMBABWEAN PROVERB

I have worked with the best producers in hip-hop, but Hi-Tek remains my absolute favorite producer to work with. His production style is a huge part of my musical DNA. He was the first producer to wrap beats around the never-ending river of rhymes that poured out of my head in a way that made them make musical sense. An astute observer, Hi-Tek never did much talking, but his music spoke volumes. Without his production my rhymes probably would've never had the right vehicle to properly drive my points home.

During the initial recording and promotion of the Reflection Eternal album, I always showed a lot of love to Hi-Tek in my songs, onstage, and in interviews, but not until much later in my career did I truly understand his importance in my life. Both of us are stubborn visionaries in songwriting, and while we both love the same type of hip-hop, we spent a lot of time arguing over how to create it. My approach to hip-hop was that of a curious outsider whose ambition to compete with the greats placed me in a circle of the best doing it. As the son of professors, I didn't grow up break-dancing or writing my name in graffiti on a wall, I grew up appreciating hip-hop for its connection to the poetry of the Black Liberation Movement. It took me years to get out of my head and allow the music to flow thru me naturally. Hi-Tek was first and foremost a B-boy who grew up dancing. He was raised around hustlers, and his father was a soul singer who fronted his own band, the Willie Cottrell Band. Our different approaches to creating music were reflected in our different upbringings. While I had a lofty and academic approach to creating songs, Hi-Tek was more guttural, focusing solely on the vibe.

If the vibe wasn't right, Hi-Tek wouldn't create. Many times he would begin working on a beat that I would love, then he'd scrap it and tell me he wasn't feeling it while I was writing to it. Other times he would tell me to be less wordy or intricate. Back then I dismissed this criticism as Hi-Tek's not understanding the point of my rhymes. I now know that whether he understood the point of a rhyme was irrelevant; he was solely focused on how it hit the ear. Working on the Reflection Eternal album in such proximity for two years almost made us dislike each other. Neither of us would bend, which meant that the only ideas that made it out of the lab were the very best ones. I often compare making that album to Superman's crushing pieces of coal in his hands to make diamonds. Our creative friction helped create a great body of work.

My primary goal on *Train of Thought* was complete lyrical domination. I wasn't focused on what the fans wanted, I wasn't focused on hit singles. I just wanted other MCs to hear me and say I was the best. I would write entire songs to those Hi-Tek beats, scrap them, and start over, never satisfied with what I came up with. On songs that featured other MCs, like "Ghetto After-life," featuring one of the greatest lyricists of all time, Kool G Rap, I would damn near torture myself in the booth to get the lyrics, flow, and cadences right. On "Down for the Count," featuring Rah Digga and Xzibit, I wrote my verse over and over for days and recorded in the booth for twelve hours straight. I rapped so much that day I lost my voice that night and had to take a couple of days off before continuing.

"Love Language," the first of the many hip-hop ballads I would come to be known for, was dedicated to and inspired by Darcel, who had given me two beautiful children in Amani and Diani. The first verse is me trying to reconcile with the music industry's pulling me away from Darcel romantically, so it references night-clubs and the fights that couples go thru as they grow with each other. The second verse reaffirms my commitment to love, and the third verse, written at a Jamaican hotel called the Rockhouse, with its references to coral reefs and floral pieces, is me reminding my-self who Darcel was to me and why I fell in love with her in the first place. Being back in Jamaica while working on *Train of Thought* for the first time since I went with Darcel and Amani taught me how important location was to writing for me. From that moment until now I often visit the Caribbean at the start of an album to get my mind right.

Science fiction movies like *Blade Runner* show us that memo-ries separate human beings from machines, and the lyrics to the song "Memories Live" was me coming to terms with my mortal-ity. This song taught me how to write to the beat; before working with Hi-Tek I was writing to the beat in my head and trying to fit the words into spaces where they did not necessarily belong. Tak-ing my cue from the Ann Peebles sample the beat was built around, I started "Memories Live" as a letter to my son, but ended it by correctly predicting that this album would somehow get me to

Africa. Along the way, I came to terms with my parents' splitting up. Even though this had had a huge impact on me, I had hardly spoken about it. I used "Memories Live" to explore how I felt about it and to say to my parents how proud I was of them for deciding to put the mental health of their children ahead of their relationship.

"Africa Dream" is the song that best captures how differently Hi-Tek and I felt about creating music. Although he would eventually agree with me, Hi-Tek did not at first like the beat he created for what would become "Africa Dream." After watching him scrap so many beats that I liked, I finally put my foot down when I heard this one. "Africa Dream" was one of the last songs we recorded for *Train of Thought*, and I think Hi-Tek had probably had enough of my complaints, so he allowed me to record on the beat and to put it on the album on two conditions. First, he would not be listed as the track's producer. Second, he would be allowed to put a track on the album that I did not like called "Big Del from da Nati."

Big Del was, and is still to this day, one of Hi-Tek's greatest friends. Back then, Big Del was working at a Big Boy restaurant in Cincinnati and would come to the studio after work to smoke, drink, and vibe with us during recording sessions. I loved having Big Del around, but for Hi-Tek it was more than that. Big Del helped to create the exact vibe Hi-Tek needed in order to create. Big Del's opinion was highly valued because Hi-Tek felt that Big Del represented an impartial third-party voice as well as the average consumer who would decide whether to purchase our album. Hi-Tek understood better than I did that my quest for complete lyrical domination meant nothing if the vibe wasn't right, and Big Del helped Hi-Tek to vibrate higher.

As much as I loved Big Del's energy, I felt that *Train of Thought* was my first true lyrical statement to the world, and the short freestyle that Big Del dropped over "Big Del from da Nati" didn't cut it for me. I felt that Big Del's lyrics, like the song's title, were too simple and literal. By the time the album dropped, I realized that simple and literal was exactly what was needed to balance out the intensity of what I was doing lyrically. Hi-Tek used my challenge as an opportunity to give *Train of Thought* a much-needed lighthearted breather of a song. Meanwhile, I used the track he begrudgingly let me have to create "Africa Dream," a song intended to create the full experience of all Black music in one track. It starts out with African drums played by a friend of mine named Delwynn who I went to junior high school with, accompanied by Weldon Irvine on keys. The first words on "Africa Dream" are from a Zimbabwean proverb because African proverbs are in many ways the first hip-hop lyrics.

When Hi-Tek and I turned *Train of Thought* in to Rawkus, they didn't quite jump for joy. Jarret and Brian seemed to like the album well enough, but they were looking for a single they could push to radio, and according to them, Hi-Tek and I had failed to record one. Still high from the success at radio they had had with Pharoahe Monch's *Godzilla*-sampling monster jam, "Simon Says," Jarret and Brian had switched from the "independent as fuck" mentality they co-opted from Company Flow and were now chasing hit records. To me, songs like "Move Somethin'," "Love Language" (featuring Les Nubians), "Too Late," and "Touch You" (featuring Piakhan) were potential hits that could garner airplay with the correct promotion. Still, Jarret and Brian refused to accept the album until we recorded one more song that could be a potential single. As Hi-Tek and I prepared to shoot the video for "Move Something," we went back to Electric Lady to record one more song, "The Blast."

The concept behind "The Blast" was Corey Smyth's. Throughout the recording of *Train of Thought* Corey tried to convince us that we needed a song that would teach people how to pronounce my name, which he found people to have difficulty with during his representation of us. Hi-Tek had had the track for "The Blast" since before I met him, and I had written rhymes to it before but never completed them. When Hi-Tek played the track in Electric Lady that night, Corey stopped and said, "That singing in the sample sounds like it's saying, 'Kweli.'" This was the seed. I wrote down *you pronounce my name Kwa-lee, any questions*, and by the end of the night, "The Blast" was born.

Train of Thought was epic and sprawling. I took all of my frustration, pain, hopes, and dreams and spread them out over the album's twenty tracks. *Black Star* introduced me to the music industry, but *Train of Thought* was my official statement of arrival as an MC. The video for "Move Something," which featured a cameo appearance by Dave Chappelle, dropped shortly before the album and created a small buzz, but it would be the Little X–directed video for "The Blast" that would capture people's attention and make them take Hi-Tek and me seriously. As we geared up to drop the album and the video for "The Blast," Corey approached us with an idea about a tour called Spitkicker.

20

~~~

Spitkickers

It's important we communicate
And tune the fate of this union to the right pitch
—COMMON, "THE LIGHT"

The guys in De La Soul understood the power of a collective; they excelled at artistic collaboration. As original members of the famed Native Tongues crew, they knew that power came in numbers, and Dave Jolicoeur from De La Soul came up with the name for a new crew: Spitkicker. Dave saw what was happening with the Rawkus artists and recognized the potential for it to be bigger, so he got with Corey to make Spitkicker an official crew. The original Spitkicker crew were De La Soul, Common, Pharoahe Monch, Biz Markie, and Reflection Eternal, Hi-Tek and me. Once the crew members were established, we put together a nationwide Spitkicker tour that rolled out in the summer of 2000. Besides Biz Markie, all of us had albums that had either dropped or were about to drop. De La Soul had just dropped their fifth album, *Art Official Intelligence*. Pharoahe had just dropped his solo debut album, *Internal Affairs*. Common's *Like Water for Chocolate* dropped right before the tour began, and *Train of Thought* dropped right as the tour ended.

Putting Hi-Tek and me on tour with seasoned acts like De La Soul, Common, and Biz Markie was like throwing a baby into the pool to teach it how to swim. I was riding on tour buses to perform in different cities every night. Because I had yet to master breath control, I was screaming into the mic nightly, losing my voice after every show. I would perform until I was drenched with sweat, while drinking liquor and smoking weed to excess. I would party every night after the show, going out to nightclubs, trying to pick up women. I was going thru a mushroom phase as well, so I shroomed a lot on the Spitkicker tour. Like a merry band of pirates the Spitkicker crew ran thru town after town, collecting the spoils of our victories. I learned a lot by watching De La and Common every night. By the end of the tour, I was a far better performer than I was when we first left. However, the most important lesson I learned from the Spitkicker tour is that you have to maintain your health while traveling.

We were in a small club in Pittsburgh on the last night of the tour. After a month on the road I had a fever of 102 degrees and I was more exhausted than I could ever remember being in my life. Lying in my hotel bed on a rainy night minutes before the show, feeling sickly, I was trying to psych myself up for one more hit, but it wasn't working. I decided to eat the last of the mushrooms I had. I figured that if I got really high, the show would go by more quickly. I figured wrong. By the time I got to the club, the combination of the mushrooms and my fever had me tripping balls. During my set, I felt as if the audience was onto me, and I began to panic. I walked over to the DJ set and whispered to Hi-Tek that I didn't feel well, apologized to the audience, cut my set short, and ran three blocks in the pouring rain back to the hotel. When I got in my room and looked in the mirror, I was startled because I did not recognize the person staring back at me. I looked like a zombie. I spent a few minutes staring at myself in the mirror, trying to find me, then took a cold shower to try to bring my high down. When that didn't work, I lay in bed and stared at the ceiling, scared to fall asleep out of fear that I would not wake up. I called my mom to tell her I loved her and I missed her in case this was my last night alive. Yeah. I was tripping.

When the Spitkicker tour ended, I slept every day for a week straight. I had no desire to leave the house, and every time I woke up from one of those deep sleeps, I was drenched in sweat. The entire area around where I slept would be soaked. Darcel was worried. Fearing I had contracted something nasty, I went to see a doctor, who told me I was simply exhausted and that sweating was my body's way of trying to release the many toxins I had put in it while touring. Still, the tour was an amazing experience. I knew I loved to travel, and I had traveled quite a bit by then for a twenty-four-year-old man, but living on a tour bus and being in a different city every night was a rush I had never felt before and one I couldn't wait to feel again.

My next opportunity to tour arrived almost immediately. On October 17, 2000, the album *Train of Thought* arrived in stores, but was also available online. The internet had begun to change the dynamics of the music industry in a major way, and while forward-thinking artists and entrepreneurs were embracing it, the industry was trying to get as far away from it as possible. The business model of the music industry in the year 2000 was that all money being made from music belonged to the industry. Artists were treated like employees by managers and label executives and were given limited access to pertinent information. The less informed you kept an artist, the easier it was to take advantage. The internet, however, allowed artists to have access to information and resources they had never had and connected them with fans and like-minded artists without ever having to leave the house. By 2000, the communities of artists that challenged one another in the way that the Greenwich Village MC scene of the early 1990s challenged me existed online rather than in the parks. Underground rappers who couldn't get on mainstream radio had a new outlet in internet radio, magazines were becoming less relevant for their failure to keep up with the speed of the now, and aspiring MCs were battling one another in the comment sections of their favorite blogs.

This climate fostered the rise of Okayplayer.com. Started by Ahmir "Questlove" Thompson and the writer Angela Nissel, Okayplayer started out as an online fan club for the Roots, but by the summer of 2000 it had evolved into the main hub for an artistic community that included but was not limited to the Roots, D'Angelo, Bahamadia, dead prez, Common, Q-Tip, Erykah Badu, Slum Village, the Jazzyfatnastees, Jaguar Wright, Hi-Tek, and me. Rawkus was behind the curve with online marketing, and neither Corey, Hi-Tek, nor I was familiar enough with the internet to take it seriously, so we turned to the good folks at Okayplayer .com to help us engage with our fans online. I felt honored to be considered a part of such an incredibly talented group of artists, and I was grateful to the Okayplayer staff for going above and beyond to make sure that Hi-Tek and I had some sort of proper online representation.

While album sales did not reflect this, *Train of Thought* was an immediate critical success. Music reviewers loved it, and fans loudly declared it to be a proper follow-up to the cherished *Black Star*. So when the Okayplayer tour got ready to roll out in the fall of 2000, I was asked to come out and rep for Reflection Eternal. The tour would consist of the Roots playing for a revolving door of Okayplayer-affiliated acts, so to save money, I went on the tour while Hi-Tek stayed in Cincinnati. Alongside the Roots, I toured the country for two months straight, often doing two sets a night with the Roots as my backing band. This was a dream come true.

Beyond enjoying my own time onstage, I got to see some of the world's best hip-hop and soul music acts nightly during that tour. Bahamadia, a legendary female MC from Philadelphia and the first "famous" rapper that I ever recorded with (see "Chaos," from Rawkus's *Soundbombing II*), brought Phat Kat out as a hype man, and together they opened the set by going back and forth with fierce rhymes. The Jazzyfatnastees, a singing duo from Los Angeles who worked closely with the Roots, would be up next and add sweet melodies to the hip-hop-centric Roots set. Next up, T3 and Baatin from Slum Village would hit the stage doing Roots-backed sections from their classic underground album, *Fan-Tas-Tic, Vol. 1*. The group's producer, J Dilla, preferred to stay in his home-town of Detroit working on music and only came to a couple of shows. Bringing us back to soul and R&B, Philly's own Jaguar Wright would stalk the stage next armed with a bottle of Jack Daniel's in one hand and righteous fury in the other. Jaguar's songs were often filled with a mix of pain and anger, and her voice was so powerful, it matched the emotion in the songs every night. After Jaguar, I came on and did a medley of selections from my Black Star and Reflection Eternal albums, which set the stage for M1 and stic.man of dead prez to come on and rock songs from their powerful debut album, *Let's Get Free*.

Every night we would run the set in this order, then repeat it with different songs while the Roots performed some of their fan favorites in between the transitions. The encore for every night was a rousing rendition of dead prez's revolutionary club classic "It's Bigger Than Hip-Hop," with all the performers onstage at once.

Once word of the tour began to spread, the shows only got bigger. Guest artists such as Guru from Gang Starr and Big Daddy Kane would sit in with us on various nights. Even though the Okayplayer tour was a full month longer than the Spitkicker tour, I did not get sick because I heeded the lessons. I curbed the smoking and drinking, only partaking in these vices after the show rather than throughout the day. I slowed down the partying. Whereas on the Spitkicker tour I was rolling with a bunch of dudes all day, I rode on the bus with the Jazzyfatnastees and Jaguar, the women, on the Okayplayer tour. I found that having feminine energy around me all day made me curb my appetite for meeting strange women at night. When a bunch of dudes hang out all day, their testosterone levels are thru the roof by the night, and they start competing for the attention of women.

By the end of the Okayplayer tour my home life had fallen apart. Even though I curbed some of the bad habits I picked up on the Spitkicker tour, it was too little, too late. I was giving too much of my time and energy to other women, taking my focus away from Darcel and my children. I had proven incapable of being faithful on tour, which weighed heavily on me. I was selfishly trying both to live a flashy "rap life" and to be a family man. Darcel remained the same, always having my back, but I was changing. I was outgrowing our relationship, and I had to make a decision. Either I had to focus on fixing my relationship or I would have to let Darcel go.

Instead of returning home after the tour, I booked a room in the newly built Hudson Hotel on Fifty-Eighth Street in Manhattan. I stayed there for about two months while I prepared for my next adventure, a spot on tour with R&B stars Erykah Badu and Musiq Soulchild that was set to roll out in February 2001. Hi-Tek and I were both asked to go on this tour, but he declined, deciding instead to focus on producing new tracks at home in Cincinnati.

While touring was becoming profitable for me, Hi-Tek felt that his time was more efficiently spent in the lab. I was forced to find a tour DJ, and being that I would be touring with two R&B singers, I decided to add backup singers to my stage show. After a few weeks of auditions, I hit the road supporting Erykah Badu on the Mama's Gun tour with a new DJ, DJ Chaps, and two wonderful singers named Stephanie McKay and Tiffany Mynon.

Mama's Gun by Erykah Badu may be my favorite album of the "neo-soul" era, and I'm sure touring with her during that album's release has something to do with how I feel about it. Having already captured the music world's attention with the jazzy riffs and Five Percenter philosophy that made up her debut album, *Baduizm*, Erykah used *Mama's Gun* to let us know just how serious a musician she was. Working closely with producers such as J Dilla of Slum Village, Erykah crafted instantly classic tracks that seemed to defy space and time. She had recorded *Mama's Gun* during an emotional breakup, and every night onstage I would watch her relive those emotions thru song. Touring with De La Soul and the Roots solidified my hip-hop credentials and taught me a lot about live shows, but touring with Erykah was a master class in becoming who you were when you wrote the song. Seeing Erykah perform "Green Eyes" every night, which is a song about dealing with the jealousy one feels when one's ex-partner moves on to a new love, touched me in a particularly personal way. I felt as if Erykah had perfectly captured what Darcel had been trying to convey to me lately, and that song made me more compassionate about Darcel's situation.

After the Mama's Gun tour I had a renewed passion to connect with my family, but I also knew I no longer wanted to live with Darcel. Our relationship was becoming a thing of the past, so I began to focus on coparenting rather than trying to fix us. I wanted the freedom to come and go as I pleased, but also the feeling of love you get from seeing your family every night. I ended up renting an apartment not far from 42 St. Marks Avenue. Anytime I wanted to see Darcel, Amani, and Diani, all I had to do was walk half a block. This living arrangement, as selfish as it was, was perfect for how I was living at the time. I could maintain the appearance of being a father who lived with his children while living like a bachelor. I still spent a lot of time with Amani and Diani, but whenever things between Darcel and me got too intense, I could escape to my apartment. It was, for a short time, the illusion of the best of both worlds.

21

The Strange Land

I had crossed the line. I was *free*; but there was no one to welcome me
to the land of freedom. I was a stranger in a strange land.

—HARRIET TUBMAN

It had been two years since I went to Cuba with members of the Malcolm X Grassroots Movement, but I still performed annually at MXGM's Black August concert, which raised
money that continued to pay for activist-style community services
all over the country and to provide support for political prisoners.
In 2001, MXGM decided to throw three Black August concerts in
South Africa. The prediction I made at the end of "Memories Live"
had come true within a year. We would start our trip in Durban
during an international conference on racism, head to Cape Town,
and then end in Johannesburg. In August 2001 I left for Africa
with Jeru the Damaja and his DJ Tommy, Black Thought from the
Roots, stic.man and M1 from dead prez, and Boots Riley from
the revolutionary Bay Area hip-hop group the Coup. Also traveling with us were respected journalists and activists like Monifa

Bandele, Rosa Clemente, and dream hampton, but what was especially exciting to me was that my younger brother, Jamal, would be coming as well.

Jamal and I were close growing up. Being close in age made us best friends until I hit puberty and began to be more interested in impressing my peers than my family. As I began cutting class in high school and running around getting high, Jamal stayed in the books and was at the top of his class regardless of which class he was in. As I became less interested in baseball and then sports altogether, I gave Jamal my baseball card collection, which he enhanced and maintained nicely. This stoked his interest in sports, and he approached it as methodically as he did everything else in his life. All thru high school and college Jamal could recite any sports statistic like a machine. By 2001, Jamal had graduated from Harvard University and parlayed his sports knowledge into a journalism job at the Cadillac of sports magazines, *Sports Illustrated*. He was his own man now, and I was looking forward to getting to know the adult Jamal on a different level. Being with my brother on my first trip to Africa was special for me.

When we arrived in South Africa, the international conference on racism was in full swing. Leaders from around the globe were at a hotel in Durban to discuss policies that would foster racial equality. As the conference became critical of the Israeli government's treatment of Palestinians as second-class citizens, General Colin Powell, the U.S. representative in town for the event, walked out in a show of solidarity with Israel. This action did not endear Americans to the South Africans attending the conference. Having lived under the brutal foot of apartheid until recently, South Africans recognized what was going on in Israel as apartheid, and the United States, with all the tax dollars it sends to Israel, was Israel's coconspirator in this unacceptable practice. Our Black

August tour group was scheduled to speak to a group of journalists during the conference about hip-hop's role in activism, but after General Powell walked out, the questioning at our conference became more pointed.

As young musicians from America, many of us were out of our element at this conference. While some of the questions were about music, many of them were about America's role in policing and oppressing the world. These South Africans wanted to know not only how we were combating injustice at home but what qualified us to speak to them about injustices they had been fighting long before we arrived. As we tried to explain that we were there in solidarity with them, we got a lot of pushback. People mentioned how the jeans and sneakers we were wearing cost more than the income of entire villages in Africa. They brought to our attention that we were probably charging too much money for the average South African to be able to attend our concert. As the conversation got heated to the point of shouting, Rosa Clemente and dream hampton tried to steer us in a more positive direction, but it wasn't working. Not until stic.man from dead prez stepped up did things start turning around. Stic was the quietest of all of us. He had spoken little for the whole trip, being a quiet observer instead. When he did speak, it was humble, measured, insightful, inclusive, and right on time. Stic accurately conveyed what the South Africans were trying to get us to understand, while explaining to them that we were there to learn, not lead. This was the first of many lessons I have since received on being a good ally. Good allies do not declare themselves to be such; a good ally knows when to listen.

After listening to and learning from our South African brothers and sisters, we decided to lower the entrance fees at all of our South Africa shows. We spent a couple of nights in Durban before heading to Cape Town for our first show, at a small nightclub. The people were extremely gracious and welcoming. This show didn't feel any different from underground hip-hop shows that I had grown up going to in New York. Seeing how hip-hop had empowered people of color all over the planet, but especially in the motherland, was wonderful. After Cape Town we headed to Johannesburg, where we visited the home of Winnie Mandela. Somehow MXGM secured the Johannesburg train station as the venue for Black August, and we put on an incredible show for thousands of South Africans. Because many people who lived in the townships could not afford the Johannesburg show, the day after, we set up a free show in a plaza in the middle of Soweto. The response we received from the people was amazing. One shoeless boy came up to ask me how Amani and Diani were doing. A fan, he had both the Black Star and Reflection Eternal albums and had heard me rap about my kids. It blew me away that he didn't have any shoes, but he had my albums.

After spending two weeks traveling thru South Africa, our group headed back to New York City. We landed on September 9, 2001. As incredible as my African trip had been, I was looking forward to getting home to my family. I missed Amani and Diani immensely, and Amani was starting preschool that year, so I wanted to help him navigate this experience. On September 10 I spent the evening at 42 St. Marks Avenue and stayed the night. As Darcel took Amani to school the next morning, I stayed to watch Diani. I tried to start my day by making some business calls, but my cell phone wasn't working. Certain areas of the apartment had bad reception, so around 9:00 a.m. I stepped out onto the block to make my calls. I immediately noticed an eerie, quiet energy in the streets. The people passing by seemed more intense than usual, and they were moving pretty fast, even for New Yorkers. Still trying to get cell reception, I stopped a dude walking by me who was trying to get reception on his phone. I said,

"You ain't getting reception either, huh?" His response? "We are under attack! Look!" He pointed down the street in the direction of Manhattan. From St. Marks Avenue, I had a clear view of the Twin Towers of New York City's World Trade Center, which were about two miles from the apartment. They were engulfed in flames. It was September 11, 2001.

While I claim no religion, being given a traditionally Muslim name at birth has endeared me to Muslims all over the world. Being a Black man with a Muslim name has given me a firsthand view into the xenophobia that many Muslims experience globally and has helped me to be more compassionate to the struggles that many Muslims face. I choose not to identify with a religion, but I have a great respect for Islam. I like that true Muslims consider Islam a way of life more than a religion, and that they acknowledge prophets of other religions as worthy of respect. Some of the most intelligent, compassionate, and gracious people I've ever met have been Muslims, and I can see how Islam, when studied properly, can lead to intellectual and spiritual enlightenment. A great many critiques can be made about how some people interpret Islam regarding basic human rights, but I find practitioners of other religions who pretend that the Quran is worse on human rights than the Bible to be hypocritical. These holy books have far more in common than many people think.

Long before 9/11, anti-Islamic sentiment in America had reached a boiling point. The events of 9/11 simply gave many American bigots a twisted justification for their hatred of Islam. People who only see terrorism when it's done by brown people or when it's done in the name of values they hold dear often ignore context. The Middle East is in turmoil, and many there have reason to hate the United States. U.S. imperialism has destroyed many lives, and the U.S. government has never been above terrorism to achieve its goals. The circumstances that led to the events of

September 11, 2001, were put into place long before Osama bin Laden was born. For any student of history, this is crystal clear. I was a bit surprised when so many Americans, including some of my peers in the hip-hop community, adopted bandwagon patriotism and lined up behind the Bush administration's childish and dangerous response to our national threats.

Upon seeing the Twin Towers on fire, I ran back into the house, grabbed Diani, and headed to Amani's school to get him. My mom had beat me to the punch, arriving at the school minutes before I did, so I headed to her house to get Amani, then went back to 42 St. Marks Avenue and met up with Darcel. Once I knew the family was secure, I headed back out into the street to try to get some firsthand information. I had been paying attention to the news, but in the early hours after the attack so many rumors and conflicting stories were flying around that I decided to shut it off until the journalists stopped speculating and had some real info. Realizing I wouldn't be able to get a taxi and that public transportation would be a no go, I hopped on my bicycle and headed down Flatbush Avenue toward Manhattan. Walking up Flatbush was a wall of people who had crossed the Brooklyn and Manhattan Bridges on foot, many of them covered in soot and dust. The crowd of people was too thick for me to make any headway, so I rode to my homie Rich Mason's crib in Bed-Stuy. Rich had roof access with a nice view of downtown Manhattan, so I figured I could pay attention to everything that was happening from up there. I ran into Jeru the Damaja upon arriving at Rich's crib; apparently Jeru had the same roof idea. We all spent a few hours on the roof watching the city burn, listening to news reports and trying to figure out exactly what new world we were facing.

We had never before seen an attack of this magnitude on American soil, so many Americans, facing for the first time the possibility that terrorism could affect their lives, retreated to fear. People I knew and respected surprised me by, at best, enabling xenophobia, and, at worst, by being outright racist. Some claimed to act this way in the name of patriotism, some claimed it to be pragmatism, but none of it was pleasant.

22

~~~

Wake Up, Mr. West!

I'm not the hero. I'm the guy in the crowd
making fun of the hero's shirt.
—SETH MACFARLANE

Black Star was my introduction to the world. Reflection Eternal was proof that I could hold my own as an MC. My debut solo album would have to prove that I wasn't a fluke, that I was an exceptional MC and here to stay. Would I be able to turn in a classic piece of work without a producer as talented as Hi-Tek overseeing it? *Quality* gave me the opportunity to fully realize the music in my head without any roadblocks. However, sometimes roadblocks keep you from danger.

DJ Scratch, who produced "Shock Body," was the first producer to land a placement on *Quality*. I took a Megahertz track down to Jamaica to find the reggae superstar Super Cat and throw him on a song called "Gun Music"; I ended up finding his young brother Junior Cat, who is on the song with Brooklyn's own Cocoa Brovaz. I enlisted Bilal to help me record a version of my favorite ballad, Eddie Kendricks's "Can I," which I called "Talk to You (Lil' Darlin')," and I flew to Los Angeles to record "Put It in the Air" with DJ Quik. On "Stand to the Side," one of the two *Quality* songs produced by the late, great J Dilla, we brought a piece of wood into the studio for Savion Glover to tap on. I didn't care that you couldn't see him when you listened; I was trying to incorporate all types of Black music into one hip-hop opus.

Quality starts with Dave Chappelle doing a civil rights character he made up on the spot over a beat produced by the Fyre Dept, which puts the listener in the same space they were in when they heard Dave doing his Nelson Mandela impersonation on the intro of the Reflection Eternal album. Lyrically, I knew I had to top what I had already done with *Black Star* and *Train of Thought*, but I was also coming into my own as a songwriter and I was starting to have more fun with my craft. I was taking the lessons I'd learned from working with Yasiin and Hi-Tek and was finally creating my own uninhibited musical vision. On the Megahertz-produced "Rush," I talked a lot of shit over rock guitars, and on "Joy," featuring Mos Def, I may have created hip-hop's first dedication to doulas while detailing the birth of Amani and Diani. On "Won't You Stay," produced by Supa Dave West and featuring my good friend Kendra Ross, I stepped up my hip-hop ballad game by trying to put myself in the shoes of the women who are in love with musicians, for better or for worse.

The most interesting development of the *Quality* recording sessions was my burgeoning relationship with a young producer named Kanye West. One night late into the recording of the album, Kanye walked thru the studio door looking for Yasiin Bey. Yasiin had said he was showing up to record vocals for "Joy" that night, but he had yet to arrive. I invited Kanye, who I had never met, to wait for him. When Kanye mentioned that he produced,

I asked him to play some tracks. When he pushed play on that CD, my jaw dropped. Not since Hi-Tek had an unknown producer played something for me that literally gave me chills. This was some of the best hip-hop I had ever heard, yet no one knew about it. Two of the tracks Kanye played for me that night made it onto *Quality*, "Good to You" and "Guerrilla Monsoon Rap," featuring Kanye, Black Thought, and Pharoahe Monch.

Kanye's star began to rise after that initial recording session. In September 2001, Jay-Z dropped his career-defining masterpiece album, *The Blueprint*, with the lead single, "Izzo (H.O.V.A.)," and many of the album cuts produced by Kanye. Kanye can be seen in the video for "Izzo," mean-mugging and showing off his tats. As fans of the art began to dissect *The Blueprint*, they began to understand that Kanye and Just Blaze were the producers responsible for Jay-Z's new but instantly classic sound. However, the more people began to check for Kanye West beats, the more he tried to explain that he was a rapper who only started to produce so that he could get his raps out there. *The Blueprint* secured Roc-A-Fella Records a dominant spot in the hip-hop food chain of the early 2000s, and as one of the main architects of its sound, Kanye became the go-to guy for not just Roc-A-Fella artists but any hip-hop or R&B act looking for a hit that dripped with authenticity. Often showing up at events dressed like a walking contradiction of styles with his blinged-out Roc-A-Fella chain, Polo sweaters, and Louis Vuitton book bag, Kanye relished every opportunity to spit in the face of those who said hip-hop artists had to fit in neat little packages. By keeping his rhymes unflinchingly honest and staying on top of his production chops, he was the first artist to be embraced by the underground and mainstream fans in equal measure.

—m—

Golly, more of that bullshit ice rap
I gotta apologize to Mos and Kweli
—KANYE WEST, "BREATHE IN BREATHE OUT"

Kanye gave me a beat CD the week after I turned *Quality* in to Rawkus for shipping. One of the tracks on the CD was based around snippets from a live recording of Nina Simone's classic song "Sinnerman." Kanye took Nina's haunting vocals and made an intro with them, then he chopped her piano playing to hip-hop perfection. The moment I heard it, I made it my mission to get this track. This was only a year after we first met, but within that year Kanye had gone from the guy who would offer me any of his tracks to the guy doing songs with Mariah Carey, to whom, he told me, he'd promised that beat. I asked him to keep me in mind if she changed hers, and I called him once a week to ask him about it in case he forgot. After about a month of my harassing him, he finally agreed to give me the beat.

When I first wrote to the track that would become "Get By," it was in four-bar intervals that ended with the refrain "just to get by." I wrote a bunch of those and kept the ones I liked, and that's what became the heart of those verses. After I laid them, I invited Kanye to the studio to listen. His idea was that this song should be hip-hop gospel, and he began to improvise the chorus, singing in a high-pitched wail that was meant to give me an idea of what the person singing the hook should sound like.

The melodies of the "Get By" hook that Kanye came up with are infectious, but the hook is the lyrics:

Just to stop smoking, and stop drinking
but I been thinking, I got my reasons
just to get by

Everybody has vices; I find it hard to trust people who say they don't. Anyone who has been thru any struggle can identify with the hook of "Get By." To bring out the gospel that Kanye was looking for, he wanted to use the Harlem Boys Choir. He didn't even have a deal yet and he was already thinking big. The Harlem Boys Choir was too expensive for me, and Kanye used them on his own track, "Two Words," from *The College Dropout*. No matter. I had my own secret weapon, Kendra Ross, my good friend whose father let us record some of *Black Star* at his studio. Kendra brought some of her singer friends to the studio to complete Kanye's gospel vision. Abby Dobson, who I've worked with extensively throughout my career, is one of the voices on the hook, along with William Taylor and Vernetta Bobien. Chinua Hawk translated Kanye's high-pitched wail into a run for the ages that my fans love trying to duplicate at the shows. The moment the song came together, I knew it was special.

"Get By" was massive out of the gate. The song was extremely well crafted. I was an underground favorite and Kanye West was becoming the face of hip-hop. DJ Enuff began to play "Get By" on his trendsetting mix show on New York's Hot 97, which led to its being added into the rotation. Big Von from KMEL in the Bay Area jumped on it around the same time, and by getting "Get By" to spark off in the country's two biggest hip-hop radio markets, we got the video played all over BET and MTV, which led to radio play on every hip-hop station in the nation. I asked Jay-Z to get on the remix, and he agreed, via two-way pager. After not hearing back from him for two months, I received a cryptic text from Jay that said, "What's your email address?" Moments later,

I had the recording session of a Jay-Z verse to "Get By" in my inbox. When I ran into him again later that year, I insisted on paying for that verse. Jay refused to take my money. He informed me that he charges entire recording budgets for a verse and that he was giving me that verse out of love for the culture.

Jay-Z was far from the only rapper willing to lay a verse on "Get By." Busta Rhymes was also gracious enough to send me a remix verse thru email days after the song came out. When I sent my rough Jay-Z/Busta Rhymes "Get By" remix to Kanye for approval, he was in the studio with Yasiin, and they both added verses. Before I even heard their verses, Kanye was up at Hot 97 with DJ Enuff, playing "his" remix on air. Snoop Dogg added a verse to what became a West Coast version of the remix. And 50 Cent used the beat for one of the many mixtape songs he dropped in 2003. "Get By" was becoming a monster hit that I could not control. I needed to stop fighting it and let it be great.

By the spring of 2003 "Get By" was a bona fide hit, and MCA Records had been absorbed by Universal Music Group's Geffen Records. Aided by the hottest names in hip-hop, the "Get By" remix seemed like an unstoppable force of nature. That was, until it landed on the desk of Def Jam executive Lyor Cohen, who contacted Rawkus to find out why Def Jam's most profitable artist was giving credence to this underground movement by doing songs with the likes of me. While Jay-Z had graciously agreed to record a verse for me out of respect for the craft, Roc-A-Fella Records' contract with Def Jam at the time stipulated that Def Jam had to give permission for all Jay-Z feature appearances. Lyor Cohen did not approve of Rawkus or Geffen making any money off Jay-Z. A cease-and-desist letter was sent to all radio hip-hop DJs and radio stations, which scared them out of playing the remix; it went from almost two thousand weekly spins to zero in a week's time.

My success has never been defined by what was playing on the radio, and I was blessed that "Get By" also helped with the shows. After it dropped, my show became one of the hottest commodities on the hip-hop touring circuit, along with acts like the Roots, De La Soul, and Common. While I was opening for Common as he toured his *Electric Circus* album around the country in 2003, Kanye asked if he could come on tour with me. Kanye was already becoming one of my favorite artists. He was struggling to get a record deal, and I was struggling to understand why. To my ears, the bars he went around spitting to anyone who would listen were pretty impressive. The rest of the industry seemed to be so blinded by his superb production that they couldn't even hear his rhymes; they were too busy trying to get his beats from him to care.

I heard most of Kanye's 2003's *College Dropout* on Common's *Electric Circus* tour during the spring of 2003. I also heard the rhymes for "Gold Digger" and "Hey Mama," songs that didn't get revealed until Kanye's *Late Registration* album from 2005. Herein lies the genius of Kanye West. Everything the man says is going to happen, does. He is the concept of manifest destiny reworked as a Black boy from the South Side of Chicago. He is the living, breathing definition of speaking truth to power. When he first played "Hey Mama," now my favorite Kanye song, for me, I implored him to drop it immediately. His response? "Nah, that's going on my next album, *Late Registration*." Here he was without a deal for his first album, and he was saving heat for the second one, and it was already named. When I first heard him say in "Jesus Walks" "here go my single, dawg, radio needs this," a full six months before he had a deal, I thought he was being audacious at best. I also did not think that a hip-hop single about Jesus would get any play. I was wrong on both accounts.

When Kanye hopped on my tour bus in 2003, he was already

saying he was going to be the biggest hip-hop artist in the world. He told everyone that his first three albums would be *The College Dropout*, *Late Registration*, and *Graduation*. Most folks nodded and smiled, while others outright questioned his sanity. Kanye was unbothered. He was like a firecracker, always energetic and always ready to rhyme. I would bring him out halfway thru my set to do his verses from "The Bounce" and an early version of "Two Words," then we would go back and forth rhyming for a few minutes. At times Kanye would walk up to the DJ, stop the music, and spit a cappella a new rhyme he was working on. He would interrupt my set and change its direction. I was the first person Kanye said "I'ma let you finish, but . . ." to.

People sometimes say to me that I put Kanye on. I didn't put Kanye on—he put himself on. When I brought him on tour with me, it wasn't a favor. I did it because he was talented and he made my show hotter. I had homeboys who rhymed that I didn't bring on tour with me because I didn't feel they were as passionate about it as I was. I think Kanye may have been even more passionate than I was, which is saying a lot. He may be the most passionate person I ever met. Kanye West is so passionate about what he does that those who lack passion in their lives feel threatened by him. When he went on CNN and said that George Bush didn't care about Black people during the aftermath of Hurricane Katrina, he vocalized what many of us felt at the time, and he meant it. No other Black celebrity as big as Kanye was then would've dared say something like that in public. Kanye West has proven thru his lyrics and public statements that he has a deep, deep love for the Black community he was raised in.

The more control Kanye West got over his output, the more "conscious" his output became. As an MC heavily influenced by Common, dead prez, Yasiin, and me, and the son of a college professor, Donda West, Kanye applied his lessons heavily on many songs throughout his career, such as "All Falls Down," "Lost in the World," "Murder to Excellence," and many more. On *Yeezus*, an album that Kanye unconventionally marketed by projecting his face on sixty-six buildings across the world, he upped the conscious ante by rhyming intelligently about the causes of our pathologies rather than the symptoms. By comparing himself to King Kong on "Black Skinhead" he simultaneously critiqued those who feel threatened by his success as a Black man and made a nuanced commentary on the public's perception of his marriage to Armenian-American reality TV star Kim Kardashian. On "New Slaves" he talks about the prison industrial complex with an informed flow that people would expect to hear from an underground activist MC like Immortal Technique before they heard it from the world's biggest pop star. By declaring himself a god on "I Am a God," Kanye brings the influence that the Five Percenters have had on hip-hop full circle. Kanye became the MC that the hip-hop purists say they wanted, the MC able to balance the debauchery with the content while keeping the music fresh. However, once you belong to the world at large, the hip-hop purists begin to feel betrayed.

Kanye ended up getting his deal with Roc-A-Fella/Def Jam Records, but not until he put out the song "Through the Wire" and paid for the accompanying video himself did they take notice and begin to support him. "Through the Wire," which was built around a sample of Chaka Khan's classic "Through the Fire," featured Kanye West literally spitting thru the wire, struggling to get the rhymes out while his jaw was wired shut as a result of a 2002 car accident. It is one of the most impressive hip-hop performances ever captured on tape. The song became his first hit, and he did it without the help of any record label. His story sold the song, and its success helped create the buzz he needed to drop his debut album, *The College Dropout*.

By 2004 Kanye was so in demand as a producer that spending time with him was a feat in itself. The days of getting CDs full of Kanye West beats were over, as he preferred to create on the spot, not just because all his beats would immediately sell but also because it helped him to create more organically. When he visited one of my sessions for my *Beautiful Struggle* album, rather than give me a beat that was already done, he created the beat and the hook for what was to become "Get Em High" as I watched. Not only was that skeleton of a beat not the vibe I was looking for, I didn't want to do a song about smoking weed. Kanye passionately tried to sell me on the beat, to no avail. Instead, I chose a beat that was fully realized and had John Legend singing the words *I try* over and over on it. I replaced John with Mary J. Blige and "I Try" was born.

Three months after that *Beautiful Struggle* session I was on tour in Europe while Kanye was in New York putting the finishing touches on *The College Dropout*. On a December day I received a frantic call from him; he needed a verse from me on his debut album, but I had only one day to turn it in or else it wouldn't make the album. I was in Copenhagen, Denmark, so I booked a studio after my show that night and opened up the email that contained the song he wanted me on. It was "Get Em High." By putting this song on his debut album Kanye found a way to get me to rap to the beat he originally made for me.

Not only did Kanye succeed at getting me on that beat, but by not making the song about weed even though weed references were in the chorus, he expanded my understanding of what the song could be. Everything he rapped about on "Get Em High" was real. He was hanging out on BlackPlanet.com back then, and people thought he and Damon Dash were assholes. By rhyming about how he used my name for "picking up dimes," he teed me up nice and helped me find subject matter for my verse. After sending Kanye the verse thru email, I didn't hear the song again until it came out. The day *The College Dropout* dropped, I was so excited about it I had my tour bus stop at a Target first thing that morning to purchase my copy. As I listened to the final version of "Get Em High" for the first time, a feeling of dread welled up in me and a look of horror crossed my face. My verse was placed in the song a bar later than where I laid it, which threw the flow I was going for completely off.

When working on music thru email rather than in person, it becomes easy to get creative signals crossed. Hip-hop beats are four-bar loops, so instead of my verse starting on the first bar, it came in where the second bar would be. To this day, it doesn't sound quite right to me. I don't know if it was the fault of the engineer on my end or the engineer on Kanye's end, or if it was just where Kanye decided to place the verse upon hearing it, but I had to quickly go from the horror of realizing that the verse would sound off to me forever to begrudging acceptance of it. The album was already out; there was no going back. When I got Kanye on the phone that day to find out where the breakdown in communication happened, he didn't know either, but he did say he loved the way it sounded. As I braced myself for critics to start saying I sounded off, the opposite occurred. People loved the verse and the song, and my place on one of the greatest debut albums in hip-hop history was cemented. To this day I perform my verse on that song all over the world, and people go crazy when they hear it. Either Kanye heard something I didn't hear or I had to chalk it up as a beautiful mistake.

On *The College Dropout*, Kanye introduced the world to his contradictions, and he's utilized them for the content of his songs for the rest of his career. For every "The New Workout Plan" there was a "Spaceship," for every "Good Life" there was a "Diamonds from Sierra Leone," and they are all excellent pieces of music.

Kanye displayed an affinity for Black history, pornography, the working class, and the 1 percent, sometimes all in the same verse. As one of the first hip-hop superstars to be equally influenced by the artists on Rawkus and Roc-A-Fella, he straddled the line and brought those two worlds closer together.

Everybody has contradictions—why should artists be different? Because the artist's platform can be so much bigger than the average person's, artists are often held to a higher standard in the eyes of their peers. The responsibility of this expectation falls on the artist, not the consumer of art, but too often the consumer fails to realize that the artist can be a victim of the same pathologies as those that he/she is making the art for. I challenge this expectation because I think that contradictions in artists should be celebrated. I don't want my art holier-than-thou, I want it eye level. I can remember KRS-One being called contradictory by hip-hop journalists all the time because he often switched his philosophical outlook and did so publicly. These contradictions make KRS-One a more genuine artist to me, and it is KRS-One's name that will remain thru history, not his critics'.

My theory about contradictions and my support of Kanye were put to the test when I saw him support Donald Trump, first onstage at a concert, then later standing next to him in front of Trump Tower with a fresh blond do. As much as I wanted to embrace this obvious contradiction, I could not. Everyone has a line in the sand, and fascism is mine. From the time Donald Trump kicked the journalist Jorge Ramos from a press conference while on the campaign trail to his attempt to ban Muslims and his "many sides" defense of Nazis marching in Charlottesville, Donald Trump has never proven himself to be anything but a fascist. In my eyes, no normalization of this behavior should be tolerated. Even if we put aside the time Trump called Black people lazy, the time he called Mexicans rapists, the time he called Elizabeth Warren Pocahontas, the time he was caught on tape admitting to sexual assault, and all the terrible things he said and did before his presidential campaign, we are still left with a reality TV star who once body-shamed Kanye's wife, Kim Kardashian, by talking about her body in a disparaging way on *The Howard Stern Show*.

Kanye West was not the only Black entertainer who disappointed me by standing next to Donald Trump. The Hall of Fame football player Jim Brown, the comedian Steve Harvey, and the singer Crisette Michele, all highly respected by the Black community and by me, all made the trip to the Trump White House to offer an olive branch to the Donald. If you were a celebrity with a modicum of success before 2017, you were probably in a room with Trump at some point. Celebrities are often sheltered and can relate to other celebrities more quickly than they can relate to the average citizen. Given their hyperbusy schedules and disconnect from what average working-class or poor people go thru daily, celebrities can often miss things that others don't have the luxury of avoiding. For this reason I engage a lot on social media and show up in the flesh at community-organized events that push for justice and equality. Without knowing the fast-moving, ever-changing language of the activists who do the work whether or not the camera is on them, it is easy to have lofty, high-minded goals that may take earned celebrity privilege for granted. My belief is that the Black celebrities who were cherished by the community and wanted to give Trump a chance were operating with the best of intentions. However, when it comes to oppression, intent does not matter, only results do. That the road to hell is paved with good intentions is not just a saying. I don't believe these celebrities were operating from an informed place.

A year and a half into Trump's presidency, it became clear to me that anyone still supporting Trump was being willfully ignorant. I'd assumed that Kanye had changed his mind about Trump when he deleted his pro-Trump tweets, but that assumption was proven false when Kanye, responding to my criticism of his support for the conservative YouTube personality Candace Owens, told me that he loved Donald Trump. Earlier in the year, Candace Owens, a Black woman, trolled me on Twitter, suggesting I was not equipped to debate her on a YouTube channel called *The Rubin Report*, a place where white supremacists go to pat one another on the back. When Candace Owens came after me, I was called nigger, monkey, and various other racial slurs for weeks by her cultlike followers. Kanye, to my disappointment, did not seem to mind my being treated this way by the followers of a woman he chose to uplift.

Later that week, Kanye repeated his love for Trump to Ebro Darden, a personality on New York's Hot 97 radio station. When Ebro made Kanye's feelings public, Kanye spent a couple of weeks doubling down on his love for Trump with shortsighted tweets and bizarre interviews. Using right-wing catchphrases such as *diversity of thought* and pushing white-supremacist talking points about Black-on-Black crime and slavery's being a choice, Kanye pushed himself further and further away from the community that embraced him while he was coming up and found a home with the same right-wing white supremacists that damn near called for his death when back in 2005 he said that George Bush didn't care about Black people.

As a friend of Kanye's I found myself in the unique position of being able to relay to him directly how the community felt, but I'm not sure he heard me. It's hard to tell a self-made man who has accomplished as much as Kanye has that he is doing "him" wrong, but freedom has never been free. Kanye's push for his personal freedom comes at the expense of Black people, and he is now being weaponized against us by people who will turn against him when he stops parroting their talking points. I think Kanye is smart enough to wake up and realize this one day, so I will be praying for the day he comes back home. As Dave Chappelle has said onstage, Kanye is still ours. Even the ugly parts we do not like.

While I cannot support Kanye while he supports Trump and various other white supremacists, I never stopped respecting Kanye as a man, and I don't think I ever will. That being said, as long as he supports Trump, I will not be able to support his music. This saddens me because the music that Kanye has made has helped to make our lives brighter, and he has previously used his music to shine a light on the tragedies that poor and oppressed communities go thru. He is the antihero who became a hero despite himself. So the question is, who are you? Are you the hero, or the guy in the crowd making fun of the hero's shirt?

23

Family. Matters.

You cannot have relationships with other
people until you give birth to yourself.
—SONIA SANCHEZ

The moment I recorded "Good to You" over Kanye's
Al Green sample flip, I rushed straight to Rawkus Entertainment
declaring that I had a hit record. I played it for Jarret and Brian,
but they weren't that impressed with it. Kanye had yet to make a
name for himself, and Jarret and Brian liked "Waiting for the
DJ." I stood my ground and forced a single release of "Good to
You," but Rawkus never supported it as a single, so it went nowhere. It was clearly done just to appease me and give them time
to figure out their actual rollout.

For "Waiting for the DJ," Jarret and Brian went all out. They
flew Beverly Bond and DJ Enuff to Los Angeles from New York
to be in the video, in the hopes that would translate into some
New York City club play. I flew with Beverly on the flight to Los
Angeles, and she mentioned that I should have the Los Angeles–

based DJ Eque do a cameo in the video. I wasn't familiar with Eque, but Beverly said she would be a good look, and I trusted Beverly. When Eque, real name Cynthia Bonier, showed up, she had on little makeup, a Nike tracksuit, and a baseball hat, but her casual look did not take away from her beauty. Raised in Houston, Texas, she had a youthful, freckled face, an awesome smile, an irresistible Southern charm, and a sexy country twang that made me chuckle every time she spoke. She was extremely beautiful, so I asked her for her phone number, making a mental note to reach out to her the next time I was in California. I didn't have to wait long.

About a month after the "Waiting for the DJ" video was released, I ran into Eque at a *Vibe* magazine party at some hotel in Manhattan. She was cohosting a TV show called *Vibe TV* with the R&B producer Bryce Wilson, and she was in New York doing press, looking stunning in a tight red dress. Seeing Eque with her hair done and noticing how the dress hugged her curves, I could not believe this was the same tomboyish girl who had appeared in my video. I must have done a noticeable double take because Eque laughed and said, "You didn't even recognize me, huh?" The next day, I took her out on a date, and the following week I invited her to come spend the weekend with me in Miami while I was hosting a party at a nightclub.

There is nobody in the world like DJ Eque. She is unique in many ways, and she was filled with more fiery passion than all the women I had dealt with before put together. Raised by her single mother in Houston's notorious Third Ward, she was accepted to the University of Texas on a basketball scholarship when she was seventeen years old, and by the time she was twenty-three she'd moved from Texas to Oakland, California, with her new baby daughter, Kyara, in tow to pursue her dreams of being a hip-hop DJ. Eque got her big break deejaying for the Bay Area rapper Tha Poetess, eventually moving to L.A., where she became one of Los Angeles's premier nightclub DJs and an in-demand tour DJ, rocking shows across the country deejaying for Uncle Luke of 2 Live Crew fame, Erick Sermon, Queen Latifah, and many more. She masterfully navigated this sexist music industry while single-handedly raising a daughter and commanded respect for her DJ skills, not for her body or for her looks. This impressed me.

By December 2003 I had my first bona fide rap hit in "Get By," a beautiful new girlfriend, and a ton of respect from both people in the music business and underground fans who appreciated solid lyricism. I had begun working on a new album, which I would call *The Beautiful Struggle*, which boasted features from musicians I admired, like Mary J. Blige, Faith Evans, Common, Anthony Hamilton, and more. I felt that I could do no wrong and that God was favoring me. That Christmas, I was extragenerous with the gifts. Every year, my family celebrates Christmas at my home, and this year was extraspecial. I got the biggest tree I could find, and Eque did exceptionally well cooking for the family under my grandmother's suspicious eye. Darcel and I seemed to be on good terms that day as she dropped Amani and Diani off at my apartment for the first of their two Christmases. However, later that night, when Darcel informed me that she wasn't coming back to pick up the children, I had to make some important life changes, quickly.

While I was living my dream career, Darcel was struggling to find her artistic voice and her place in society. We were no longer together, but she was living in the house I grew up in, making it awkward for her to begin a new relationship. Finding work also seemed to be hard for Darcel, so I was still taking care of her as if she were living with me. In 2002, Darcel wrote a novel that was loosely based on her life called *Dana Dances on Paper*. Impressed with her tenacity and sensing that it would help her get on her feet, I helped Darcel publish and sell this book. However, when I refused to pay for the second printing after the first printing sold out, Darcel and I got into a heated argument. Despite my investment, I had seen no profit from *Dana Dances on Paper* and I felt that her asking me to continue to pour money into it while she made all the profit was unfair. Darcel took this to mean I wasn't supporting her writing, and by extension that I wasn't supportive of her. I decided to give her an ultimatum. I told Darcel that if she got a job, any job, I would give her money for the second printing. I didn't like that Darcel was seemingly dependent on me, and I was trying to use this book situation to motivate her to do for herself. She got a part-time holiday job at a store in Brooklyn's Kings Plaza mall.

The ultimatum may have been the straw that broke the camel's back. Darcel clearly felt stifled, and that Christmas night she decided to do something about it. She felt that it wasn't fair that I got to travel and live my life, doing what I wanted to do, while she had to stay home to raise the kids, so she called to tell me that going forward, the children would live with me while she tried to get her life together. There wasn't a discussion; she simply said that she wasn't coming back to pick the children up, and that I had to find a way to deal with that. She left the keys to 4709 Avenue K with the children and moved all of her stuff to a single room she rented somewhere with the money she made from her mall job. This bold play shocked me for many reasons, the first being that Darcel was such a great mom who loved her children dearly. However, I could not imagine a life of feeling stifled, of not seeing who I wanted to see or not being where I wanted to be.

Since Eque was my girlfriend, having her help me raise Amani and Diani seemed to make the most sense. However,

Eque's attitude toward my children and my situation with Darcel was cautious to say the least. A Texas girl living in Los Angeles, Eque didn't much care for New York winters, and asking her to play mom to children she had known for less than a year when she had her own daughter to raise was a tall order for a woman whose career demanded that she also be able to travel extensively. I knew Eque could help out here and there, but I still needed someone I could depend on to live in that house and completely hold things down. One day on the phone with Makeba—the first person who had really supported my hip-hop career, and who was living at her mother's house in South Carolina with her nine-year-old-son, Jahaad—I expressed my frustration with Darcel and my whole situation. As Makeba has been known to do since the day I met her, she came thru for me in a big way and offered to move from South Carolina back to Brooklyn to help me out.

Makeba was my angel during those months. Without having a partner to help me with Amani and Diani, I would have had to change the entire way I ran my career, and I do not think I would have continued to be successful if not for her. For holding me down in the manner in which she did, I owe Makeba more than I can ever give her. The nurturing nature that first endeared me to her when we met back in 1994 was on full display, and Makeba took to mothering like a fish to water. She loved my children as if they were her own and helped me to provide needed stability for them amid a sea of confusing, emotional decisions. I also owe Jahaad a great deal for becoming such a good friend to Amani and Diani during such a rocky time. For the next few months we would become an unconventional but tight-knit family.

My refusal to help Darcel out at all during the months the children were living with Makeba and me did not sit well with Darcel and made her realize that the only reason I had always given her money was because the children lived with her. So in May 2004, Darcel declared that she wanted Amani and Diani to live with her again. I did not agree. With Makeba's help, I felt that after Darcel's sudden departure I had successfully stabilized the home where my children had lived all of their lives. They each had their own room and they were doing well in school. I had no plans to allow Darcel to uproot them and undo the work Makeba and I had put in. If Darcel had been able to provide the same level of home stability that Amani and Diani were already experiencing, I would have had no problem with their living with her, but I knew that wasn't the case. When Darcel realized that I wasn't budging in my position, she sued me for custody of our children and child support.

When Darcel first left the kids with me on Christmas night back in 2003, several people in my life told me to take her to family court and get legal custody of my children. I was staunchly against this. Whatever problems Darcel and I had were family problems, and I felt that the state needn't be involved. It takes a village to raise a child, and all of my trust remained in the village, not the government. It mattered not to me that whoever went to family court first would have the upper hand; I simply could not bring myself to ask the state to create a set of rules that Darcel and I should have been capable of following on our own.

Family court was a terribly sobering experience. I quickly learned that the fathers who showed up in family court before me didn't quite make it easy for me. As at the hospital where Amani was born, people at family court dealt with fathers as if they were all deadbeats. It didn't matter that I was giving Darcel thousands of dollars a month before she left the kids with me, nor did it matter that Amani and Diani had spent the better part of a year under my supervision. Darcel was the mother, and in family court, for good reason, the mother is always given the benefit of the doubt. For a mother to assert that a father is unfit for custody of their children, all she has to do is suggest that the father is not around. The onus is on the father to dispel said accusation. To claim that a mother is unfit for custody, a father has to prove that the mother is messing up badly, like violence-and-drugs bad. In front of the judge, Darcel and I had two very different stories about who was taking care of the kids. The judge went with Darcel's version and forced me to pay her thousands, even though the kids had been living with me for the majority of the year.

Now that I was giving Darcel money again, she was able to get a slightly bigger apartment, and Amani and Diani went back to living with her. This was right before school started, and since I no longer needed Makeba to help me with my children, she moved to Los Angeles with Jahaad and enrolled him in school there. She always wanted a better quality of life for Jahaad, and California seemed to have more opportunities for them to flourish. We said tearful goodbyes, and Makeba exited my circle for a second time. As I think back, what she did for me during that year was amazing. She put everything she had going on down to come be a family with me when I needed a family for Amani's and Diani's well-being. Writing this book has allowed me to reflect on the people who have come in and out of my life in new ways and helped me to realize that I owe more gratitude to many of them than I've given them. Makeba is the best example of one of these people. Without her help and support I would have failed at my mission.

When Amani and Diani moved back in with Darcel, and Makeba and Jahaad left for California, the need for me to live at 4709 Avenue K was diminished. I decided to sell the house. I remembered visiting this house back in 1987 with my parents and meeting the old white couple that owned it and sold it to them. At that time, the Dominican family next door was one of only two families of color on the block. Now, no white people were left in the neighborhood. In fact, hardly any American-born families were in Flatlands anymore; it was all Caribbean. While this gentrification made the neighborhood definitely more vibrant and colorful, this house was still in a two-fare zone, far away from the heart of the city and inconvenient to commute back and forth from. The house at 4709 Avenue K had belonged to my family for twenty years. It was my parents' first major purchase together. My brother and I were raised there, and it provided a home base for us long after we became adults. My children were raised there; Makeba and her son spent time living there. It was sad for me to sell a house that had given so much to my family, but it was time.

In 2007, after buying a house in Los Angeles and asking Eque to move in with me, I asked for her hand in marriage. By being a fixture of the Black Hollywood scene, we had become a "power couple," and while I wasn't sure I was ready to be married, I felt that a woman as beautiful and as talented as Eque still deserved to be married. She definitely had a right to question my commitment to her. On the surface, I was doing all of the right things. I took her on fabulous vacations, I bought her all of the clothes and jewelry she wanted, her nails got done, her hair got did, and she had all the bags and all the shoes that allowed her to keep up with the Hollywood elite, but I still found myself sneaking around with other women. My cheating became public knowledge after Eque, who had grown up in a violent household, tried to physically fight me over my infidelities one too many times. Instead of confronting her about the violence, I blamed myself as the cause of it and would try to make up with her. By 2009, I was ready to cut the other women off and try to settle down. Eque and I set May 9, 2009, as our wedding date.

The best advice I got about weddings was from my friend JuJu, who said that the wedding was not really for us, it was for everyone else. I knew Eque loved me and she knew I loved her. The marriage was to make this love real in the eyes of people who were not us. We were known as a party-going couple, so I wanted to make our wedding the best party of the year. I rented a Bel Air mansion owned by Master P and got Hennessy to help pay for the ceremony. I flew both of our families and friends in from all over the country and I got Ahmir "Questlove" Thompson to DJ. My daughter, Diani, was the flower girl and my brother, Jamal, was my best man. Our guests ranged from Karlie Redd of Love & Hip Hop to Queen Latifah, representing the most diverse cross section of Black Hollywood possible. Not one to turn down a gig, even on my wedding day, I booked a show with the Roots that night, which became the official after-after-party for my wedding.

Despite the ceremony itself being beautiful, my wedding day was filled with drama from top to bottom. I wasn't used to wearing suits and didn't realize until two hours before my vows that I didn't have a belt that went with my suit. My father, Jamal, and I made a quick trip to a local Men's Wearhouse that was interrupted by a heated argument I got into on the phone with rapper Xzibit. Xzibit had been upset that Strong Arm Steady, a group he invested some money in, signed with my label, Blacksmith, and he had expressed some anger over this on Twitter, which led to us yelling at each other on my wedding day. Later on during the reception, Eque's mom and dad, who didn't normally get along and hadn't seen each other in years, began drinking together. By the time Eque and I got back to the house where we were all staying, her parents were fighting each other.

Some people ask for forgiveness for the things they say while they are drunk, explaining that the alcohol makes them say things they don't mean. I find the opposite to be true. In my experience, alcohol is a truth serum, liquid courage if you will, that numbs you to the point of saying what you really mean regardless of the repercussions. Eque's parents had a lot of history between each other, and a lot of negative stuff was said. When the fight became physical, Eque and I had to separate them and then get rid of all of the alcohol in our home. While Eque took her father to a nearby hotel, I tried to calm her mother down and get her to go to bed. She was too upset and inebriated to hear me, and she began to direct her angry words at me and the women in my family, women she had met for the first time earlier that day. I knew she couldn't mean the hateful things she said about them because she didn't know them at all. I also knew that she was trying to hurt me with her words. I could speculate about why but I will never know for sure.

Lying in bed that night, I started to really think about my future. Is this the life I wanted? Is this what I had to look forward to? Would Eque and I end up like her mother and her father? I understood that Eque came from a violent environment, but I had also seen her make great strides toward being a better communicator over the years. Eque and I loved each other's company and we had many of the same interests, but we definitely had very different ways of dealing with hurt feelings. That night I decided that the situation with Eque's parents must have been a test and I was going to try my best to honor my vows. But as Yoda says, "Try not. Do or do not. There is no try." If trying is failing, I failed to honor my commitment to Eque.

By 2013, the stress of our relationship had taken its toll on me and I was spending less and less time at our home. When I look back at pictures of myself during this time, I do not like the way I look. I wasn't happy, and I wasn't making Eque happy. It seemed like we were becoming enemies, so I decided to separate myself from that relationship so that one day we could work on being friends again.

24

Blacksmith Music

If skills sold, truth be told
I'd probably be, lyrically Talib Kweli
—JAY-Z, "MOMENT OF CLARITY"

In the year since my first hit record, "Get By," had dropped, I went from having a great relationship with the mother of my children to having to fight in family court for the right to see them. Splitting my time between dating Eque and spending time with Amani and Diani, I was living on both coasts, frantically flying from New York to Los Angeles and back every week. I had toured with acts like Jay-Z, N.E.R.D, and the Black Eyed Peas, and I was gearing up for a tour with the Beastie Boys, all while trying to finish recording *The Beautiful Struggle*. I was firing on all cylinders, trying to strike while the iron was hot. The world as I knew it was coming apart at the seams, but I was ferociously at work building a new world to replace it. Things I once assumed to be true I could no longer depend on or take for granted.

During the recording of *The Beautiful Struggle*, Jay-Z retired from the music business for the first of many times. Having ruled the hip-hop and R&B charts for ten summers straight, Jay-Z was claiming he was retiring at the top of his game to forever cement his legacy as the best to have ever done it. When he announced that his swan song would be called *The Black Album*, the hip-hop nation collectively waited with bated breath for what we thought would be the last collection of hot sixteens we would ever hear from our beloved Hov. As songs began to leak from *The Black Album* in the final days before its release, I received a call from Busta Rhymes telling me that Jay-Z had mentioned me in a lyric on a song called "Moment of Clarity." Busta played the song over the phone and congratulated me for the mention.

Even though we were all peers who fiercely competed with one another, Busta knew just as well as I did how significant a moment this was for the culture. Along with artists like Common and Yasiin Bey, I had worked hard to get my brand of conscious, lyrical hip-hop to be respected by the gatekeepers of the mainstream. Jay-Z was the official representative of the best that mainstream hip-hop had to offer. When it came to being relevant in hip-hop's mainstream, Jay-Z was the Holy Grail. Jay-Z's mentioning me and Common on "Moment of Clarity" marks the moment when the lines that separated what was considered underground and what was considered mainstream began to blur. Previous notions of what was "hot" were challenged once Jay-Z admitted that the artists that he looked to when it came to craft were the artists that most of the industry tried hard to ignore. The mere mention of my name in a Jay-Z song gave me industry credibility that years of making great hip-hop had not. I was leaving the realm of artist and entering the realm of celebrity. Soon, it became cool to say you were a fan of mine whether or not you were familiar with my music.

It has been debated whether Jay-Z was taking shots at Common and me with these lyrics. Is he suggesting that the way we rap is not profitable, therefore dissing it? I didn't see these lyrics as anything but high praise. I felt that if an artist as respected and prolific as Jay-Z, on a song called "Moment of Clarity," where he speaks of his father for the first time in a song, on an album that he said was his last, had the way I rhyme on his mind, that's gotta be a good thing. Hearing "Moment of Clarity" for the first time was definitely a "Mama, I made it" moment for me. I felt that I must be at the right place at the right time. I also felt that I needed to capitalize on this moment by responding to the lyric, and I quickly asked Common to meet me at Right Traxx Studios on Forty-Seventh Street in Times Square, where we recorded the song "Ghetto Show" over a Supa Dave West beat. I used my verse to playfully toss Jay-Z's lyric right back at him, and Anthony Hamilton showed up to sing a hook that made the entire song fall into place.

> *If lyrics sold then truth be told, I'd probably be,*
> *just as rich and famous as Jay-Z*
> *Truthfully I wanna rhyme like Common Sense*

Jay-Z's mention of Common and me on "Moment of Clarity" was the first of many events that ushered in a less stringent way for fans to look at hip-hop and its subgenres. For years, artists and true fans of the craft had been able to judge art on its merit rather than on what was trendy, but since hip-hop had become big business, a concerted effort had been made by the labels and the media to separate hip-hop fans into warring factions, the underground versus the mainstream. Besides doing records that would fit in underground and mainstream formats simultaneously and shouting out Common and me on songs, Jay-Z, for his part, had also begun doing concerts with the Roots crew as his backing band.

When given the opportunity to interview anybody he wanted by the editor of *XXL* for the magazine's fiftieth issue, gangster/pop-rap icon 50 Cent chose to interview me, to the surprise of many. Mainstream America had recently become fans of 50 Cent, but 50 Cent was a fan of Talib Kweli and Hi-Tek.

This underground meeting the mainstream converged nicely when the homie Dave Chappelle, who had recently become one of the most famous comedians in the world due to the success of Comedy Central's *Chappelle's Show*, decided to film a concert in Brooklyn featuring all of his favorite artists and call it *Block Party*. Inspired by the Wattstax concert that commemorated the Watts riots of August 1965 and working closely with my manager, Corey Smyth, Dave used his own money and his relationships with artists to throw one of the best parties Bed-Stuy had ever seen. *Block Party* was very much like a caffeinated version of the Okayplayer tour, with the Roots as everyone's backing band and Dave playing host and ringmaster, improvising jokes between each musical performance. Handpicked by Dave Chappelle himself, *Block Party* performers included me, Common, Yasiin Bey, Kanye West, Jill Scott, Erykah Badu, dead prez, Big Daddy Kane, and Kool G Rap. All of the stellar performances led up to *Block Party*'s main event, the reunion of the Fugees, who by 2004 had not performed together for seven years. By using his platform as one of comedy's most famous to showcase his favorite artists and to get the Fugees back onstage together after so many years, then filming it and putting it on sale, Dave Chappelle proved that the so-called underground hip-hop movement had arrived and was indeed a force to be reckoned with.

My fourth and final album with Rawkus Entertainment, *The Beautiful Struggle*, was released in September 2004. My journey from the release of my first single, "Fortified Live," to *The Beautiful Struggle* had taken many twists and turns. I was once the darling of the fastest-growing, most cutting-edge hip-hop label to emerge in years, but now I had to compete with big-box Interscope acts such as Gwen Stefani, 50 Cent, and Eminem. I became a small fish swimming in a big pond. Rawkus tried to maintain their independence for as long as they could, but by 2004 both Jarret and Brian were ready to move on to other ventures. The underground hip-hop scene wasn't what it used to be, and the artists that Rawkus had initially found success with, acts like Mos Def and Company Flow, had moved on years before.

I took my competition seriously and was determined to prove my mettle in the business, so for *The Beautiful Struggle* I took full advantage of working with a bigger budget to turn in an album that would be respected simultaneously by the music industry as well as the underground. Hi-Tek returned to my musical mix to produce three cuts on the album ("Back Up Offa Me," "Work It Out," and the title track), but a track was also produced by the chart-topping team of Pharrell Williams and Chad Hugo, known as the Neptunes ("Broken Glass"). Both Faith Evans and Mary J. Blige appear on *The Beautiful Struggle*, on "We Know" and "I Try" respectively, making it the first album to feature them both since the Notorious B.I.G.'s *Life After Death*. As a Brooklyn rapper who cut his teeth in the Bad Boy era, I was proud of that, but some fans felt alienated by the influx of R&B-flavored hip-hop I was introducing them to. I was attempting to broaden my fan base without alienating the fans I already had, and I had mixed results.

Lyrically, I felt I was on top of my game and only getting better. On songs like "Never Been in Love" and "Broken Glass," I was more confident in my storytelling, and on songs like "Work It Out" and "A Game," which was produced by Antwan "Amadeus" Thompson, that newfound cockiness was on display. My flow, which I had still been developing on my first three albums, began to feel more comfortable. I was becoming a more polished musician as well, learning how to better incorporate my vast musical inspirations, but many fans of my first three albums like the rough version of me better. This is where I first started to understand the difference between large parts of my "hip-hop purist" fan base and myself. When *Black Star* dropped in 1998, I was the new kid on the block, the cutting edge, but by 2004 I was an established industry artist. I was also getting older than many hip-hop fans, so while their influences were strictly boom-bap-style 1990s hip-hop, as a 1970s baby I was still inspired by the lush sounds and arrangements of rhythm and blues. On *The Beautiful Struggle* I wanted to impress more than hip-hop fans, and for the first time I had the resources to try.

I was in Europe on tour with Kanye when *The Beautiful Struggle* dropped, then I joined the Beastie Boys on their Challah at Your Boy tour. This was more like a carnival, with the Beastie Boys bringing a circuslike feel to the show thru costume changes and transitioning fluidly back and forth between live instruments and straight-up rocking two turntables and a mic style with the legendary DJ Mix Master Mike. Before I touched the stage, a dog act would go on, Bob's Amazing Mongrels. Ad-Rock had seen these dogs doing tricks on TV and in classic Beastie Boy style decided that they would be the opening act for the tour. Getting to travel thru the United States and then some European dates with the world-famous Beastie Boys in the last years of Adam "MCA" Yauch's life is an experience I do not take for granted.

While "Get By" was acknowledged as an iconic hip-hop record, none of my albums were gold or platinum in 2005, and after "I Try" failed to chart well as a single, Interscope shut down the marketing and promotion budget for *The Beautiful Struggle*. Never mind that they didn't spend any money on radio promotion for "I Try," Interscope still decided to cut their losses long before my project ever had a chance to compete. Refusing to give up on the album, Corey and I spent our own money on radio promotion for the Just Blaze–produced "Never Been in Love." Corey, Just Blaze, and I flew up to Toronto, Canada, to work with a young director named RT on a vision I had for the "Never Been in Love" video. It would be a mash-up of two of my favorite musical scenes from movies, the performance of "A Heart Is a House for Love" from *The Five Heartbeats*, and when Jim Morrison performs "Light My Fire" on *The Ed Sullivan Show* in *The Doors*. We then set up and paid for a radio run where I glad-handed DJs across the country, trying to get them to play the song in the mix. It worked.

Seeing how effective Corey Smyth and I could be without being handicapped by a major label in control of the purse strings gave me an idea. What if we never had to ask for permission to roll out a single? What if we weren't dependent on someone else's money and schedule to put out the music we wanted to put out? Blacksmith Management as a company was in a better position to take advantage of trends in the culture than many major labels were. It was time for us to step up and get off the major-label hamster wheel. The more time I spent signed to a major label, the less relevant I was becoming as an artist. Everything in me told me to push back against this. I had the creative vision down; I just needed a partner to help with the legwork. I thought Corey would excel at this.

After a couple of months of talking about it, I convinced Corey that we should sever our ties with Interscope and start our own label. I suggested that we call it Blacksmith Music. I was reading a lot of Dan Brown books and I was fascinated by ambigrams, words that when flipped upside down remained the same. Dan Brown had famously used an ambigram for the word *illuminati* in his book *Angels & Demons*, and when I showed it to Corey, he tracked down the artist who created it for Dan Brown and had him draw up a Blacksmith ambigram. Once I saw this logo, I knew we were onto something big. In my mind, Blacksmith Music would pick up right where Rawkus had left off.

The first project ever put out by Blacksmith Music was an album I recorded in 2005 called *Right About Now: The Official Sucka Free Mixtape*. *Right About Now* was just that—where I was musically at that moment. I called it *The Official Sucka Free Mixtape* because I was too nervous to have it judged as a straight-up album. With songs like "Ms. Hill," which was a dedication to the legend of Lauryn Hill, and "Drugs, Basketball & Rap," featuring Planet Asia, which was more of a street-style record than my fans were used to, I was taking chances that I had never before taken. For the promotion of *The Beautiful Struggle*, I recorded two mixtapes, *The Beautiful Mixtapes*, volumes 1 and 2, which featured artists like the Game, Killer Mike, Ludacris, and more. These mixtapes found me experimenting with all different types of styles, but the mixtapes were free. Asking fans to pay for my experimentation was a different level of trust.

Corey and I put out *Right About Now* thru a one-off distribution partnership with Koch Records, then at the beginning of 2007 Corey secured a more stable deal with Warner Bros. Records to distribute Blacksmith Music records. Not only would we be putting out Talib Kweli albums, we would now have the opportunity to sign other acts. Immediately, I thought of Jean Grae, my friend from my Washington Square Park days. Jean had grown into one of my favorite MCs, yet she wasn't signed to a label. As if by divine meddling, Jean and Corey were also good friends, drinking buddies who used to party together years before. Blacksmith Music seemed like the perfect home for Jean Grae, and we secured a budget to release an album she was working on with the producer 9th Wonder called *Jeanius*.

Besides Jean Grae, Blacksmith Music also signed a group of West Coast MCs called Strong Arm Steady. Consisting of the MCs Phil Da Agony and Marvin "Krondon" Jones III from Los Angeles and Mitchy Slick from San Diego, Strong Arm Steady was a collective I met thru Xzibit that was putting out critically acclaimed, well-received mixtapes at an amazing clip. With Jean Grae and Strong Arm Steady behind me, I felt poised for reinvention. I began to take the whole crew on tours, feature them on my songs, and include them in all of my promo. I became a soldier for Blacksmith Music, confident that my new crew would make huge waves in this business. I had Blacksmith merch pressed up, and I started and maintained a website called yearoftheblacksmith .com. I produced a series of mixtapes with the Blacksmith artists and began spending any extra money I had on studio time for the crew. However, when I would try to visit the Blacksmith office we asked Warner Bros. to set up for us, they would treat me as if I were merely an artist signed to Blacksmith Music as opposed to one of its founders and owners.

Blacksmith Management belonged to Corey Smyth, but Blacksmith Music belonged to both of us. We were co-CEOs of the company with equal rights. On top of that, Corey wasn't working on Blacksmith Music, the label, I was. Corey and his employees in his New York office were efficiently running the management company, but none of them had the knowledge or the resources to do any of the label work. This led to several arguments between Corey, his staff, and me. I was writing songs, recording albums, paying for studio time for Blacksmith artists out of my own money, running the website, touring over two hundred days a year, and was still the only one doing any label work whatsoever. So when employees of Warner Bros. continued to treat me as if I were Corey's employee, I went straight to the top and got a meeting with Warner's president at the time, Tom Whalley. I needed to find out not only why I couldn't get in the office, but why there never seemed to be any money for Blacksmith Music projects.

By the time I finally met with Tom Whalley, I had been signed to Warner Bros. for over a year. This was the opposite of my experience with the heads of Rawkus, whom I had met in the hood years before signing with them. Tom was gracious enough; he invited me to his home and seemed genuinely excited about me as an artist. It was Corey Smyth and Blacksmith Music that he was confused about. Tom said that he thought Blacksmith Music was Corey's pet project that had nothing to do with me. Apparently, Corey had received money to develop Blacksmith Music, but after a year it seemed to me that we had little or nothing to show for it. So when I asked Tom to give me more money for a Strong Arm Steady video, he was surprised and asked about the money he had already given to Corey for Blacksmith. When I went into that meeting I thought I was going to enlighten Tom Whalley about how he was disrespecting me as an artist. I left questioning my relationship with my manager, partner, and best friend of almost ten years.

To be fair, for years I went out of my way to not be involved in my own business. I shied away from any official meetings and convos, preferring to be a creative artist and allow management to handle everything else. I didn't sign my own checks or read my contracts, and I placed my trust completely in the hands of another man. This, I was about to learn over the next few years, was a mistake. As much as I had learned from Corey, as great an ear as he had for talent, and as great a friend as he was to me, I should never have been so dependent on another to handle my business affairs. When I confronted Corey about the money given to him by Warner Bros. for Blacksmith Music, he ran down a list of costs for running his Blacksmith Management office and explained that most of the money went to paying rent and employees. I had a problem with this because I thought that money was supposed to go to the label, not his management company. After also factoring in that not only had Corey not discussed this with me, but that Blacksmith Management didn't seem to me to be doing any label work at all, I felt like Corey might not have always had my best interests in mind.

This news was hard for me to swallow. For years I'd leaned on Corey and followed his lead, even when people told me not to. Blacksmith Music was my idea, and my understanding was that the money that he received for it was given to him based on Warner Bros.'s interest in me as an artist, not in Corey Smyth as a manager or Blacksmith as a label. I felt betrayed, but not to the point of wanting to end the relationship. Beyond the business, Corey had been a great friend to me for many years, and the show money was still rolling in lovely. We'd started this Blacksmith Music thing together, and for the sake of Jean Grae and Strong Arm Steady, I wanted to see it thru to the end. I had asked Jean and Strong Arm Steady to trust me as an artist and a CEO, and I planned on making good the promises that Blacksmith Music had made to them.

25

Shadows of Tomorrow

Yesterday belongs to the dead
The past is yesterday.
Today is a preview of tomorrow.

—LORD QUASIMOTO, "SHADOWS OF TOMORROW"

The first album to be released from Blacksmith
Music's partnership with Warner Bros. Records would be my
fourth solo album, *Eardrum*. My plan was for the album, already
sprawling in nature by the fall of 2006, to be the one that defined
my career. The first single, the Kwamé-produced "Listen!!!," had
been released in August 2006 with a graffiti-inspired video, but I
was still working on the album, so this release was a bit premature.
Determined to work with hip-hop's best producers, I scheduled
sessions with such folks as Pete Rock, Hi-Tek, and Kanye West,
but when I received seven CDs full of beats from Madlib of Ox-
nard, California, my direction for *Eardrum* changed dramatically.
Somehow, Madlib had the sound that perfectly captured where I
was musically.

I first worked with Madlib, real name Otis Jackson, a year before we actually met. Just like Dilla's before him, Madlib's beat CDs were making the rounds thru the industry and landing in the hands of the highest-caliber MCs. The work Madlib released thru Stones Throw and Blue Note Records as a solo act, as a member of the Lootpack with Wildchild, DJ Rome, and his brother Oh No (real name Michael Jackson), and as the cartoon alter-ego Quasimoto had firmly established him as a cult favorite among beat heads and vinyl collectors. Eventually, I would end up rapping alongside Madlib on a project he created with J Dilla called Jaylib, but in 2006, I was still just a fan with some exclusive unreleased heat.

As I began to record *Eardrum*, I was sitting on about one hundred unreleased Madlib beats. His sound was as clean as it was dusty, as original as it was sample heavy, and as awkward as it was graceful. After experimenting with working with more high-profile artists on *The Beautiful Struggle*, a more underground artist like Madlib seemed like the perfect producer to jump-start the recording of *Eardrum*. The only problem was, there was too much great music. Madlib would create an entire series of tracks by just sampling blaxploitation-era movies, then he would move on to rock and roll, then Afro-Brazilian music, then reggae, and so on. What he did with these samples was so cinematic I would often get caught up in listening to the beats and it would distract from my writing. To remedy this, I painstakingly chose my favorite ten out of the hundred I had and only listened to those. When I finally began to write to these tracks, my only reservation was that I couldn't have an entire album of Madlib beats. After laying down a couple rhymes, the why quickly turned into why not, and I put *Eardrum* on hold to focus on recording an album produced entirely by Madlib. To honor the *lib* in both of our names, I called this project *Liberation*.

Madlib is as elusive as a person as he is prolific as a producer.

Getting Madlib on the phone was a feat. In my experience, the most creative balk at being always available. They value their time and understand how the walls they put up block out enough noise for them to express themselves with the clarity they are looking for. I've heard stories that Bill Murray only accepts movie scripts by fax. Madlib is the Bill Murray of hip-hop.

Liberation took me a week to record. I holed up in my basement with my engineer Dave Dar the week before Christmas 2006 and recorded my rhymes in mostly one take. The Queens rapper and future *Love & Hip Hop* star Consequence owed me a favor for a song I did with him, so I emailed him the track for "Engine Running," and he sent back a fire verse. Candice Anderson, who was singing backup for me at the time, laced "Happy Home." I also threw my kids, Amani and Diani, on "Happy Home," which added to the family narrative that ran thru the song. Strong Arm Steady, who would later do their own album with Madlib, called *In Search of Stoney Jackson*, joined Chace Infinite and me on "The Function." After I finished recording I emailed the album to Madlib, all ten songs at once. His text-message response was one word: "Dope!"

One of the elements that added to Madlib's production style was his ear for obscure loops, sounds, and voices to sample. This gift was also a curse for me, because it would be hard to release an album full of uncleared samples without facing lawsuits. I had become a big enough artist to make the radar of anyone trying to get paid from the illegal sale of a song with uncleared samples. To get around the sample-clearance issues for *Liberation*, I decided to release it for free. I quickly fell in love with the poetry of releasing a free album called *Liberation*, and I knew the fans would absolutely love it. Rappers signed to major labels in 2006 were not releasing any free music online, much less entire albums, and I knew this move would be lauded as revolutionary by the fans, even if it was hated by my business partners. I texted Madlib two days before New Year's Eve 2006 to ask him if he would be okay with putting out *Liberation* for free at midnight on New Year's. I suggested that we frame it as a holiday gift to our fans. This time I got a three-word response: "Bet. Let's go!"

At midnight on January 1, 2007, *Liberation* was released thru my Myspace page as a free download. For a "cover" I used a googled image of a Banksy painting of the hood version of the Vietnam memorial statue in D.C. The reviews for the project came in fast and fantastic. My fans were either hailing *Liberation* as a continuation of my stellar output or a triumphant return after the seemingly more commercial sound of the *Beautiful Struggle* album. Madlib's fans were excited about free music from their hero, and many were experiencing me as an MC for the first time. I was gaining new fans who listened to the type of hip-hop I did but who had long ago dismissed me as nothing but a cog in the major-label machine. We did not announce the free release until the day of, even to our respective managers and record companies. Corey Smyth and Madlib's manager, Egon, scrambled to figure out how we could capitalize on *Liberation*, while Warner Bros. and Madlib's label, Stones Throw, seemed confused about how to respond to it. Warner Bros. began questioning my interest in my deal with them and asked me if I was serious about *Eardrum*. Stones Throw took a more direct approach, putting the album out for free as a Stones Throw release on their website.

Until *Liberation*, I hadn't realized how many people thought of me as a mainstream artist. Sure, I had a couple of mainstream hits with "The Blast" and "Get By," but I started out rapping in the parks and dropping singles on Rawkus Entertainment. Even though technically I had been signed to a major for the last two years, I still saw myself as the kid who hosted open mics at Nkiru Books. No matter what the sound of *The Beautiful Struggle* was, having an album with the likes of Mary J. Blige, Faith Evans, the

Neptunes, Kanye West, and John Legend on it made me look like a mainstream artist to the casual listener. At the very least it seemed as if I were trying to go mainstream. The truth is, music has never been a political decision for me. I go get who the song asks for, not who some A&R says is hot. This did not matter to many Madlib fans, who prided themselves on being anti–corporate hip-hop. To my surprise, many of his fans either had not heard of me or found it surprising that I would even work with an artist as underground as Madlib. To me, it always seemed like a perfect fit.

I released *Liberation* for free for another reason also. For the first time since "Get By," I felt I had something to prove to hip-hop. I did *The Beautiful Struggle* for me, to explore my newfound fame and relationships. I had *Eardrum* coming down the pipeline, and before I would ask fans to spend money on it, I wanted to earn the respect of the community that some said I had lost by making *The Beautiful Struggle* musically accessible to those who weren't necessarily invested in underground hip-hop. My music will forever be an honest expression of me; it is never done for the fans. I didn't have fans when I first started creating music, so I would never let the desire to have a fan base be the reason I create. But if you work hard enough at it, you get what you pray for, and I had received support and respect from hip-hop fans in droves throughout my career. I was financially secure enough now to be able to give something back, so I gave what I was best at giving, my art. I made my money not by bowing to industry conventions but by being myself. The spirit moved me to give *Liberation* away for free, and so far the spirit had not told me any lies.

If the music business was a boxing ring, then *Liberation* would be the jab that set up the knockout punch that was to become *Eardrum*. *Liberation* allowed me to give my original underground hip-hop fan base exactly what they wanted: dusty samples coupled with rhymes about what hip-hop meant to us. It was a pretty good display of my skill set, but one that I could practically do in my sleep. I recorded and wrote *Liberation* in one week, and as fun as it was, it did not provide the artistic challenge I was looking for. With *Eardrum* I intended to marry the lessons I learned from recording *The Beautiful Struggle* with the lessons I learned from recording *Liberation* and find the perfect balance of musical authenticity and inclusiveness. This is why the first song from *Eardrum* is called "Everything Man."

I approached recording *Eardrum* with a ferocious energy. "Everything Man" begins with the legendary poet Sonia Sanchez speaking over African drums about what it is like for her to listen to my music. This is followed by two minutes of me rhyming about how I try to be and often fail at being everything to everyone. "Hostile Gospel," my second collaboration with Just Blaze, was about how this music is my church and how my rhymes are prayers. While touring with the Black Eyed Peas, I developed a great working relationship with will.i.am, who produced two of *Eardrum*'s standout cuts, "Say Something," featuring Jean Grae, and "Hot Thing," which featured will.i.am himself. Kanye West produced and added a verse to "In the Mood," which also featured another one of my musical heroes, the great Roy Ayers. Musiq Soulchild turned in a soul-stirring hook for the DJ Khalil–produced "Oh My Stars," my MC mentor KRS-One joined me on "The Perfect Beat," and Madlib produced three of *Eardrum*'s songs. I even had the hip-hop icon Pete Rock on board for two tracks, "Stay Around" and "Holy Moly." *Eardrum* was twenty tracks long and featured many of the artists I considered to be the best at this craft because I was recording it as if it were my last statement to the world.

On songs like "Stay Around" and "More or Less," which was produced by Hi-Tek, I was beginning to assess my place in the music business. I felt that the perception people had of me was different from the reality, and I was eager to gain control of it. I was hyperaware of the critiques that had been made about my loquacious rap style and beat choice, and I used this album to prove that I was everything the critics said I was not. I was also focused on team building, so I used "Say Something," featuring Jean Grae, and "Go with Us," featuring Strong Arm Steady, as showcases for my Blacksmith Music crew. On "Soon the New Day," produced by Madlib and featuring, at Questlove's suggestion, the pop/jazz phenomenon Norah Jones, I detailed a conversation I had with a girl in a Detroit nightclub. On "Give Em Hell," featuring Lyfe Jennings and Coi Mattison, I explored my relationship with religion in the most in-depth way I possibly could. Even though by the time I recorded *Eardrum* I was solely writing lyrics if I was inspired by music, the lyrics to "Give Em Hell" were the first I had written in some time that I felt worked just as well as spoken word as they did as rap lyrics. I ended up using these lyrics as my poem during my second HBO *Def Poetry Jam* appearance.

The critiques I received for my choice of featured artists on *The Beautiful Struggle* didn't make me stay away from popular, mainstream artists; in fact, they had the exact opposite effect. With *Eardrum*, I set out to prove that I could work with the most mainstream artists on the planet and still deliver a stellar album that hit all of the "real hip-hop" benchmarks. In addition to working with Norah Jones and having will.i.am assist with two songs, *Eardrum* also featured Justin Timberlake on "The Nature." Having an album that featured pop stars like Justin and Norah right along with underground hip-hop acts like UGK and KRS-One perfectly captured where I was at artistically in 2007. I was straddling both worlds effectively. *Eardrum* debuted at number two in the country on *Billboard* the August week it dropped, right behind *High School Musical*. To do better than me on the charts that week, you had to be able to look, sing, and dance like Zac Efron. My hardcore fans also loved it, and I felt vindicated in my vision.

26

Independent's Day

Stash more cash than Bert Padell, inhale
Make you feel good like Tony Toni Tone
—THE NOTORIOUS B.I.G., "ONLY YOU (REMIX)"

Growing up in a house with educators, I learned how to think critically, respect history, and understand my responsibility to my community. I learned the values of hard work and education. Teaching is a labor of love because teachers are grossly underpaid and you must love it to be good at it. My parents were good at teaching, but never had the opportunity to make the large sums of money I did by doing music. When your cash flow is wildly unpredictable, some days you are up and some days you are down. Without proper financial guidance it becomes hard to maintain stability and reckless spending becomes the norm. Perry and Brenda Greene couldn't teach me how to navigate large sums of money because they didn't have experience with that. When I see how many of my peers in hip-hop have the same financial issues, I suspect that my experience is pretty common.

When your name starts to ring bells in the music business, the holy trinity of artist relations comes sniffing around you: managers, booking agents, and business managers. A good manager will plug you in with good booking agents and business managers but will also know when it is time to make the necessary changes as your career grows. My manager, Corey Smyth, had a relationship with the William Morris Agency thru his management of De La Soul, so I began my career with them on the booking side. Corey also found a mentor in Bert Padell, an old-school business manager who had a firm called Padell Nadell Fine Weinberger. Bert, who began his storied career as a batboy for the New York Yankees during the 1950s and ended up as one of the most famous and powerful accountants in the music business, liked Corey's energy and gave him an office within PNFW headquarters on Fifty-Sixth Street. Naturally, one of Corey's first moves on my behalf was to set me up as a client of this firm.

While Bert Padell brought me into the firm, the accountant assigned to me pushed most or all of the work for my account onto a bookkeeper. The first bookkeeper I had got sick and let a lot of bills rack up; the second one seemed just plain incompetent. By this time the smart move would have been for me to leave PNFW, but I was too young and naive to realize how badly they were messing me up. After a couple of years I realized that I should be getting better service, but then I was introduced to Michelle Faieta, a bookkeeper who actually took an interest in keeping me informed about my bills and my account. I stayed with PNFW until Michelle left in 2008.

The average business manager in the music business makes 5 percent of every dollar you bring in. For this payment, the managers are to make sure your books are in order and to give you sound business advice. However, many of these firms are so big that if you are a new client, you can get lost in the sauce. They

naturally spend far more time on established clients who are paying all the bills with the firm's 5 percent of their huge sums. If
you are not one of these priority clients, you will get the short end
of the stick.

Once a year, around tax time, I would get a letter from PNFW
saying I needed to pay my taxes, but other than that, there was
no communication that I recall. I didn't know how money worked,
much less taxes. I thought a dollar was worth the paper it was
printed on, and the only taxes I had ever paid were taken out of
my Nkiru Books paycheck. I wasn't responsible enough to pay my
taxes or to even understand the trouble that would come by not
paying them. My question now in retrospect is, if it wasn't my
business manager's job to navigate me thru this, then what was I
giving them 5 percent of my income for? I could've fucked my
money up by my damn self without having to pay anyone to do
it for me. I now understand that the ignorance of young people
from the hood who somehow come into a lot of money is quickly
preyed on by these business managers who know the game. By
the time I got to PNFW, Bert Padell was a superstar accountant
who hobnobbed with Madonna and Diddy.

How could I think I wasn't with the right firm? To be fair, Bert
helped me get a loan for a house by flexing his weight on a phone
call, and he was great about remembering to call you and sing
"Happy Birthday" on your born day. I would pick up the phone,
forgetting what day it was, thinking there was some issue
because Bert himself was calling, and he would begin loudly and
immediately—

"*Haaaapppyyyy biirthhdaayyy tooo yooouuuu!!!*"

As nice as these birthday wishes were, they didn't help me at
tax time. PNFW charged a lot but, it seemed to me, provided the
bare minimum of services. I was mistaken to put my trust in them
and to allow anyone but myself that much control over how my

finances were handled. Purchasing a failing bookstore with Yasiin didn't help either. I naively thought that having a business manager absolved me from having to comb thru the details of my account, and I was good at rapping, so whenever money got low, I would just go out and rap some more to make more money. However, because of the negligence that abounded (including my own), I was never able to catch up with previous tax debts. If you ever wondered how rappers can make so much money and end up in so much tax trouble, this is how.

These days I've raised my financial IQ and pay attention to every dollar that comes in and leaves. Having to pay tuition and mortgages has forced me to stop coasting on my lyrical talent and actually plan for the future. I have since done the work to get competent financial people on my team. I still have tax debt to catch up on, and I have come close to being one of those rappers you see in the press who owes millions to the IRS. Maybe I should go ahead and become a Moor.

If I was going to survive in the new industry, my management could no longer get 20 percent of all profit. Now that I was bringing a lot more work to the table on my own, I told Corey I could only give him 20 percent of things he brought in. This deepened the rift that was beginning between Corey and me. The business that Corey had taught me no longer existed. The business model was changing daily, and as a recording artist I had no choice but to pay close attention to these changes. Independence was key at this point, so every move I made from now on had to get me closer to ownership.

In the spring of 2009 Hi-Tek and I headed to Negril, Jamaica, to start the recording of the second Reflection Eternal album, *Revolutions per Minute*. This was my third trip to Jamaica to start an album, and this time I also brought Eque, Res, and Graph Nobel with me. I rented a house on the beach, and Dave Dar flew in to engineer the sessions for us. For three weeks we spent our days sunbathing and swimming, and we spent our nights recording, going to reggae concerts, and eating great Jamaican food. We recorded most of the vocals on that Jamaican trip, and Hi-Tek and I flew back to Cincinnati to mix and master the album. The night we landed in Cincinnati, we got arrested.

Still high, literally and figuratively, from our Jamaican trip, we decided to go straight to the studio from the airport and start mixing immediately. Feeling proud of what we were working on, we hopped into Hi-Tek's old-school Lincoln and headed to a local nightclub for a few drinks. Hi-Tek's Lincoln was like a club in itself. The pretty car was covered in lavender candy paint and sitting high on twenty-four-inch rims. It attracted a lot of attention, especially when Hi-Tek let the music bang out of the trunk. After partying at the club for a couple of hours, we jumped back in the whip and headed across the Ohio River to Hi-Tek's Covington, Kentucky, studio, the Tek Lab, with the new Reflection Eternal project blaring loudly out the speakers. As we pulled into a gas station on the Kentucky side for snacks, a police car pulled up on us and an officer hopped out to tell us our music was way too loud. Even though we cooperated and immediately turned it off, the police decided to make Hi-Tek do the drunk test. He failed. Our interaction with the police went downhill from there. After a harsh exchange of words, I was searched and they found weed in my jeans. Hi-Tek and I were both detained.

Hi-Tek and I had gone our separate ways after the difficulties of recording *Train of Thought*. After spending damn near every day together for three years, we definitely needed some space apart to grow. For two years, Hi-Tek and I didn't speak to each other, and we didn't begin to rebuild our friendship until we began working on *Revolutions per Minute*. The trip to Jamaica helped, but I felt as if we connected as more than friends—as brothers—that night in the drunk tank in Covington. Our bond has largely been unspoken, but being locked up together was a metaphor for how we felt then about our careers. *Train of Thought* had tethered our destinies together forever, and the tribulations we faced that night made our bond stronger. It anchored us and reminded us of our purpose.

Some of the best lyrics I've ever written are found on *Revolutions per Minute*. *Train of Thought* was my favorite album lyrically up until then, and I was trying hard to outdo myself. "In This World" felt like an instant classic, and we did a video for it immediately. When Hi-Tek cut up the Jay-Z "truth be told" lyric over the hook, it felt as if this time around we were bringing the mainstream into our world. When I said, "I paid my dues kept the receipt for taxes," that reflected how what I'd learned business-wise was starting to creep into my lyrics. On "Ballad of the Black Gold" I tackled the history of oil companies in Nigeria, hardly a ripe subject for a pop song. On "Lifting Off," I dealt with my addictions to controlled substances thru song in a real way for the first time in my career. My responsibilities on the album were more than lyrical; I was now documenting my path to maturity.

The rollout for the new Reflection Eternal album suffered due to poor management. Warner Bros. was always more interested in me as a solo artist than they were in Blacksmith Music artists or the Reflection Eternal project, and it showed in the way they handled the marketing and promotion for *Revolutions per Minute*. We had to fight for every dime, and it was often a struggle to even get label people on the phone or to commit to a meeting. There was no radio budget, no real budget for marketing and promotion. Blacksmith Music, both Corey and I, had to make sure we had people in the Warner building that we could trust to push things thru for us. We failed miserably at this.

On May 18, 2010, *Revolutions per Minute* was released to the world thru Blacksmith Music/Warner Bros. By my standards it was a stellar piece of work and Hi-Tek and I had shown a lot of musical growth since *Train of Thought*. It had great features like Bilal, Bun B from UGK, and Estelle from the U.K. On "Just Begun," which also featured Yasiin Bey, we introduced J. Cole and Jay Electronica to many fans. It was critically acclaimed, debuted at number 18 on *Billboard*, and sold twenty-one thousand copies in its first week. Still, I knew we could have done much better with the rollout. The first Reflection Eternal album, released ten years prior in the year 2000, was listed as Talib Kweli and Hi-Tek Are Reflection Eternal. As a solo artist I had released four studio albums and a bunch of mixtapes since 2000, so I had a quantifiable sales history. As a group, Reflection Eternal had no sales history at all, and without sales history, retailers will provide limited support. I thought it was extremely important to keep the group name consistent, and I made this point to Warner Bros. over and over, in many meetings and on many emails. No matter what I said, I continued to see the group being promoted by Warner Bros. as Reflection Eternal rather than Talib Kweli and Hi-Tek Are Reflection Eternal.

Warner Bros. promised that the album would be listed as Talib Kweli and Hi-Tek Are Reflection Eternal, but when it dropped, that was not the case. If the album had been listed under Talib Kweli, our first-week sales would have doubled. This was a huge mistake. If that wasn't bad enough, a small label called Babygrande, which once did a deal with Hi-Tek, cannibalized our release date with a surprise simultaneous release of a Hi-Tek compilation. This release confused fans, who were looking for a new album from Hi-Tek and me rather than some compilation hastily put together by some culture vulture trying to profit off our hard work. I was so livid at the incompetence surrounding the *Revolutions per Minute* rollout that I immediately requested to be dropped from the Warner Bros. roster. My request was accepted.

For the first time in my career since I signed that Rawkus deal in 1997, I was an unsigned artist. Not knowing where my next check was coming from was daunting but necessary for my growth. I had become too dependent on other individuals to make sure my family and I ate. I considered firing Corey, but I didn't feel confident in my ability to navigate my career by myself and still felt I needed a manager's help, so I met with other managers in the business to see what my options were. Rich Nichols, the Roots' longtime manager, gave me some great advice, but with the Roots transitioning from a touring group to the house band for Jimmy Fallon's new TV show, *Late Night with Jimmy Fallon*, Rich's hands were pretty full. It was Blue, who managed Outkast for years, who gave me the advice that helped me chart my course. Blue reminded me that as a man I was responsible for making sure my career went the way I wanted. Blue explained that as a manager he is only as good as what his artist is able to provide, and that from what he could see, Corey had done a good job with me, and maybe it was now my turn to step it up.

Blue was right. Corey was a great guy with a great ear who had supported me for years. He had become one of my best friends. But over the years I noticed that Corey wasn't any better with money than I was, and as I grew, the gulf between what Corey and I knew industry-wise had decreased dramatically. Corey knew what he knew, which was booking shows and keeping artists on the road, not running labels. Blacksmith Music was a great idea, but it was my idea, not Corey's. Because he was so close to me, I expected Corey to automatically understand my vision, but he had his own vision. I was thirty-four years old, and nobody knew more about what my career needed than I did, and no one was in a better position to make it happen. Rather than sever the relationship, I

decided that I would become so fiercely independent and knowledgeable about the business that Corey would have no choice but
to follow my lead.

   While I was conflicted about my business relationship with
Corey, the sense of freedom I felt from no longer being associated
with a record label was rejuvenating. While I was by no means a
rich man, by staying true to myself with the music, I had earned a
huge amount of cultural currency, which I knew would come in
handy for the rest of my life. I felt the same way I did when I first
stepped on the SOB's stage to perform at the Lyricist Lounge almost fifteen years before. I was grateful that I still had something
to prove, except this time it was more for myself than for the
world. I had spent a career trying to become one of the best MCs
in the eyes of other MCs, and I had achieved that. The questions
I had for myself were: What was I going to do now that I had
achieved my original goal? What were the accolades really worth,
and how would they feed my family? I hadn't realized how stifled
I felt dealing with the major labels until I left them. Now that I
was no longer tethered to the industry, I felt I could breathe easier. So I took a deep breath and plotted my next move.

27

Knowledge of Wealth

> Anyone who has traveled so far will not easily be
> dragged again into the world.
>
> —JAMES BALDWIN

When Blacksmith Music was founded, I thought I knew a lot about the business, but I still had so much to learn. I learned that I had been taken advantage of as an artist by my labels and my management far more than I had realized. When I began to go back and look at old contracts, budgets, and marketing plans, I realized that ever since Rawkus sold out to Geffen in 2002, I never had a fighting chance to compete. Fans often think of the music business in romantic terms. They think all you have to do is be good enough to make a hit, and if your music is good enough, you can compete. Now that I was asserting myself as more than just the artist and involving myself in every aspect of the business, I saw just how far away from a meritocracy it was. It wasn't even close.

Rawkus believed that the music of the artists they signed was every bit as good as the music on mainstream radio, and they spent money to prove it. Rawkus used to throw decadent, elaborate parties for DJs to convince them to play Rawkus records. They flew us around to city after city, making us shake hands with and do drops for the mix-show DJs. They spent hundreds of thousands on music videos and indie radio promotion so that the networks and radio stations would have no excuse not to play our music. But when the Rawkus artists got dumped onto major labels, the majors didn't care at all. They had artists who they invested far more in, and they looked at Rawkus like that underground shit that doesn't need a radio budget because it's for the "lyrical" heads anyway. These major-label folks had a lot of preconceived notions about who Rawkus artists appealed to, and when Jarret and Brian were no longer around to stand up for us, we got put on the back burner, shelved, or dropped. It's not that artists like Pharoahe Monch and Kool G Rap and me were no longer making great music, it's that no one was willing to invest the money it would take to get the word out to the people that this music existed.

By September 2010 I felt so liberated by not being a signed artist that I began working on an album that I intended to sell by myself. I was six albums deep into my career, and I'd made such a name for myself that I asked myself, why do I even need a label? Fans were now buying more digital music than they were physical, which meant that I didn't need to spend the money it would take to press up physical copies for people to buy it. I had industry relationships and a studio in my North Hollywood crib, so what was stopping me? With the exception of *Liberation* with Madlib, I had gotten used to needing permission to record and release an album. The realization that I didn't require any was rejuvenating. I called the burgeoning project *Gutter Rainbows* and got busy.

Coming off an album produced entirely by Hi-Tek had me

antsy to explore what I would sound like working with some of my other favorite hip-hop producers, so I dove right in. By that November I had recorded fourteen songs over beats by producers like M-Phazes, 88-Keys, Khrysis, and Ski Beatz. Jean Grae guested on the Oh No–produced "Uh Oh," and Kendra Ross showed out on the S1-produced "Wait for You." Outasight appeared on the 6th Sense–produced "Ain't Waiting," Nigel Hall hopped on S1's "Mr. International," and one of my favorite MCs, Chace Infinite, appeared on the Maurice Brown–produced "Self Savior." When I sent a rough copy of *Gutter Rainbows* to Dru Ha, the head of Duck Down Records, who was also running a DJ crew called 1200 Squad, it was to try to get his DJ crew to support the project, but upon hearing it, Dru had bigger ideas. Dru had spent years partnering with larger companies for distribution of albums from his storied Duck Down roster, and by 2010 he was ready to throw his own hat into the distribution ring. As the Boot Camp Clik–affiliated label head behind classic Duck Down albums such as Black Moon's *Enta da Stage*, Smif-N-Wessun's *Dah Shinin'*, and Heltah Skeltah's *Nocturnal*, Dru knew firsthand how hard it was to sell Brooklyn-based underground hip-hop in a rapidly evolving mainstream environment, but somehow Duck Down had survived every era and remained relevant. Now, Dru and his younger brother Noah were starting a distribution company called Duck Down Distribution, or 3D for short.

When Dru found out I planned on putting *Gutter Rainbows* out all by myself, he proposed a partnership between his new company, 3D, and me that would allow 3D to be the distributor for the album. This meant I was the label, so I needed to come up with a name. I called my label Javotti Media, named for my grandmother Javotte Greene. I had fond memories of spending weekends at my grandma Javotte's house in New Rochelle, a house that my father had bought for his family with money he made as a child actor. Javotte was an accomplished actor and singer, and I remembered waking up often to the sounds of her singing opera in the hallway. Javotte possessed a creative soul, and her creativity had been reborn in me. Plus, I knew that naming my label after my grandma would make it way harder for me to put some bullshit out in her name.

Gutter Rainbows, all in all my ninth studio album, was released on January 25, 2011. It sold almost as well during its first week as *Revolutions per Minute* had, which proved to me that I didn't need to be affiliated with a major label like Warner Bros. to move units. Dru Ha's team at 3D was a fraction of the team that a multinational corporation like Warner Bros. had, but they worked harder and smarter and got way better results while spending far less money. *Gutter Rainbows* is still one of my least-known albums, but the album showed me the power of independence. Within three months of its release, I received my first royalty check from the sales of *Gutter Rainbows*. That was the fastest I'd ever been paid for an album I released. I was kicking myself for not going the indie route sooner.

While I began building Javotti Media with the help of Dru Ha, Corey was working on a deal for Blacksmith Music to release content thru Capitol/EMI Records, which would later become Caroline Distribution. I began recording an album that would come to be known as *Prisoner of Conscious*. One of the first songs I recorded was "Before He Walked," produced by E. Jones and featuring Nelly and Abby Dobson. Many considered Nelly to be the opposite of me, a commercial artist with radio hits who fans of underground, lyrical hip-hop were supposed to despise. Yet, Nelly was one of the most gracious dudes I had met in the business. We often spoke about collaborating on a song, and one night back in 2011 Nelly stopped by my North Hollywood crib to kick it while he was working on a film. We spent the whole night talking about music and the perceptions people had of us as artists. I fondly recall introducing Nelly to the music of J Dilla and Madlib that night. He had heard of both but wasn't familiar with either. After a marathon all-night session of listening to Madlib and Dilla music, Nelly and I began working on the E. Jones track that would become "Before He Walked."

mm

Music gave me knowledge of self,
And now my knowledge of self done gave me knowledge of wealth
—NELLY, "BEFORE HE WALKED"

With Nelly as my first recorded feature, I knew that *Prisoner of Conscious* was aptly titled. I never thought of myself as a prisoner of anything, but I knew that many fans and industry types had relegated me to a box. This box prevented me from doing songs with artists like Nelly, regardless of what the song was about or how good it was. This box was death, and I would use this album to break out of it. For inspiration for the album, I flew down to São Paulo to immerse myself in Brazil's African-based rhythms and to catch a concert by the Ethiopian jazz pioneer Mulatu Astatke. While in Brazil I tweeted that it would be dope to do a song with the Brazilian singer and actor Seu Jorge, whose career I had been following since his fantastic work in films like *City of God* and *The Life Aquatic with Steve Zissou*. Within five minutes, Seu Jorge's manager tweeted me back, and that night Seu was in the studio laying down his parts for the Terrace Martin–produced "Favela Love."

Busta Rhymes spazzed out on the RZA-produced "Rocket Ships." Melanie Fiona added vocals to the Saadiq Bolden–produced "Ready Set Go." Marsha Ambrosius made the J. Cole–

produced "It Only Gets Better" come alive, and my old friend Rubix resurfaced to go back and forth with me on the Oh No–produced "High Life," which also featured a hook performed by a Sierra Leone–based artist named Bajah. However, a verse from an unknown MC named Kendrick Lamar would get me the most attention when we began to roll out *Prisoner of Conscious*.

Back in 2010 Eque and her friend Devi Dev were running a radio show out of my North Hollywood home studio called *Left Effect*. *Left Effect* featured Devi Dev interviewing the most exciting artists emerging out of the Los Angeles underground hip-hop scene, while Eque played the music. During most of their shows I would stay inside the house, but one night while I was smoking outside at the back of the house while *Left Effect* was being recorded, I overheard a gravelly voiced MC spitting rhymes that seemed far from amateur. Dude was going off! That night Eque and Devi were having the group U-N-I as guests, and they brought their homie Kendrick Lamar with them. Hearing Kendrick rhyme made me want to go inside and pay more attention. I already knew the U-N-I dudes, but Kendrick I had never heard, and his style automatically reminded me of those Washington Square Park ciphers I was raised by.

I got Kendrick's number that night, and a year later while he was in New York doing early promo for his yet-to-be-released debut album, *Good Kid, M.A.A.D City*, he stopped by the studio I was working at to kick it. After hearing a song I was working on called "Push Thru," which already featured a verse from the New Orleans MC Curren$y, Kendrick jumped on it. Curren$y was killing the rap game with his independent hustle, releasing a series of marijuana-laced albums that were creating a cultish fan base, but when Kendrick laid his verse on "Push Thru," I knew the record held a special place in the culture. Knowing that Kendrick was about to blow up for real, I quickly scheduled a video shoot for

"Push Thru." For years, from Kanye West to J. Cole and Jay Electronica, I had been early when it came to releasing my collaborations with MCs that I knew were bound to blow up later. With this Kendrick Lamar feature, I got the video done but then waited to release it until the world caught up with my opinion of him as an artist.

I had worked on *Prisoner of Conscious* for two years and I was extremely proud of it, but when I was ready to turn in the finished product to Capitol/EMI, I could not because the Blacksmith Music staff had failed to turn in the proper paperwork. Without proper clearances and agreements, an album cannot be sold. I was frustrated. This meant that even though the album was completed by the summer of 2012, it wasn't going to come out until the next year. I was never shown an accounting for how Corey had spent the money Capitol/EMI had given us to record *Prisoner of Conscious*. These constant disappointments with Blacksmith Music and Management became too much for me to bear. In December 2011, I told my good friend Corey Smyth that I was no longer interested in working with him in any capacity.

Deciding to split with Blacksmith Management after thirteen years was one of the most difficult decisions I ever had to make. Blacksmith Management provided a comfort zone for me, and Corey Smyth had become one of my best friends. As disappointed as I was in the way he'd handled my career during the last few years, he had been integral to setting up the career I was currently enjoying, and he had been there for me as a friend thru situations beyond music business. My realization that as an artist I had outgrown him took a long time. An even harder realization was that I'd outgrown Corey years before I made this move.

28

Dillagence

I taught them everything they know, but not everything I know.
—JAMES BROWN

Ryan Leslie is a genius. I knew this before I had the chance to work with him, but only in the abstract. As a Harvard-educated producer/singer/songwriter famous for his work with such artists as Kanye West and 50 Cent, Ryan made a couple of hit records but also made his mark on YouTube, frequently giving out industry advice and letting people into his creative process on his channel. By the start of 2013, Ryan was a completely independent artist who was trying to figure out how he could have access to the same analytics and consumer data that the people who sold his music had. Realizing that companies such as Apple and Amazon were using emails to market directly to fans, Ryan came up with a way to get the emails of his fans anytime they bought his music. With the help of his team at his company, Disruptive Media, Ryan Leslie built ryanleslie.com, a website where once you provided your email address, you could buy Ryan's music and whatever else he felt like selling.

I first worked with Ryan on a song called "Outstanding," which would appear on a 2012 mixtape I did with DJ Z-Trip called *Attack the Block* and later as the bonus cut to 2013's *Prisoner of Conscious*. The summer that *Prisoner of Conscious* dropped found Ryan reaching out to me to discuss a business opportunity. My experience with Blacksmith Management taught me to communicate about business thru email, but Ryan insisted we meet in person. After playing phone tag for a month or so, Ryan finally caught up with me at Javotti headquarters one muggy August night and began to explain what he was doing with ryanleslie.com. He completely revolutionized the way I saw selling music.

Since watching comedians like Louis CK and Aziz Ansari set up websites to sell their comedy specials, I had always been intrigued by the idea of cutting out the middleman. Comedy was easier to sell than music because comedians don't need other musicians, engineers, studios, and so forth to produce content, but additionally, setting up a site that allowed people to buy music directly from it was expensive. Ryan and his team figured out how to do it at a low cost. As if showing us the website weren't convincing enough, Ryan received a notification on his phone that someone had just made a purchase at ryanleslie.com. To show us just how interactive the site was, Ryan looked up the phone number of the person who had just bought the album, called him, and thanked him on the spot. I was looking at the future of direct-to-fan relationships, and it was beautiful to see.

Besides music, Ryan was also selling unique interactions. One could purchase VIP access to a Ryan Leslie show, hang out with him in the studio, or even invite him over for a pizza party. Ryan was taking what Prince had done twenty years before with his New Power Generation fan club and giving it a face-lift for the millennial generation. After his presentation, I asked what I thought to be the most important question: How much would it cost Ryan and Disruptive Media to build a site like this for me? Ryan told me that he had wanted to present this idea to me in person because he thought of me as the artist he knew of who could benefit from it the most. Disruptive Media was offering to build my site for free in the hopes that I would find success with it and further spread the word. This was an incredibly generous offer. I didn't know Ryan that well, and I'm sure that he had artist friends he knew way better than me that he could have made this offer to, but he was showing me that he had paid attention to my artistic journey. Within two months Disruptive Media built Kweliclub.com for me, and I am forever in Ryan Leslie's debt for being able to see that I was a great vessel for this idea.

In October 2013 I was still promoting *Prisoner of Conscious*, but the prospect of selling an album directly to the fans without a middleman was burning a hole in my psyche. While touring with Macklemore and Ryan Lewis that fall, I began working on an album called *Gravitas*. With my engineer Federico "C Sik" Lopez along for the ride, we would set up mobile studios in the amphitheater locker rooms across the country that were used as dressing rooms for the tour. My goal was to get an album up and out on Kweliclub.com for the Christmas season, hoping it would bring in some much-needed holiday cash. The excitement of selling direct to fans plus the motivation to be done for Christmas had me working frenetically on *Gravitas*, and other than the week it took to record *Liberation*, the month it took me to record *Gravitas* was the fastest I had ever completed an album.

To create *Gravitas* I called in favors for production and features, and I put the album up for presale on Kweliclub.com in late November 2013. Big K.R.I.T. recorded on "Demonology" in one of those locker rooms. Gary Clark, Jr., jumped on that song at the last minute as well. Oh No was *Gravitas*'s anchor, producing three songs, "Rare Portraits," "Wormhole," and "Art Imitates Life," which featured Black Thought, Rah Digga, and ALBe Back. Wu-Tang Clan's Raekwon the Chef showed up for a guest appearance on the Thaddeus Dixon–produced "Violations," and the Under-achievers trade bars with me on the Statik Selektah–produced "New Leaders." *Gravitas*'s crowning achievement, however, is "Colors of You," featuring Mike Posner, produced by the late, great J Dilla.

James Yancey, aka Jay Dee, aka J Dilla, was born in Detroit, Michigan. Raised in a household full of soul and R&B music, he came of age at a time when hip-hop culture had taken over the consciousness of Black youth. A fan of the warm, jazz-influenced boom bap of early-1990s hip-hop, J Dilla set out to emulate producers such as Pete Rock, Diamond D, and Q-Tip and created a style that would astound his heroes and quickly place him on their level. After initially working with Detroit artists like Phat Kat, Amp Fiddler, and Frank N Dank, J Dilla found interna-tional fame with a group called Slum Village. Started by a group member named T3 and featuring an unhinged, spiritual MC called Baatin, Slum Village was anchored by J Dilla's pro-duction and rhymes, and their demo tape floated thru industry circles under the name *Fan-Tas-Tic, Vol. 1*. I first heard it while working with Hi-Tek on *Train of Thought* in Electric Lady back in 1999.

Q-Tip and Questlove were early champions of Slum Village, and while all three MCs held their own, J Dilla's beats impressed them the most. Soon, Dilla was producing songs for A Tribe Called Quest, the Roots, Erykah Badu, Common, and me. He scored a big hit when he ghost-produced "Got 'til It's Gone," a Janet Jackson song that featured Q-Tip, and Slum Village began working on *Fan-Tas-Tic, Vol. 2*. That album was like gospel to me. The way that T3, Baatin, and J Dilla attacked those Dilla beats was liberating. They were so good at using their voices and flows as instruments that the lyrical content was almost secondary. For years, I had focused so much on lyrical content that my flow began to feel stiff. I wasn't enjoying recording as much as I should have. Listening to Slum Village made me want to just melt into the music. I studied the way the three would bounce on those Dilla tracks and applied what I learned to my own style.

J Dilla was our spiritual leader. He is to hip-hop what James Brown is to soul and what Bob Marley is to reggae. However, Dilla was never a high-minded hip-hop purist. Contrary to popular belief, J Dilla was not a backpacker. Just like Hi-Tek, who was also from the Midwest, Dilla liked driving his Cadillac truck to the strip club. Dilla's lyrics were full of sex and marijuana, but his superior dedication to the art of hip-hop gives many hip-hop purists the urge to paint Dilla in a revisionist light. When it came to those beats, however, playtime was over. Nobody got busy on that MPC drum machine the way Dilla did, and watching him work is one of my greatest musical memories. When I wanted to get Dilla on *Quality*, he insisted I fly to Detroit to work with him. When I landed, I was picked up at the airport by Frank and Dank, both decked out in full-length furs. They led me to a cocaine-white limo that was waiting outside. I felt as if I were going to the prom.

As soon as I got in the limo, Frank Nitty from Frank N Dank poured a glass of Hennessy for me, lit a fat blunt, and told me that Dilla had asked them to take me for a tour around the city before we got to work. It was important to Dilla that I felt Detroit's energy before we worked together, and spending time with his homies was a part of that experience. After some local food and another visit to the liquor store, I was taken to the attic that Dank refers to when he says "the penthouse suite on top of my mom's crib" in the song "Pause." There we waited for Dilla to pull up in his Escalade, playing those thumpers he was known for. Dilla drove me to an apartment he'd just bought with his rap earnings from working on albums for A Tribe Called Quest and Busta Rhymes. The Detroit-born drummer and producer Karriem Riggins came thru, and I watched the two of them work on beats in the basement while the Grammys were playing on a huge TV in an upstairs room. The irony was that Dilla was nominated for more than one Grammy that night, for his work with Erykah Badu and the Roots. Rather than be in Los Angeles at the celebration, Dilla was in the basement working on new music and helping me craft songs for *Quality*. The fame and accolades weren't important to Dilla. The vibe was.

On *Quality*, Dilla produced both "Stand to the Side," featuring Vinia Monica, Novel, and Savion Glover, and "Where Do We Go," featuring Res, but in 2001, he was not yet known outside industry circles as the legend he would become. While becoming that legend, Dilla would produce "Roll off Me," from my 2005 album *Right About Now*, and ask me to jump on the song "Raw Shit," from his collaborative album with Madlib, Jaylib's 2003 *Champion Sound*. As Dilla's name was becoming synonymous with the best hip-hop had to offer, thrombotic thrombocytopenic purpura, a rare blood disorder, was taking its toll on his body. This disorder would hinder Dilla in traveling and appearing in person, but for years he kept it a secret from everyone but his inner circle. My relationship with Dilla was definitely more musical than anything else, but we had mutual good friends, like Dave New York and Common. When Dilla's condition worsened, he moved to Los Angeles and lived with Common, who was spending time in Cali to develop his film career. J Dilla found a network of friends and family, such as his mom (Ma Dukes), Common, and Dave New York, in Los Angeles to support him during his final years. On February 10, 2006, James Yancey, aka J Dilla, joined the ancestors. J Dilla's death marked the end of an era, but the beginning of his untouchable legacy. Three days before he passed, Stones Throw released his final opus, a collection of beats called *Donuts* that Dilla created from his hospital bed. Knowing that his time on earth was coming to an end, Dilla put his entire heart and soul into *Donuts*, and as incredible as his output already was, it may be his best work.

When Dilla passed, the value of his music instantly went up, and there was a scramble for ownership of his estate. Naturally, those close to Dilla knew that he would want all of his music and proceeds to go to his mom, Ma Dukes, but legally it wasn't that easy. In 2013, after years of legal wrangling and maneuvering, Ma Dukes finally retained control of Dilla's estate. When I made a trip to Detroit, Ma Dukes and Frank Nitty let me go thru some of those vintage Dilla beats and allowed me to use one on *Gravitas*. Featuring another artist from Detroit, the homie Mike Posner, the J Dilla–produced "Colors of You" would become one of my favorite songs I've ever recorded. Once I decided to add this song to *Gravitas*, I knew the album was complete. *Gutter Rainbows* had proven that I could make money by selling my music independently, but *Gravitas* was an even bolder step. This would be the first time I was trying to sell an album completely outside the music business. I would be asking fans to forget about the containers they normally received music in and come buy a container from me. This was a risk, but without risk, greatness does not exist.

29

~mm~

Twitter Fingers

Fools multiply when wise men remain silent.

—UNKNOWN

Every living person is privileged in some way, for the alive have privilege over the dead. People who live in what are callously referred to as first-world countries are privileged to have access to resources that people in poorer nations ravaged by imperialism do not. Because we live in a patriarchal society, every man has male privilege that no women enjoy. Because we live in a society that values the lives of white people over the lives of people of color, every white person is privileged to belong to a group that is given the benefit of the doubt more often than other groups.

As a straight American male, I was born into at least three oppressor groups. As an artist who has achieved a modicum of fame, I have earned class and celebrity privilege that most will never experience. That makes me a member of additional oppressor groups. As a compassionate person, it's important that I recognize all of my privileges, earned and inherited. When I don't, I participate in oppression either deliberately or by default. Being a member of an oppressor group doesn't automatically make you a jerk; you only become that jerk when you refuse to acknowledge how you benefit by being a member of the oppressor group you are part of.

One of the most pervasive privileges to have is white privilege. As a person of color I know this because I know what it feels like not to have it. Race is a social construct with no basis in biology, but its implications have very real consequences. Race as a concept was invented by Europeans who sought to justify the kidnapping, torture, and enslavement of generations of Africans during the Atlantic slave trade. One could say that race was invented so that people could be racist. Tribalism, nationalism, and other isms that divided people existed long before racism did, but because racism was invented for profit, none of these other isms have been nearly as successful at dividing human beings.

Being tribal, being violent, and projecting our fear and insecurities onto others are all natural human behaviors. When we engage in those behaviors, we become our base selves and we are operating on our lowest vibration. Positive communities are important because positive communities challenge us to be and do better. When challenged to do better, we become better and operate at a way higher vibration or frequency. By being born into a family of academics who focused on culture and put education first, I was blessed, and privileged to be a member of a positive community from birth. The confidence, knowledge, and experience gleaned from being a member of this community led me to discover additional positive communities once I began the journey of becoming my own man. Finding friends like Rubix, JuJu, and John Forté led me to an artistic community in Washington

Square Park that challenged me to develop the skills I use to feed my family.

Freestyling in the park as New York City descended into night was like flying thru space. I was astral traveling without ever leaving the ground. The people watching those ciphers back then were seeing glimpses of my best self. Those park sessions were the primordial stew that my career crawled up out of, so it amuses me when I hear people like Javotti Media artist NIKO IS say that he got his start battling on the internet. Using message boards and comment sections of early hip-hop sites like 88hiphop.com and Okayplayer.com, some artists who were getting their start in the early 2000s were spending more time making names for themselves in digital artist communities than they were in physical ones. Battling was no longer something a rapper needed to do in the flesh.

mm

Always got something to say like an okayplayer hater.
—TALIB KWELI, "GET 'EM HIGH"

Ahmir "Questlove" Thompson is my internet godfather. If it wasn't for Questlove, I would not have the presence on the internet that I do. I didn't even own a computer, not a laptop or a PC, until around 2004. I bought my first laptop to stay in touch with fans of mine who visited Okayplayer.com, and Questlove's interactions there were the catalyst for me. After learning how to navigate the site, I began reading comments that fans posted on the boards. That was a rude awakening. I soon found out that Okayplayer.com was not the warm, fuzzy community I had previously thought it was.

Prior to 2004, my experience with Okayplayer.com was based

around interactions with the staff who ran it and the artists that the site promoted. It felt good to be a part of an artistic collective, and I enjoyed the idea of having a place online I could call home. Little did I know that strangers were being invited into this home. These strangers were rearranging the furniture and not using coasters. Due to my ignorance about how comment sections and boards worked, I was shocked at how rude, callous, and at times hateful some of these so-called fans could be online. Fans I met in real life were always gracious to me. They had to look me in my eye and shake my hand. These online fans, however, cloaked themselves in anonymity and used that as an excuse to write things about artists that they would never say in person.

One fan in particular was using Okayplayer.com to attempt to start a boycott of my music. Apparently he was upset that I missed some in-store appearance and took it personally enough to try to shut down my career. Obviously, he didn't have the power to get this boycott off the ground, but that didn't make his actions any less disrespectful to me. On principle, having a member of a community that I helped build even attempt to take food out of my family's mouth was something I wasn't going to tolerate, and I thoroughly overreacted to the whole affair.

Upon finding out that this guy was using Okayplayer.com to try to organize a boycott of my music, I jumped on those boards and began to lay into him with the full fury of a mama grizzly fighting to save the life of her cub. I was genuinely hurt by these actions and all in my feelings about it. The fans noticed. To my surprise, many fans refused to take my side on the issue. They felt I was doing way too much and they stood in solidarity with their fellow consumer. This was the first time in my career that I realized some people no longer saw me a part of the underground hip-hop community that I identified myself with. Having delivered two mainstream radio hits by this time, I was seen as a successful artist, the other. I was no longer the underdog that the underground cheered on. To these kids posting on these boards, I was now a part of the establishment.

Not getting the support from the Okayplayer.com community, the only internet community I had felt a part of at that time, made me disengage from the internet altogether for a while. When Myspace came out, I was lured back in. With a focus on music, for many years Myspace was a godsend for independent artists trying to connect directly with fans. Myspace allowed me to circumvent many of the obstacles that the music industry had up. It gave me the opportunity to begin my exit from the industry so that I could build industry around myself. I took to Myspace like a fish to water.

In 2008, a month after Barack Obama was inaugurated as the first Black president of the United States, I joined Twitter at the suggestion of Questlove. Questlove felt that Twitter was the perfect platform for how my brain worked, and he would mention it to me often. He was correct. When I first joined Twitter, I followed the lead of Questlove and Jean Grae until I developed my own voice. Once I did, I began having daily conversations and forming relationships not just with fans, but also with people I never thought I would meet much less become friends with— people like Ellen Barkin, MC Hammer, and Deepak Chopra. Anthony Bourdain would give me restaurant recommendations when I tweeted at him from the road. For a time, even my favorite author, Paulo Coelho, was following me on Twitter.

Since 2008, Twitter engagement has been a part of my daily routine. My seeming omnipresence on Twitter has been confusing to many of my friends and foes alike, and sometimes people make it their business to tell me that they think I could be managing my time better. I find it interesting that the people who offer me unsolicited time management advice are always people I am far more productive than. In fact, when I run into the people I admire and look up to, one of the first things many of them tell me is how much they enjoy my Twitter feed. This makes me happy because I thoroughly enjoy my experience on Twitter. As a working artist I have the privilege of creating my own schedule, which means I don't often participate in activities that I don't enjoy or find rewarding. Twitter is no exception.

During my first few years on Twitter, the interactions between me and my fans seemed a lot less toxic than they would later become. That's because back then it was mostly just my fans following me. When my Twitter follower count was less than 100,000 people, the conversation would often be about music, movies, jokes, and memes. When the conversation became about social justice, the people participating in it weren't there to tear anyone down. Even in disagreement, there was respect. As my follower count went up, there began to be many who visited my page not out of respect for me, but out of the desire to follow and eventually tear down a celebrity. If you look at the mentions of people with millions of followers, droves of the comments are negative. The more famous you are, the more people hate you. The difference between me and most celebrities is that I made a choice to respond to a lot of this hate. I do this fully realizing that my responses bring more hate to my door while also realizing I am uniquely built for this. Many of these people who tweet at me anonymously online are lonely and just need interaction and engagement. They will take it any way they can get it, even if it's negative.

To be clear, I could care less if people hate my art. That's not the hate I respond to often. Opinion about art is subjective and I count the best to ever do it among my fans. The hate I never ignore is hate of humanity. As the Obama era was winding down, there was a shift in the attitude of the country that was easy to miss if you were the type who tries to convince people that online hate and bigotry are fake and to be ignored. When the deaths of Trayvon Martin and Mike Brown pushed groups like Black Lives Matter into the forefront of the national conversation, white racists who were promised a life of entitlement began to show up in my mentions far more often. These racists were the target audience of online white-supremacist personalities like Ben Shapiro, Steve Bannon, and Milo Yiannopoulos. They were grown-up GamerGaters who were now adults and starting to realize that real life was not at all like video games. They didn't like the one life they had, so they began to blame people of color, women, immigrants—anyone but straight white males—for their lot in life.

The racists who now show up daily to harass me, my fans, my friends, and my family on Twitter started out passive-aggressively a few years back. There were many faux-polite but still racist comments about "all lives matter" and "why can't I say nigga too?" There were ubiquitous whataboutisms like "what about Black-on-Black crime" and "what about Chicago" being tossed my way on the regular. That kind of willfully ignorant pearl clutching seems almost quaint now compared with the type of mean-spirited trolling racists began to engage in when Donald Trump announced his campaign. By essentially starting his campaign with the words "Mexicans are rapists," Donald Trump gave hateful bigots a green light to tell us how they really felt. The better Trump did on the campaign trail, the more empowered these bigots became. As a New Yorker, I was well aware of Trump's long history of sexism, racism, cronyism, and all-around bigotry, but once he took his act on the road, the entire world got to see these qualities, and boy did America eat it up. As a reality TV star, Trump was comical. As a serious contender for president of the United States, Trump was downright dangerous.

One of the biggest red flags of Trump's campaign for me was when it was reported that Trump, a notorious Twitter addict, had retweeted neo-Nazi accounts not once, but seventy-five times by the time he was halfway thru his campaign. This was a huge story that was not picked up by any major news organization besides *Fortune* magazine. A year later, those same Nazis got online and organized the pro-Confederate Charlottesville rally, where they shot at people, beat people up, and murdered Heather Heyer in broad daylight. A day later, President Trump called those neo-Nazis "very fine people."

I thought that news would catch and that would be the end of Trump's popularity. Instead, nobody cared, and Trump became even more popular. Neo-Nazi accounts began making me and other prominent social-justice activists on Twitter their main targets during this time. You could tell they were neo-Nazis by the way they would retweet other neo-Nazis and tweet about how Black people had low IQs, white genocide, or the purity of the white race. They would name their accounts after famous Nazis and often add 88 to their names, which is Nazi code for *Heil Hitler.* (*H* is the eighth letter of the alphabet.)

The neo-Nazi accounts create the narrative pushed by racists who often don't even realize they are racist. This is where sites like Breitbart.com came in. These ultra-conservative sites began presenting white-supremacist propaganda as actual news. Knowing that white supremacists were his base, Donald Trump hired the executive chair of Breitbart News, Steve Bannon, to run his campaign. Foreign spies are well aware that many Americans believe anything they read online, so Russian spies started accounts to promote false information. These lies would be mixed in with the bigotry found on sites like 4chan and Reddit. These lies would then be taken very seriously by sites like Breitbart, InfoWars (another Trump favorite), and others, until this fake news would end up on

Fox News, being pushed by people like Sean Hannity. The generation that grew up with the internet at their fingertips has not been
taught how to properly vet and research sources, so many of them
believe anything that confirms their existing bias.

Once Trump won the election, the amount of bigotry spewed
at me online increased dramatically. The passive-aggressive whataboutisms continued to occur, but now I was being called a nigger or a monkey several times a day on a daily basis. I've been
called a nigger more times since Trump has been president than
I had for my entire life. Racists were now routinely posting what
they thought was my home address, pics of my mother, my
children, and Eque, making disparaging remarks. They invented
lies about my family, my friends, my height, my career—anything
to distract from the fact that they lose the arguments they show
up to start with me. I would be harassed in waves by coordinated
groups of bigots, sometimes even bigots from my own community. However, no matter how relentless it gets, I'm still right there,
fascinated by every minute of it. In the era of Uber, Google, and
Amazon, social media is a battleground for the soul of America.
People order food, find dates, go to church, and attend school
online. I think it's foolish to tell people that everything counts
online except for bigotry.

There are many people who are highly critical of my Twitter
engagement. They say that I spend too much time on Twitter and
that they are concerned about how dealing with so much of the
toxicity online affects my spirit. They say that I will never be able
to educate bigots and that by responding to bigots I share my
platform with them. To that I say I am not trying to educate a
bigot or save a bigot's soul. I am trying to confront, expose, and
destroy bigots. I don't speak to them, I speak *thru* them, to *us*. To
the person who quotes Jay-Z to me and says, "A wise man says
don't argue with fools, cuz from a distance you can't tell who is

who," I say that if you're too far away to see who the fool is, come closer. Invest time in gaining context for what you are speaking on. I was taught that being pro-Black meant combating white supremacy anytime it showed up, in any space or context. So when I see the Twitter trolls start pushing certain right-wing talking points, I pay attention.

When some account starts whining about socialism, communism, globalism, and/or white genocide, those are all tells. The person who does this has been immersed in white-supremacist propaganda and taught to hate everything the Nazi hates. Surely, you should choose your battles wisely, but in the digital age, when many people spend a majority of their free time online, I think that choosing to battle bigotry in digital spaces is a wise decision.

I do not expect everyone to engage on Twitter or any other social network as often as I do. The amount of engagement I participate in can be overwhelming for normal people, I get that. I, however, am not normal. I am exceptional. Not only do I thoroughly enjoy the discourse, it sharpens me as an MC. Having to fit my thoughts neatly into 140 and later 280 characters has made me a more efficient writer. Having my worldview and ideology constantly challenged has made me a better human being. Thru my interactions on Twitter I've learned how to be a better ally with oppressed people. I've learned how to respect the experiences of others in a way that I hadn't in the flesh. Twitter is far from perfect. Twitter is run by human beings, many of whom have no understanding of how bigotry has shaped our country, and so, intentionally or not, they absolutely coddle bigots who use their platform to spread hate. Twitter has also taken the time to reach out to influencers like me in efforts to make their platform fairer. They try to get it right and fall short often. With that said, I think, for me personally, the pros of being on the platform still outweigh the cons.

I also understand that the conversations I facilitate on Twitter around activism and social justice are meaningless if they remain solely on Twitter. A movement is nothing without boots on the ground and flesh in the streets. So if social networking or online interaction ain't your jam, that's fine by me until you come to my social network page telling me how to behave. It's a common misconception that I cannot take criticism. The opposite is true. I love criticism. It's criticism that makes me better. I'm not perfect. I'm far from perfect. But I'm damn good at what I do and I don't speak on things I don't know about. I have nothing to hide and I lay out who I am on the table in a very transparent way. This attitude allows me to fruitfully engage with anyone on any level. This is how you stop the weapons that are formed against you from prospering.

When people criticize activists, they better be able to show their activism. I've never driven for NASCAR, so I wouldn't show up at the Indianapolis 500 to tell a race car driver how he can win the race. How would I know? I wouldn't. Before you go online to tell an activist to ignore injustice, before you go online to tell someone who is more successful than you how to live their life, examine your own works. Examine your own life. Then go work on that instead. You don't have to like me or be like me online, but what I won't let you do is come and tell me how to be me. If you question me, I'm going to question you. Having this platform in my hand at all times is a privilege. I plan on always using every platform available to me to highlight what the underprivileged go thru, and I will never stop. My track record is ironclad on these beats, it's ironclad on these streets, so why would it be any different in these tweets?

30

~~~~~

Defenders of the Dream

I think the importance of doing activist work is precisely
because it allows you to give back and to consider yourself
not as a single individual who may have achieved whatever
but to be a part of an ongoing historical movement.

—ANGELA DAVIS

At my core I am a connector, an observer, a documen-
tarian, to quote Yasiin Bey. I am proud to have contributed to the
vast canon of Black cultural arts, and I understand the importance
of connecting the music to the community and using my platform
to voice struggle. However, I am hardly the first to do so. One of
the greatest examples of an artist who remains connected to the
struggle is Harry Belafonte. As a young calypso singer in the 1950s,
Harry Belafonte scored the first million-selling, platinum single
with "Day-O (The Banana Boat Song)," which was an impressive feat for a person of color in those times. The ability to sing
was just one of Belafonte's many talents. Along with putting out
hit records, he danced in Broadway shows, starred in many movies,

even worked with my grandmother and the namesake of my label, Javotte Greene.

Harry Belafonte wasted no time leveraging influence for advancements in the civil rights struggle. He was one of the biggest stars on the planet but was also one of the first celebrities to show up in such places as Selma, Alabama, to march with the people while they demanded freedom and equality. Famous for chartering a plane from Los Angeles to bring Hollywood stars to Dr. Martin Luther King's march on Washington, D.C., in 1963 and always on the right side of history, Harry Belafonte went beyond the photo ops to align himself with and create organizations dedicated to changing oppressive policy.

When I was recording *Prisoner of Conscious* in 2012–13, I decided that I could not give the album that title without being more consciously involved in spreading information about actual political prisoners and making sure I connected with grassroots activists when I traveled the country performing. I took advantage of an opportunity to visit one of my biggest inspirations as a writer, the famed political prisoner Mumia-Abu Jamal. Mumia is a journalist who was on death row for thirty years, many of them spent in solitary confinement. Even though his lawyers successfully had his death sentence vacated, Mumia remains in jail for life, charged with the murder of a police officer despite mountains of evidence that suggest otherwise. Any rational, compassionate person who reviews Mumia's case can see clearly that he was framed for this murder due to his affiliation with the Black Panthers and MOVE, organizations that routinely stood up to racist policing in Philadelphia back in the 1970s. When I worked at Nkiru, we sold many books about and by Mumia-Abu Jamal, but his most popular was *Live from Death Row*.

I went to see Mumia along with my good friend the activist Autumn Marie Griffin, the activist and writer Johanna Fernandez, and Catherine Peyge, who was, at the time, the mayor of Bobigny, a French city that named a street after Mumia in a show of solidarity. He was older and smaller than he looked in the pictures I had seen, and noticing this immediately moved his persecution from abstract to actuality in my mind. The pictures I saw of Mumia were taken years ago, and these institutions were working overtime to suck the life out of him. As world-weary as he looked, Mumia's spirit knew no bounds. He was clearly connected with current events, and it seemed that incarceration gave him a clearer, more nuanced view of many of the things we discussed. From the presidency of Barack Obama to the new album by Kanye West, I had the honor of getting Mumia's take on the world that tried so hard to move on without him. If Mumia could remain this engaged, this passionate, this relevant, all while fighting for his life in prison on behalf of his people, then clearly I wasn't doing enough. Visiting Mumia-Abu Jamal in prison made me want to do far more than just make songs about the struggle. I had done that for years, but I could do better. There is no comfort or convenience in Mumia-Abu Jamal's life. As we see from the comments of many celebrities of color in interviews that prove just how disconnected from the people fame and wealth have made them, even the strongest mind can easily be seduced by convenience. I work hard and I like to enjoy the fruits of my labor, but I could not allow myself to be so comfortable that I no longer relate to the struggles of everyday people. How could I continue to properly document the struggle if I wasn't on the front lines?

A month or so after my Mumia visit I was blessed to be a part of a core group of artists and influencers of color invited to a meeting hosted by Mr. Harry Belafonte himself. This meeting was designed to connect artists and entertainers with activists and organizations and to introduce us to a new organization called Sankofa, which would be helmed by Mr. Belafonte, his daughter

Gina Belafonte, and Raoul Roach, the activist and son of the famed jazz drummer Max Roach. I was hanging out with Dave Chappelle when I got the call, so I brought him with me, and when we got there, we linked up with such people as David Banner, 9th Wonder, Rosario Dawson, Chuck D, and many more. Yasiin called in on a conference line from South Africa, and Jamie Foxx skyped in. All of these people made time on their calendars for this meeting, because when Mr. Belafonte calls you to arms, you show up. Upon meeting Mr. Belafonte for the first time, I was excited to remind him that he did a film with my grandmother Javotte. When I mentioned her name, he beamed and said, "Yeah, Javotte Greene, I remember her. She was beautiful."

Harry Belafonte had us eat dinner together and afterward gave us anecdotes and nuggets of wisdom he'd picked up from his storied career. He described himself as having been "in the back rooms of history" and spoke of personal conversations between him and such folks as Dr. Martin Luther King, John F. Kennedy, and Malcolm X. These tales led him up to his point, which was that he was over eighty years old and wouldn't be with us for much longer. He didn't feel the new generation was doing their part to advance our people, and he was attempting to give us a blueprint on how to be more active. Mr. Belafonte also spoke of his involvement with the Advancement Project and how for-profit prisons were destroying America. With images of Mumia-Abu Jamal still fresh on my mind and from my work with groups that support political prisoners, such as the Malcolm X Grassroots Movement, Mr. Belafonte's talk of activism combating the prison industrial complex resonated strongly with me. After the meeting, I approached Mr. Belafonte for advice on where to start. I explained that many of the people at the meeting had done this kind of work for years, but our records were not as popular or mainstream as "Day-O" had been. I told him I believed that hip-hop could and should carry these social and political messages, and in many ways always had. I told him I felt the movement needed to be younger, and it didn't have to be based around celebrity. This is when Mr. Belafonte told me about the Dream Defenders from Tallahassee, Florida.

You know the story. In Sanford, Florida, in 2012, a seventeen-year-old Black boy named Trayvon Martin was walking back home after going to the store for some Skittles. Realizing he was being followed, he turned around to confront his stalker, a half-white, half-Latino man named George Zimmerman, who saw himself as being on "neighborhood watch." Zimmerman, a twenty-eight-year-old man who was armed and had a history of violence, gunned down Martin for daring to walk home from the store in his own neighborhood. This case had clear racial implications. As the innocent, unarmed Trayvon began to be described as a thug in a hoodie by the mainstream media as a way to blame him for his own death, the community began to mobilize around what had now become a symbolic death. When George Zimmerman was tried and found not guilty, it proved what we already knew: our justice system is broken, particularly when it comes to the lives of Black people.

The Dream Defenders, a student-based group that organized in 2012 to protest the murder of Trayvon Martin, sprang up out of the anguish caused by the Zimmerman verdict. By the time Mr. Belafonte hipped me to them, they were in the midst of occupying Florida's capitol with a list of demands aimed at combating the stand-your-ground law, stopping mass incarceration, and shutting down the school-to-prison pipeline—policies in the school system designed to criminalize students of color who live in poor areas, ultimately prepping them to be wards of the state in a profitable prison system. Mr. Belafonte said that if I wanted to see youth in action doing the things we discussed during the meeting, the Dream Defenders was a good place to start. Later that night, while googling Dream Defenders, I came across a speech by the group's founder and leader, a young man named Phil Agnew. This speech was so fiery, necessary, and on point, I decided that if this Phil dude was involved, I was down. I asked my son, Amani, if he wanted to come, and he said yes, so we packed our bags and headed to Tallahassee to support the Dream Defenders' occupation of Florida's capitol.

I used Twitter to inform the group that I was on my way, and Phil Agnew offered to pick Amani and me up from the Tallahassee airport. I was introduced to a new generation of freedom fighters, a group that included Bree Newsome, the young woman who made headlines when she and her friends removed the Confederate flag from the South Carolina capitol days after the white-supremacist maniac Dylann Roof murdered those nine Black churchgoers in Charleston in 2015. I wasn't the first "celebrity" to visit the Dream Defenders; both Jesse Jackson and the writer/activist Kevin Powell had spent the night with them before me, but I was the first representative from the world of hip-hop to support them, which I think they appreciated. Hip-hop was their culture, too. I was awed by these young people and their energy. They chanted, sang, and danced the entire time. Their drive was unstoppable and their focus was laserlike. Unlike the armed terrorists who occupied federal buildings in Oregon, these unarmed students were prepared with not just supplies but legal and historical knowledge that made it hard to disagree with the policy changes they were fighting for. Amani and I stood with the Dream Defenders as they spoke to the press, we participated in their roundtable discussions, and we freestyled thru the night with them before settling into sleeping bags on the hard, cold capitol floor. By the time I joined them, those students had been living in that building for twenty-eight days. Spending one night with them out of solidarity was the least I could do.

While the Dream Defenders were inspired to occupy Florida's capitol by the murder of Trayvon Martin, three Black women were inspired by the murder of Trayvon to occupy spaces online with the revolutionary idea that Black lives were just as valuable as everyone else's and that the courts, the police, and the mainstream media are all part of a system of injustice aimed at killing and arresting people of color for profit. The activists Alicia Garza, Opal Tometi, and Patrisse Cullors started a hashtag on Twitter called #blacklivesmatter and applied it to any tweet that addressed racist policing, mass incarceration, or the fetishization and subsequent dismissal of Black death by mainstream media. Simple yet complex, #blacklivesmatter quickly resonated with compassionate fighters of racism. Those who never think about how undervalued Black life is in this society became immediately offended that someone was not reaffirming their values and pushed back with the unoriginal hashtag #alllivesmatter. If this is not a hyperprivileged, entitled way to put how you feel above people's lives, I do not know what is. Of course all lives matter. But all lives are not treated as if they matter. Unfortunately, we live in a society that values people with lighter and whiter skin over people with darker skin. This is not an opinion nor is this based on my anecdotal life experiences; this has been historically and statistically proven time and time again. People of color know it in their gut and are forced to deal with it daily. To be able to pick and choose when you want to deal with the realities of systemic oppression is a privilege that only those with white skin enjoy.

A little more than two years after Trayvon Martin was murdered by George Zimmerman, an unarmed Black eighteen-year-old named Mike Brown was gunned down in Ferguson, Missouri, by a Ferguson police officer named Darren Wilson. According to the official police report, Wilson saw Mike Brown and a friend walking in the middle of the street and asked them not to. Wilson says a confrontation ensued in which Mike Brown attempted to take Wilson's gun, and Wilson shot Mike Brown six times, killing him. Mike Brown's body was left right in the middle of the street for six hours, an unprecedented length of time to leave a dead body in public, but a helluva lot of time to get conflicting stories together. As the Ferguson community began to grieve and express disbelief not only at what had happened but at how long Mike's body was left in the street, the police preemptively suited up in riot gear and took to the streets to harass the community into not asking too many questions.

There were too many questions not to ask. If Mike Brown was trying to take Wilson's gun, how did Wilson shoot Brown while he was 148 feet away? Why six shots? Why was he going for a kill? Why was Mike Brown's body left in the middle of the street for six hours? When you combine these questions with the Ferguson Police Department's ugly history of racist practices, a history that was well documented in a Justice Department report initiated in part by Mike Brown's death, the community had much to be suspicious about. As the overmilitarized Ferguson Police Department continued to antagonize a community in mourning, a couple of skirmishes between police and the citizens who pay their salaries broke out. A few bottles were thrown, a grocery store was looted, and a convenience store was set on fire. While this was certainly a righteous anger, it was not condoned by the vast peaceful majority of the protesters or the community as a whole. The face of the Ferguson protester was not some anarchic looter; it was the average working-class taxpayer or student who had seen a pattern of racist policing take one too many innocent lives. The mainstream media, however, latched onto the sparse reports of rioting and looting and blew these reports far out of proportion.

The job of the police is to protect the status quo that pays for them and is represented well by corporate media, so it's always in the best interests of corporate media to present the official police story regardless of the fact that it's often not true. So when corporate-controlled media outlets began to paint a picture of the Ferguson uprising that was very different from what was being reported on the ground by independent sources, I took to Twitter to champion those voices, since activism must go beyond hashtags and RTs. Social media is a great galvanizing tool and wonderful for discussion. If not for social media I wouldn't be as informed as I am, but when it comes to actually changing policy, flesh needs to be involved. The Ferguson protesters were making this clear, but the irony that I was using Twitter to point this out was not lost on me. So, to put my money where my mouth was, I connected with two of my best friends, the poet/musician jessica Care moore and the activist/professor Rosa Clemente, and we headed for Ferguson, Missouri, to see what was going on for ourselves.

I didn't show up in Ferguson as a rapper or a celebrity; I showed up as a human being who wanted to show solidarity with a stand against injustice. I wanted the Ferguson community to be aware that I didn't expect to be treated differently from anyone else and that I was down to pitch in. Rosa, jessica, and I headed straight to the corner of Canfield Drive and West Florissant Avenue, ground zero for the Ferguson uprising, and immediately connected with the folks on the front line. The energy was joyous around us, and people seemed to be excited by the change that was in the air. There was so much diversity, but everyone was focused on the single cause of holding the Ferguson Police Department accountable for the death of Mike Brown. Men, women, and children of all ages and races were out there. Multicultural coalitions of clergy, mostly white groups such as Anonymous and Amnesty International, Black nationalist groups, and feminist organizations were all working in concert to hold the Ferguson police accountable for the death of Mike Brown and the many others who were unfairly killed by police before him. I was happy to see that folks like Phil Agnew from Dream Defenders and the Black Lives Matter cofounder Patrisse Cullors were already there doing the work. Seeing people that I admired and respected doing grassroots organizing in real time was a huge inspiration and made me feel I was in the right place. Knowing we were outsiders, Phil suggested I take my direction from two brothers actually from Ferguson, the St. Louis rapper Tef Poe and his good friend Tory Russell.

I had not heard of Tef Poe before this day, but after a bit of googling I learned that he was a well-respected underground rapper who lived in the area. Tef was making rap songs about rap life, and Tory had worked at a temporary work service before Mike Brown was killed, but like many others who grew up in that area, the events surrounding Mike Brown's death changed their lives forever. What makes the Ferguson uprising unique is that it wasn't started by a group of activists; these were average Ferguson residents who simply got sick of the constant police abuse and threats to their lives. For many of them, the world that existed before Mike Brown's death was impossible to go back to. This was a moment of no looking back, and it was seized by the likes of Tef and Tory. Armed with nothing but an intense love for the people, they positioned themselves on the front line and provided jessica, Rosa, and me with instructions on how to help out. They introduced us to young women who gave us Maalox for our eyes in case we got teargassed, and they told us how to move if the police advanced on us. The police kept a respectable distance from the protesters during the day while the media were buzzing about, but when the sun went down and the news cameras were put away, the police wasted no opportunity with these protesters.

People have the right to congregate in the streets they live on, and if the people are congregating to protest an injustice, this moves past a right into the territory of duty. However, under the guise of public safety, police began to physically push the people around, telling them to go home and that they did not have the right to congregate at all. As it got closer to midnight, the people in the streets had to make some decisions. Do we listen to what the police are saying and leave, or do we stay where we are? That the people of Ferguson continued to protest in the streets no matter what the police said is why the movement had traction, so we ignored the pleas from the Negro preachers the police sent in to distract the protesters and stood our ground. The people I was with lived in that neighborhood; they were already home. Seeing that the crowd was not going anywhere, the overmilitarized police put on their helmets, pulled out their batons, and got into an attack formation. Once this happened, someone in the crowd threw an empty plastic soda bottle at the line of police. This was all that they needed. With batons in the air, the police rushed toward the crowd filled with men, women, and children, yelling, "Get 'em!"

Not exactly sure which way to run, Rosa, jessica, and I broke into a slow jog along with several other protesters. As I looked back, I saw absolute chaos approaching us fast. The police were beating on and running over people, trying to arrest as many as they possibly could. They shot tear-gas canisters into the air, and the crowd frantically scattered in all directions. This was not the time to jog. I grabbed jessica's hand, she grabbed Rosa's, and we ran at full speed for another block, head-on into a group of police with their guns drawn. They yelled for us to get on the ground and threatened to shoot us if we didn't. Because we were stopped midrun, I slid on the ground feetfirst and ended up on my back with a cop's rifle poking me in the chest. jessica was on her stomach with her hands outstretched, and Rosa was on the ground with her arms around some teenagers who had been running with us, pleading with the police not to shoot the babies. After the police yelled confusing instructions at us for what seemed like an eternity, something else happening down the street caught their attention and they told us to get up and leave immediately.

While I certainly did not expect any special treatment in Ferguson, the possibility of being killed there had not entered my mind. As much as I'd waxed poetic online and in comfortable academic settings about the realities of police violence, as many times as I'd witnessed state violence in my life, I had not prepared myself to be staring down the barrel of a cop's rifle in Ferguson, my life in his hands. Naively, I thought that going to jail for participating in a protest was the worst possible outcome. In an instant, that peaceful protesters were putting their lives on the line nightly in the name of civil disobedience went from the abstract to reality. This was literally life-or-death for them, and the cause could not have been more admirable to me. I spoke with Rosa and jessica, and we decided that one day was not enough; we would stay as long as we could.

The following day we linked up with Tef Poe and Phil Agnew. Tory Russell had been arrested in the night's chaos. People were going to jail and losing their jobs, lives were being disrupted, but these same people would be back on the street the next day, marching peacefully. Every major news outlet had their best field reporters in Ferguson, salivating over the possibility of the city's erupting into violence. Mainstream media reports of a "riot" after it occurs are a given, but having a reporter on the ground for an actual riot would create a ratings bonanza for the network with the scoop. CNN's Jake Tapper and Anderson Cooper were spotted scurrying back and forth all over town. Geraldo Rivera was getting directly challenged live on TV by Ferguson residents on Fox News's skewed coverage of the uprising. On my third day there, I did an interview with MSNBC's Joy-Ann Reid, who had the actor Jesse Williams join the conversation live via satellite. However, when the sun went down, the news cameras were turned off and the police took advantage.

Though Mike Brown had already been killed while unarmed by Officer Darren Wilson, Mike Brown's family had to watch his life be even further diminished in the mainstream media. Just like Trayvon Martin before him, Mike Brown was being blamed for his own death. The police even put out a videotape of a young man they claimed to be Mike Brown stealing cigars from a store two weeks before he was shot, even though the owner of the store disputed this. Whether or not it was Mike Brown on the tape was irrelevant, because Officer Wilson had no way of knowing about that when he confronted Mike Brown. This was clearly a character-assassination campaign designed to blame the victim for his own murder. It didn't matter that Mike Brown came from a good home and knew both his parents, or that he was starting college that fall. It didn't matter whether his pants were pulled up or if he spoke properly. Respectability will not save young people of color from a society that profits from their destruction.

After I was in Ferguson for a week, CNN invited me to do an interview with Anderson Cooper. On the day of the interview I showed up along with my good friend Seth Byrd, from Brooklyn, who flew in to join the protest after hearing that I had gone. I was in a great mood and was looking forward to meeting and being interviewed by Cooper, a journalist I was a fan of. While I waited for the interview to start, CNN's polarizing personality Don Lemon skateboarded up and got ready to go on air. At this moment the producer, who I had only spoken with on the phone, called and told me I would be interviewed by Lemon, not Cooper. I told her this was fine and remained upbeat about the interview. I knew that Don Lemon was known to ruffle feathers with his commentary, but I had not watched enough of him to develop any opinion on his journalism. I was excited at the prospect of having a great conversation about Ferguson on national TV with a fellow Black man.

My excitement dissipated the moment I met Don. Upon realizing I would be interviewed by him, I went up to introduce myself. Don shook my hand, but I could tell by the way he spoke to me that he either didn't realize he was about to interview me or didn't know who I was at all. This was strange to me because in my experience people who are about to interview me at least pretend to act interested in who I am, but I also knew that Don was subbing in last minute for Anderson Cooper, so I did not take it personally. Right before we went on air, Don asked me how to pronounce my name, then the interview began. Don asked me a question, and the moment I responded to it—and I had some things to say about how CNN had covered Ferguson and how I felt that their coverage was lacking—he cut me off to tell me what was wrong with my perspective. How do you tell another man what he saw if you weren't there?

A couple of months after my visit to Ferguson, Tef and Tory visited New York and stopped by my Javotti headquarters in Brooklyn. When I asked them how they planned to continue protesting nightly as winter was approaching, they seemed undaunted, but also spoke of the realities that came along with this type of grassroots, direct-action activism. Warm clothes were needed, bail money was needed for people who were being arrested for civil disobedience, and food and medical supplies needed to be replenished. Tef and Tory explained that well-funded outside organizations were indeed in Ferguson, but the money pouring into those organizations from wealthy charitable people hardly ever made it into the hands of the grassroots organizers on the ground who were actually putting their lives on the line.

With all the bureaucratic red tape and politics that go into charity organizing, too many of these institutions are inefficient, and the money being given to them ends up being nothing more than a tax write-off for a wealthy person. However, without the actions of the protesters, Mike Brown's story would have gone away overnight. These protesters were not abstract to me; I knew these people. I'd broken bread with them, I'd run from the police with them, I'd inhaled tear gas with them. I felt a special connection to this movement, and I knew I could do more to help it. After Tef and Tory returned to St. Louis, I used Gofundme.com to set up a crowdfunding page dedicated to jail, bail, and life support for the Ferguson protesters, and I pledged to hand-deliver the money to activists on the ground. I set a modest goal of $10,000, posted the link on my social networks a few times, and prayed for the best.

Following the Ferguson uprising on social media, I began to notice an interesting shift in the collective consciousness of the nation. The values of Black Twitter, the leaderless mass of clever, hyperaware Black tweeters that define trends, snatch wigs, and clap back at anybody disrespecting Black culture, were entering the mainstream at breakneck speed. While Black Twitter already had its own celebrities by November 2013, the Ferguson uprising was making new leaders out of independent activists and journalists who were providing nuanced, yet passionate, round-the-clock coverage of what was actually happening in Ferguson as opposed to what we were being told by the mainstream media. Black Lives Matter was created specifically to combat the kind of tragedy that happened to Mike Brown and his family, so it was a natural fit for all of these posts that sought to fight injustice. Trayvon Martin's death sparked the creation of Black Lives Matter, but the activism in Ferguson around Mike Brown's death thrust this movement into the mainstream and forced those who could not care less about Black life to deal with it.

Contrary to the lies perpetuated by enemies of compassionate people everywhere, Black Lives Matter is not funded by billionaires like George Soros. Black Lives Matter uses peaceful tools such as marches and demonstrations to combat a violent police state. People of color are forced to live under the constant threat of violence from law officers who swore to uphold the law. We pay the salaries of these people with our tax dollars. The violence is perpetrated on us, not by us. That an unarmed group of Black activists that clearly uses peaceful means to combat violence is constantly accused of creating or condoning violence speaks volumes. It is an ugly commentary on our state of affairs. Talking heads in the mainstream media go as far as to refer to Black Lives Matter activists as terrorists, just as they did to Dr. Martin Luther King, Jr., when he dared use peaceful means in the 1960s to suggest that Black lives matter. While armed, antigovernment white supremacists whose actions actually fall under the legal definition of terrorism are treated with kid gloves by the Feds, we have police on Facebook encouraging motorists to run down Black Lives Matter protesters.

Racists, phony progressives, and those whose skin and/or financial status allows them to benefit from systems of oppression constantly try to misappropriate and defang the legacy of Dr. King. They prop up his "I Have a Dream" speech as proof of a utopia that will never be until they are honest about the way racism is ingrained in our psyches and institutions. They use his quotes out of context and conveniently ignore his revolutionary, anticapitalist stance. They whitewash him until he is safe enough for a McDonald's ad, and they pretend that he championed color blindness over diversity. The duty of freedom-loving, compassionate people is to reclaim the legacy of Dr. King, and to remind the world that his humanity was real and put into practice.

The year before Dr. King was murdered in cold blood by a white supremacist, he revisited the premise of his "I Have a Dream" speech when, in an interview given to NBC, he said, "That dream that I had that day has turned into a nightmare. I've gone thru a lot of soul-searching and a lot of agonizing moments, and I've come to see that we have many more difficult days ahead and some of the old optimism was a little superficial, and now it must be tempered with a little solid realism."

In a speech called "The Other America" delivered at Grosse Pointe High School in 1968, Dr. King explained why he never condemned riots:

> It is not enough for me to stand before you tonight and condemn riots. It would be morally irresponsible for me to do that without, at the same time, condemning the contingent, intolerable conditions that exist in our society. These conditions are things that cause individuals to feel that they have no other alternative than to engage in violent rebellions to get attention. And I must say tonight that a riot is the language of the unheard.

Addressing the woes of capitalism in a letter to his wife, Coretta, in 1952, Dr. King writes, "I imagine you already know that I am much more socialistic in my economic theory than capitalistic. Capitalism started out with a noble and high motive . . . but like most human systems it fell victim to the very thing it was revolting against. So today capitalism has outlived its usefulness."

Anyone who has read Dr. King's "Letter from a Birmingham Jail" would not recognize the Dr. King that corporate media tries to sell to us. In this letter, written while Dr. King was in jail for protesting against segregated businesses during the holiday season, which is exactly what ahistorical idiots like to tell people Dr. King would not do, Dr. King writes:

> I have almost reached the regrettable conclusion that the Negro's great stumbling block in his stride toward freedom is not the White Citizen's Counciler or the Ku Klux Klanner, but the white moderate, who is more devoted to "order" than to justice; who prefers a negative peace which is the absence of tension to a positive peace which is the presence of justice; who constantly says: "I agree with you in the goal you seek, but I cannot agree with your methods of direct action"; who paternalistically believes he can set a timetable for another man's freedom; who lives by a mythical concept of time and who constantly advises the Negro to wait for a "more convenient season."

In this same letter, Dr. King addresses why he chose to protest the Birmingham business district by writing, "We decided to schedule our direct action program for the Easter season, realizing that except for Christmas, this is the main shopping period of the year. Knowing that a strong economic-withdrawal program would be the byproduct of direct action, we felt that this would be the best time to bring pressure to bear on the merchants for the needed change." By paying attention to Dr. King's own words and the body of his work, we can clearly see that Black Lives Matter activists are using the same exact strategies and rhetoric in their push for freedom as Dr. King did. Not only would Dr. King not condemn Black Lives Matter, he would be right there at the mall protesting with them on Christmas.

Because the creation of the Black Lives Matter movement forced many people to deal with their own apathy, jealousy and hatred began to be directed at its founders. Alicia, Opal, and Patrisse, three Black, gay women who started a movement that was centered mostly around the lives of young Black men, were met with judgment and resistance when they made their movement more inclusive of the Black LGBT community, a community that in many ways is more oppressed than the Black hetero community. To discredit these women, misogynists and homophobes in the Black community began to use the same smear tactics that racists use. What was interesting to me was that those who did the least found a way to criticize three women who had done the most. From the pushback to the Confederate flag to the proliferation of body cameras on police to promises of policy reform from political candidates, the actions of the founders of Black Lives Matter have forever altered for the better the conversation surrounding systematic oppression.

If you are the kind of person who says things like "No one protests when Black-on-Black crime happens," not only are you spreading falsehoods, but you are acknowledging your deep apathy. For one, our community protests all the time the violence that's created by forced poverty. If you don't see it, it means you are not looking for it because you don't care to. Second, you never hear the phrase *white-on-white crime* used, even though white people murder one another at relatively the same rate that Black people do, despite facing no systematic oppression based on skin color. The phrase *Black-on-Black crime* is racist coding; it seeks to blame the oppressed for their own oppression and to perpetuate the idea that Black people are more violent without examining or taking responsibility for the causes of the pathologies you find in neighborhoods packed with systematically oppressed people. Working directly from the book of Dr. Martin Luther King, Jr., the women who founded Black Lives Matter have given us a language, platform, and framework for us to unapologetically celebrate the right to be alive and fight this systematic oppression, and God bless them for it.

On November 24, 2014, despite much damning evidence, a Ferguson grand jury declined to charge Officer Darren Wilson in the death of Mike Brown. Grand juries hardly ever indict police, which is why cops routinely face them rather than facing a jury of their peers. The prosecutor in the case had a long history of ties to the police department, which obviously worked in Officer Wilson's favor. As a chief justice of the New York State Court of Appeals, Sol Wachtler famously stated that a prosecutor could indict a ham sandwich if he wanted to. Prosecutors, by the nature of the job, work closely with police departments, and they are in no rush to get their friends and colleagues indicted. The verdict, while hardly a surprise to me, hit the Ferguson community hard. Given the levelheadedness and peacekeeping efforts of local, youth-led activist groups, there was no riot in the streets that night. Small violations of the law occurred, and righteous anger was directed at the police, but the mainstream media had no real violence to sink their fangs into. The people seemed to direct their anger into more creative releases. That night, when I posted the link to the GoFundMe that I'd set up for the protesters, donations poured in. The money continued to pour in for the next two months, and by the time we shut down the fund-raising page, we had exceeded our initial goal by $105,000 and had raised about $115,000 for the protesters in Ferguson.

As a music executive I had learned how to handle six-figure budgets, but being responsible for $115,000 of charity donations scared me. If I didn't take the time to figure out the best way to get the money to activists on the ground, it would be far too easy to muck up this money and have to explain where it went to angry donors. I put together a committee of like-minded activists and cultural influencers to help me make sound decisions in handing out the money. The initial group I put together consisted of Rosa Clemente, Autumn Marie Griffin, Phil Agnew and Aisha Alexander from Dream Defenders, Patrisse Cullors from Black Lives Matter, Hiram Rivera from the Philadelphia Student Union, the activist/organizer Liz Manne, the activist/musician Miles

Solay from the band Outernational, the actor Orlando Jones, St. Louis–based activist/organizer the Reverend Osagyefo Sekou, the Ferguson activist/organizer Diamond Latchison, and the activist/organizer Kayla Reed from the St. Louis chapter of Organization for Black Struggle. We called ourselves the Action Support Committee and communicated our ideas thru a series of email conversations.

Beyond providing bail support for jailed protesters, the Action Support Committee spent the year identifying and supporting direct actions, civil disobedience, and programs that were created in the aftermath of the Ferguson uprising. We donated money to groups such as MORE (Missourians Organizing for Reform and Empowerment), Hands Up United, and others. The Action Support Committee also threw two fundraising concerts in St. Louis on the one-year anniversary weekend of Mike Brown's death. That Saturday, we put on a rock-based concert that featured performances by jessica Care moore, Outernational, and Tom Morello of Rage Against the Machine, and that Sunday I performed at our hip-hop event, which also included performances by Immortal Technique, Pharoahe Monch, Jasiri X, Tef Poe, Common, and many more.

The Action Support Committee, or ASC, was started to support the Ferguson protesters specifically. However, the people of Ferguson showed communities all over the country that they did not have to sit idly by while police were slaughtering us in the street. From the protests surrounding the deaths of nineteen-year-old Tony Robinson in Madison, Wisconsin; twenty-five-year-old Freddie Gray in Baltimore, Maryland; twenty-four-year-old Jamar Clark in Minneapolis, Minnesota; and all other unarmed young people of color, all killed by the police, we could see that the support we set out to provide was needed in all of our cities, not just Ferguson.

The way that Black life is undervalued is not news to communities of color, but technology has allowed us to film it on our cell phones and share it on social networks in real time. In the same way that seeing violently fascist images on the nightly news of the Vietnam War and the struggle for civil rights sparked a revolution in the 1960s, the unfiltered stream of independently documented police abuse that made its way to hashtags and retweets was galvanizing millennials.

I believe that hip-hop is a vehicle for the liberation of my people. I believe that the seed of Black Lives Matter is there in Dr. King's writing and, for my generation, that it's there in the rise of hip-hop. But before this generation embraced the struggle, I thought the era of protest was over, that it was an archaic tool that we all benefited from; I failed to see the importance of it in today's times. But this younger generation proved me wrong. This was their moment and they were seizing it.

31

—uun—

My President Is Black

And although it seems heaven sent,
we ain't ready, to see a Black president.

—2PAC, "CHANGES"

On August 14, 2015, I was booked as a guest on HBO's *Real Time with Bill Maher*. A week or so before my *Real Time* appearance I decided that I would release an album that day and announce it on the program, which I hoped would bring a lot of traffic to Kweliclub.com. I was working on several songs for my upcoming album that I wasn't sure fit the album's direction, so I completed those songs and put them together as a separate project to be released free, exclusively thru Kweliclub.com. I called it *Fuck the Money*, and after I announced its release that Friday night on *Real Time*, almost one hundred thousand people headed to my site, gave me their email addresses, and got their free albums directly from me.

Fuck the Money went in many different musical directions; it is more like a compilation of songs I was working on than a cohesive album. I do a singsongy style on "Butterfly," which was produced by Kaytranada and features the Detroit singer Steffanie Christi'an. NIKO IS and TDE's Ab-Soul trade verses with me on an Alchemist-produced banger called "The Venetian." Four songs on *Fuck the Money* were produced by Antwan "Amadeus" Thompson: "Nice Things" features me on a more trap-style beat; "Fall Back," featuring Styles P, has a more upbeat club sound; "Leslie Nope" is me having fun on a track that would be perfect for a rap battle; and "Money Good," a guitar-laced, thoughtful track, ends the album. "Echoes," which was produced by Farhot and features singing from Miguel and Fall Out Boy's Patrick Stump, was recorded back in 2011, during the same session as the Miguel-featuring "Come Here." I did a video for the title track, "Fuck the Money," featuring South Africa's Cassper Nyovest, and I used the album's intro, "Gratitude," produced by Thanks Joey, as a show opener that summer.

My fascination with the spirit of collaboration has always kept me afloat in this business, and the fall of 2015 was no different. A year earlier, one of my favorite hip-hop producers, Patrick "9th Wonder" Douthit, had casually suggested that he, Pharoahe Monch, and I form a collective called INDIE 500. This collective would be formed in the spirit of the Native Tongues, who we were all greatly influenced by, and would encourage us to support one another's crews and projects as well as to work together more often. Pharoahe's label is W.A.R. Media, mine is Javotti, and 9th's is Jamla. Shortly after that suggestion, I flew to 9th Wonder's home city of Raleigh, North Carolina, to do some recording with the Jamla squad, which included a producer team named the Soul Council. Soul Council was headed by 9th Wonder himself, but cats like Khrysis and E. Jones, who produced songs on *Gutter Rainbows*, were no slouches. I arrived at Brightlady Studios, the Jamla headquarters, at the same time as the exceptional West

Coast rhyme team of Problem and Bad Lucc, who had their own independent movement going on with a label called Diamond Lane. With all of this creative energy bursting out of one studio, we recorded much of what would become the basis for a collaborative album between 9th Wonder and me, *INDIE 500*.

As a founding member of the seminal hip-hop group Little Brother, 9th developed a reputation as a curator of the culture. He would go on to be a hip-hop fellow at Harvard and a professor at North Carolina's Duke University, but it all comes from the boom bap, and 9th never strays from it. His love for the culture rubs off on the people he surrounds himself with, and spending time at Jamla felt like being at some sort of fun hip-hop summer camp. By the time we finished the album, great independent MCs like Brother Ali, Planet Asia, and Slug from Atmosphere had joined the party. K'Valentine dropped a verse, jessica Care moore dropped a poem, and NIKO IS spazzed on four of the songs.

Working closely with 9th also allowed me to witness how phenomenal an MC Rapsody is. Born Marlanna Evans, Rapsody became one of the first nationally recognized female MCs to make a name for herself on skill alone. Besides Jean Grae, there had never been a female MC who was not signed to a major who was respected by the boys in the way that Rapsody was. One of the most humble people I ever met in this business, Rapsody treated my crew and me like family when we were in Raleigh, and I felt an instant kinship with her.

For Rapsody, 2015 was a big year. She started that year by appearing as a guest on Kendrick Lamar's highly anticipated album *To Pimp a Butterfly*, delivering an incredible verse on the song "Complexion (A Zulu Love)." Shortly after *INDIE 500* dropped, Grammy nominations were announced, and Kendrick's album was up for eleven of them. Rapsody's recognition was a victory for the crew, and it was cool to see her and 9th Wonder on the red carpet at the Grammys. I knew the music industry was starting to take notice of Rapsody, but I was still surprised to see her walk into the Roosevelt Room at the White House while I was there for a meeting with President Barack Obama.

In mid-March 2016, I and fifteen other established hip-hop and R&B artists received an email from the White House asking for our participation in a meeting with President Obama. This meeting would center around criminal justice reform, but no other details were provided. I had no clue who the other artists would be, and I would not find out until the day of the meeting. All I knew was that to be invited to this conversation was quite an honor. As the first African-American president of the United States, Barack Hussein Obama had broken many barriers and achieved what I grew up thinking was an impossibility in my life- time. A pragmatist and an excellent politician, he somehow de- fied the incredible odds against him and rose from his Hawaiian birthplace to become an Ivy League–educated lawyer and a sena- tor from Illinois before he upset Hillary Clinton for the Demo- cratic presidential nomination in 2008. A Harvard man, Barack Obama reminded me of my younger brother, Jamal. Barack and Jamal possessed the same studious way of speaking and the same set of political values and shared a quiet righteousness. When Obama first campaigned in Iowa, Jamal believed enough in him as a candidate to travel to Iowa and volunteer. I'm sure I'm not the only person who felt this way, but Barack felt like a member of my family.

As a musician who is also closely associated with social activ- ism, I often warned of the dangers of being misinformed about America's voting process. Many people believe that every vote counts and that voting is patriotic. Black voters in particular are often reminded that many of our ancestors were denied the right to vote and others died while trying to change this. However, a closer examination of the process reveals a broken system that sells people the idea of change while effectively maintaining the status quo. The electoral college, set up by wealthy slave owners to ensure that states with the most land had more votes, along with the incredible amounts of money that candidates need to run, all but make certain that those who benefit from white supremacy are the only ones who can ascend to power. By beating more established politicians at their own game, Barack Obama cracked this code. While the office of the presidency, just like the work of a police officer, will always be meant to enable white supremacy, some choose to try to reform this corrupt system from the inside. I always maintained that I would vote for a worthy candidate, but I did not believe the system allowed for one. In 2008, Barack Obama changed my mind and earned my vote.

My children were also impressed with Barack. They followed the campaign closely and rooted for him the whole way. Growing up, I could not imagine seeing a Black person as president, unless it was Morgan Freeman playing him in a movie. Amani and Diani were getting to watch one of history's greatest moments play out. By the end of Obama's historic run, my children would be hard-pressed to remember a time when the president was not Black. Because of how the electoral college works, I knew my vote for Obama in New York would probably not count. New York would be sure to vote Democratic in 2008. I could not, however, ignore the pull of history. I cast my vote for Barack Obama as a symbolic gesture of progress.

Policy-wise, Obama definitely handled some situations poorly in my opinion. For example, I believe Obama deserved criticism for his dependence on drone strikes as a preemptive measure and for his support of unfair immigration regulations. People are right to resist any and all imperialist policy. However, I also feel that when you look at the racist obstructionism that Obama faced from Congress as the first Black president, it's amazing that he got anything accomplished at all. From pushing through a national health-care plan to making criminal justice reform a priority during his tenure as president, the accomplishments of the Obama administration make me confident in my belief that the country was way better off with an Obama presidency than we would have been under John McCain or Mitt Romney.

Arriving at the White House for the first time in my life in April 2016, I immediately got lost. I ended up on the wrong side of the building, and an intern was dispatched to find me. Thus I arrived in the Roosevelt Room first, while all the other artists were being gathered somewhere else. As the artists walked into the room one by one, I was immediately impressed with Obama's choices. He seemed to have assembled a pretty diverse cross section of hip-hop and R&B stars. While I sipped tea and wondered what was about to take place, in walked Rick Ross, Wale, Common, Alicia Keys, Swizz Beatz, Pusha T, A$AP Rocky, Nicki Minaj, J. Cole, DJ Khaled, Busta Rhymes, Ludacris, Janelle Monáe, Chance the Rapper, and Rapsody. This group of artists would certainly have different perspectives.

After a round of introductions, the president got down to brass tacks. Making connections between the school-to-prison pipeline and the prison industrial complex, Obama began to explain that he felt mass incarceration was the greatest domestic problem that America had. He spoke of the problems with mandatory minimums and of his plan to ban the box that makes ex-felons have to admit their criminal history while applying for jobs, a law that essentially guarantees unemployment for ex-felons. When Obama mentioned the hundreds of prisoners with minor, first-time offenses who had been released due to his executive orders, both Rick Ross and J. Cole mentioned young men they knew personally who had been released, and they thanked Obama for it. To his credit, many of the points I planned on raising around criminal justice were raised by Obama himself before I had a chance to speak on them. After laying out the meeting's agenda, Obama talked up My Brother's Keeper, asked us to publicly support it, and opened the floor for discussion.

The meeting lasted three hours. I was focused on driving the group to not just meet but to leave with some tangible commitment to a plan that could exist above and beyond the Obama administration. Obama was excited at the prospect of being free from the presidency and having a chance to participate in any activity he wanted without the weight of the office on his shoulders. I was looking forward to seeing what post-presidential Barack Obama would mean to the world.

32

~mn~

Trump's Amerikkka

Truth isn't truth.

—RUDY GIULIANI

If you grew up in New York City in the 1980s, avoiding the orange phenomenon known as Donald Trump was damn near impossible. He was everywhere, attending parties and premieres, dating fashion models. His first mention in the mainstream media ever was a 1973 story in *The New York Times* about how he was being sued for housing discrimination. Much like the gaudy, decadent TV show *Lifestyles of the Rich and Famous*, Donald Trump represented every stereotype the poor and working-class masses had about rich people in the 1980s. That spoiled, entitled, hyperviolent, sexist villain seen in so many 1980s teen comedies? Donald Trump was a father figure to that caricature. And it was fine, because as long as all he was doing was making sure poor New Yorkers of color had a hard time living in his buildings, he was tolerated. Scratch that, he was celebrated. Donald Trump, son of a billionaire slumlord and Ku Klux

Klan supporter, was seen as a symbol of the American Dream, the physical embodiment of wealth.

So when Donald Trump put out a full-page ad in the *New York Post* demanding that the Central Park Five, Black teenagers who were later exonerated by DNA testing and set free, should be given the death penalty for a crime they had yet to be found guilty of, it was dismissed by mainstream media as Trump just being Trump. When reports surfaced about Donald Trump's saying such things as "laziness is a trait in the Blacks" and "the only kind of people I want counting my money are short guys that wear yarmulkes every day," they were dismissed as Trump just being Trump.

I always recognized Donald Trump's racist dog whistles. I would cringe whenever my favorite rappers would mention him in lyrics as a symbol of opulence. When he began doing reality TV, while overseeing failed business venture after failed business venture, while declaring bankruptcy four times, Trump began to make more sense to me. He was a clown, a court jester, an empty suit. I was fine with letting him pretend to be the boss, fake-firing people on TV. Donald Trump's tangible effect on my life wasn't realized by me until he was triggered by the election of the first Black president in U.S. history, Barack Hussein Obama.

And triggered he was. Something about Obama just didn't sit right with Donald Trump, and being a famous white man, he was given an incredible platform to speak on this at length on Fox News, often. As the world's most famous birther, Donald Trump went out of his way to normalize the racist lie that Obama was not born in America. Trump offered no proof of this, other than that Obama seemed foreign to his sensibilities. If you grew up the son of a billionaire Ku Klux Klan supporter, you were promised a world in which no Black man would ever have authority over you. Barack Obama's mere existence destroyed Donald Trump's world, so he made disparaging Obama his main focus.

When Trump started his campaign by saying Mexicans are rapists and kicking Mexican reporters out of his press conferences, he was exhibiting the same behavior I saw him exhibiting when he demonized the Central Park Five. When he bullied Elizabeth Warren with that Pocahontas slur and disrespected Ghazala Khan, a Gold Star mother, I saw the same misogynist who had been famously busting into girls' dressing rooms unannounced at his pageants for years. Despite this sordid history, the GOP handed Donald Trump the nomination. Soon after, Trump would hire the executive chair of Breitbart News, Steve Bannon, as his campaign manager. Bannon is notorious for his advocacy of white supremacy. He is on record over and over advocating publicly for white nationalism. He is antidiversity, anti-immigrant, and anti-Muslim. He has been accused of saying he didn't want his children to attend school with "whiny Jews." So when Donald Trump himself RTed neo-Nazi accounts over seventy-five times during his campaign and then hired an admitted white nationalist to run said campaign, that wasn't just coincidence.

Even if people missed Steve Bannon's love of white supremacy, it was impossible to miss how Breitbart.com became a Trump cheerleading site when they were printing such stories as "Gays Need to Get Back in the Closet," "Renegade Jews," "How Birth Control Makes Women Crazy," and how the Confederate flag has a "Proud and Glorious Heritage." This is not hyperbole; these are actual Breitbart headlines. Between Breitbart.com and its louder, dumber cousin InfoWars, run by Alex Jones, Trump had the only news outlets he needed. It didn't matter that InfoWars posted stories about Obama being a demon who smelled of sulfur and hard-hitting pieces about how the Sandy Hook massacre was staged. As long as they said good things about Trump, he considered them his primary sources of info. Everything else was ironically dubbed fake news. By using his Twitter account to spread the lies he read on Breitbart and InfoWars, Trump effectively reached his core base without having to deal with the fact-checkers and investigative journalists who would call him on his bullshit. While we went high and ignored the trolls as they went low, they—especially the Russian sock accounts—used Twitter and Facebook to spread enough lies to help win Trump the election. America elected a troll as president.

By the time the tape surfaced of Trump bragging about sexual assault, I had learned my lesson. Trump's base would support him no matter what he said or did, and his base was a vocal minority that chose social media as their venue while mainstream media was busy patting itself on the back. I could no longer afford to dismiss Trump as a joke. The man was caught on tape saying he gets to grab pussy without permission because he's a star, and it somehow made him more popular with his core, family-values supporters. These people would clearly do whatever it took to win this election, even if it meant contradicting everything they claimed to stand for. Racist white people in America knew that making the most famous birther in the world president would be the ultimate fuck-you to Obama. They relished with unabashed glee the thought of electing Trump to stick it to the nigger president.

I always hesitated to compare Trump to Hitler. To jump to Hitler comparisons can come off as petty and dramatic and undermine otherwise sound arguments. That changed after Donald Trump compared those fighting against the rising tide of fascist ideals in America with the neo-Nazis and KKK members who were marching in favor of fascism in Charlottesville, Virginia, on August 12, 2017. One of these fascists, twenty-year-old James Fields, plowed into a crowd of protesters with his car, killing Heather Heyer. Fields, like many of the fascists who marched that day to protest the removal of Confederate statues, was dressed in a white golf polo and khaki trousers, the same outfit Donald Trump favors on his many, many golf outings. This is no coincidence. The election of Donald Trump had violently radicalized many racists.

Trump himself has without a doubt consistently displayed the traits of a narcissistic fascist who doesn't understand the difference between president of a democracy that has governmental checks and balances and a dictator. When I saw his first unhinged press conference, in which he disrespected a Black journalist, silenced a Jewish journalist, and told bald-faced, unnecessary lies about the margin of his victory over Hillary Clinton, I knew I was watching a Hitler moment. It wasn't good enough that Trump won the election; he badly needed us to believe that he won bigger than anyone else in history. This is so far from being true it's amazing that he even fixed his lips to trot out this lie, but lie he did. Bigly.

When challenged on this lie by a journalist from NBC, Trump's response amounted to "Well, that's what I had heard, so . . ." When no other journalist pressed the issue, when Trump was simply allowed to tell lies to the American people from that podium, when Trump was allowed to say that the buck shouldn't stop with him as president, I knew we were in bigger trouble than I thought. The politicians, Hillary, Bernie, they failed to stop Trump. The journalists are now failing to correct Trump and hold him accountable. The media has completely failed us.

The right-wing media insisted for months that Hillary Clinton was under criminal investigation over emails, when she wasn't. Obama was criticized for everything from asking about the price of arugula during a campaign stop to mentioning that his Blackness helped him relate to Trayvon Martin. The GOP congressman Joe Wilson literally yelled "You lie!" at Obama during a speech while Obama was president. The double standard that is applied to Trump is unacceptable. Donald Trump built his political career on a racist lie about Obama's being born in Kenya. Why is nobody yelling "You lie!" at Trump? If the politicians and the media refuse to hold the Trump administration accountable, the people have no choice but to.

How do we fight back? We show solidarity with marginalized groups that will be further marginalized in Trump's America. We stand with the family of Ben Keita, a Black American Muslim who was lynched in Lake Stevens, Washington. We stand with the family of Heather Heyer, mowed down by neo-Nazis in Charlottesville, Virginia, who Trump referred to as "very fine people." We show solidarity with the women who marched on Washington during 2017's historic Women's March. We show solidarity with Jewish people whose communities and cemeteries are currently under attack by white supremacists. We stand with the Native Americans who are protecting Standing Rock from the Dakota Access Pipeline. We say no to mass incarceration. We say no to the overpolicing that leads to overcriminalization of communities of color. We say no to the Muslim ban, we say no to the wall, we say no to Donald Trump, loudly and often.

In March 2017 I was so frustrated with the lack of resistance to the Trump administration that I headed to Rock Creek Park in Washington, D.C., and for a week I dedicated two to three hours of my day to standing outside and meeting with anti-Trump folks. I used social media to let people know where I would be. I chose Rock Creek Park because it was the rare D.C. location where a crowd was allowed to gather without a permit, and I chose that week in March because there was also a women's march and an anti–Dakota Access Pipeline protest going on in D.C. I wanted to attend both to show that we must combat this administration as a unified front and show solidarity with all groups that will be further marginalized by Trump's policies.

My original plan was to show up at Rock Creek Park every day until I saw some sort of real policy change, but after a week, I was inspired after meeting and forming relationships with activists in D.C. who were already engaged in doing the kind of work I was hoping to participate in. I met passionate folks from great DMV organizations like Restaurant Opportunities Center United, ONE D.C., and Dulles Justice Coalition and decided to let them take the lead on this work. As someone not from that community, it was important that I fell back and listened to how they wanted to move. The lessons I learned from younger activists like those in Dream Defenders and Black Lives Matter were starting to impact my life in tangible ways. Making that trip to D.C. restored and renewed my focus on the movement.

33

The Story of Mama

I had a lot of fights in my life. Physical ones too. I can't say I
was never scared. I was scared often. I fought thru the fear.

—BEVERLY "MAMA" MOOREHEAD, AKA TOOTS

The last time I saw my grandmother, Beverly Moorehead, aka Mama, aka Toots, was on Sunday, July 15. I accompanied my mom, Brenda Greene, to 2401 Nostrand Avenue in
Brooklyn, the apartment Mama had lived in since 1975, the year
of my birth. My mom explained to me the day before that Mama,
who had been in and out of the hospital for the last couple of
years, would not be going back to the hospital and was choosing
instead to make her transition to the ancestors from her apartment. My aunt Jo Ann, my cousin Tracy, and his wife, Neicey,
were already there, and together we talked with, laughed with,
and listened to Mama. Even though Mama had not been doing
well over the past few years, I realized on this day that I had not
done the work to mentally prepare myself for her passing, and I

wasn't sure if I was strong enough. Mama walked me thru that. Mama lent me her strength.

Mama's home was appointed in the exact same fashion as it was on the first day I had been there. Just about every wall was covered with pictures or artwork that created a living museum of her experience in this world. There was the meticulously painted portrait of her youngest daughter, Lori, dressed in her 1960s-style schoolgirl outfit. There were the dolls, so many dolls. Mama loved her dolls. There was the small but beautifully decorated black-and-white-themed bathroom. I have traveled the entire world, and I've never seen a fancier bathroom than Mama's.

And there was Mama. She couldn't stand, she couldn't really open her eyes, she was smaller than I had ever seen her, but she somehow was still radiant as ever. For most of our exchange she was completely coherent, talking about how much she loved *CSI* and how fine that LL Cool J was. She was doing impressions of my brother, Jamal, to outline how smart he is and telling me about how my mother tried to get her to visit the Anne Frank house during a trip to Amsterdam. Why would she do that, Mama wondered aloud, when she had already seen the movie? Mama wanted to find the casino instead.

It was when Mama was speaking in uninterrupted streams of consciousness that she really dropped some gems on me. She could not express enough how glad she was that she spent a year traveling the globe after her retirement. Travel, she explained, was the key to life. Travel is the best education one can get, and learning is what keeps us alive. We never stop learning. She also advised me to be wary of falling in love, because falling in love will sometimes hold you back from being who you truly are. I was taken aback at first, until I realized that she was advising me to let go of attachments. There is nothing wrong with romantic love, but the idea that we own people is false. We refer to our spouses as ours:

my wife, my husband. That language can sometimes lead us to believe that we own people or that we are owned by people, and when you make decisions with this mind-set you may not be working in your best interest. I think Mama felt that if she was "in love" in the way that she was raised to believe being in love meant, she would never have traveled and been able to discover her true self.

Every great fairy tale is rooted in a reality of pain, hardship, and struggle; a beautiful struggle if you will. This is why Mama and her ex-husband—my grandfather Lloyd Moorehead, who Mama passive-aggressively referred to as Moorehead while he was alive— were featured in the artwork of my 2004 album, *Beautiful Struggle*. The story of Mama and her three daughters contains the blueprint for a modern fairy tale. There are no white knights or damsels in distress, only a strong Black woman who left South Carolina for the busy streets of New York City to plant a family tree that would yield what would have previously been called impossible fruit. Brenda, Jo Ann, Lori, Abena, Taiwo, Kehinde, Lloyd, Jamal, and I are that fruit.

When the three daughters grew up and moved away from home to start their own families, Mama defined herself by her relationship with her grandkids. She wore the role of matriarch like a snug glove. All three of the daughters raised their families in Brooklyn, all within minutes of Mama's home, so as youths we were blessed to have Mama and her wisdom as a constant presence in our lives. God bless the three daughters for keeping us in such close proximity to their mother. It taught us the importance of staying in communication with your blood. I loved going to Mama's house every Friday night for marathon sessions of Monopoly with all the grandkids. We would play until somebody won, even if that meant playing until five in the morning. It was important to Mama that we finished what we started, always.

I will forever cherish the family trips we took together. Every Thanksgiving we would head to the Bronx to see Aunt Hazel and Aunt Jessie. We would go camping, to amusement parks, or to Lido Beach every summer for the Greene family reunion. It was on those trips to Lido Beach that I discovered my undying love for Mama's biscuits. I can taste one in my mouth right now as I write about them. As an adult I realize that "love" was really just a whole lot of butter. She would drown those Pillsbury biscuits in it.

Mama's love was a tough one, as her daughters can attest. As a single mother she had the difficult task of trying to raise them with no help, and she raised them using very traditional methods. We have not had the luxury of coddling our children in our community—ain't no time-outs. Black parents have often chosen to show their children exactly how tough the world can be to Black people by being tough at home. This is a survival instinct that I do not use to judge a parent. I wasn't raised to believe that spanking is an effective disciplinary measure, but I was spanked once in my life. It was by Mama.

Every Christmas season Mama was gracious enough to take all her grandkids to Fifth Avenue in midtown Manhattan near Rockefeller Center to see the big Christmas tree and all the animatronic dolls that adorned the windows of the fancy shops. We would stand in line in the freezing cold and walk around for hours looking at every window. As the day came to a close, Mama, who was far from financially well-off, would get us some food and then buy us gifts that we could present to our parents as gifts from us. This was an incredibly selfless gesture designed to teach her grandkids how to properly give and receive. It taught us how to appreciate what our parents did for us and it helped keep the family together. One year, after spending the whole day with Mama doing our annual Christmas ritual, I carelessly left the gift that Mama spent her hard-earned money buying for me to give to my parents on the subway. I don't remember what the gift was but I do remember the butt-whooping I received for losing it. Mama spanked me right there at the Flatbush and Nostrand Avenue junction.

I don't think my parents were happy about me being spanked, and if I recall correctly there may have been an argument about it. I still don't believe in corporal punishment, but in retrospect I'm glad I had that experience. First, if Mama hadn't spanked me, even though it was only once, I would have no experience with being spanked to even talk about it at all, so I am grateful for that. Second, and most important, hurt people hurt people. Mama lived a life I have not experienced, a life I am probably not even built for. I cannot imagine how hurt she must've been by my carelessness in that moment. Here I am receiving things I hadn't actually worked for, and I couldn't even be bothered to remember to carry them off the subway with me. Sure, I was a child, but Mama didn't treat us like children; she tried as best she could to give us the respect we deserved as intelligent human beings. She didn't hide truth from us, even if it was ugly, which truth often can be.

As my music career started to yield some positive results in my early twenties, I was happy to receive the support of my family. It was the love from my family that helped drive me to become successful at my craft; we are a confident bunch, and after I sold some records I was certainly impressed with myself. However, no matter how many records I sold, no matter how many stages I graced or TV appearances I made, Mama would always tell me I could be doing way more. Mama wasn't particularly religious, but she kept us grounded and would eventually help me learn how to pass on any praise I received to the most high. "You're not living up to your full potential," she would say. "You can do way more than rap—you can be a lawyer, a teacher, you can write and direct movies and plays," she would say. Initially, I would be dismissive of this rhetoric. In my mind, Mama just didn't understand hip-hop and how powerful it was, so she didn't have the capacity to understand just how hard it was to fund my business and just how well I was doing for myself. I couldn't have been more wrong.

It's not that Mama didn't understand or respect hip-hop, it's that Mama understood *me* and respected *me* more than I even understood or respected myself. Mama loved music. She loved great songs, she loved to dance. Even though she was born long before hip-hop was in vogue, she was never an old fogey about it; in fact, she always embraced hip-hop as valuable Black music. Years into my career, whenever I would visit Mama, she would tell me how often she watched BET and would weigh in on issues that affected the hip-hop community. She would tell me which rappers she liked, which rappers she didn't like, and ask me if I knew them. It amused her that people gushed over her when they found out she was my grandmother, because in her mind I could be way more than a rapper and she couldn't understand why they were so impressed.

Now, in the second act of my music career, I finally get what Mama always knew. I *am* way more than a rapper. I *can* do way more with my life. I *do* have far more potential than I was giving myself credit for. This is why when Yasiin Bey and I bought Nkiru Books, Mama, who was retired, came daily to volunteer and help us run the store. She understood that the bookstore was a more true manifestation of who I could be, and by supporting me in that endeavor she endeared herself to the young people I was running the streets with at the time, essentially becoming "Mama" to all of them as well. The life of an entertainer doesn't last forever, and Mama was preparing me for the future, a future that she knew she would not be on earth to see. In this sense, she was a visionary.

When a young Barack Obama decided to run for president after being a senator for only four years, I immediately knew he would become our first Black president. Presidential races are essentially popularity contests, and there was no politician more popular than Barack Obama in 2008. Obama was a dream come true for older Black people who had experienced the deep-seated racism of the Jim Crow, pre–civil rights era. For them, Obama represented the happily-ever-after part of the fairy tale. When I saw the effect Obama's campaign had on my grandmother, whether or not I agreed with how the system worked became secondary. Being a part of history and voting for the first Black president, helping that dream to come true, became the goal.

And what an effect it was. Mama's love for all things Obama could not be understated. She began calling herself the Obama Mama, and the name stuck. She had the Obama T-shirts. She had the Obama campaign buttons. She not only had Barack Obama dolls, she had Michelle Obama dolls as well. Mama was always happy, always in good spirits, but I cannot recall seeing her happier than she was the day Barack Obama became the first Black president. Being able to tell Obama about how much my grandmother loved him was an awesome experience.

After the meeting I attended at the White House in 2016, I found myself alone for a short period of time with the president in the Oval Office. This was the perfect opportunity to get something signed for my grandmother. Earlier that day I had ripped a page out of some magazine that had a picture of Obama on it and put it in my pocket for this occasion. When I pulled out my meticulously folded magazine page, Obama said, "You ripped that out of a magazine? That's ratchet." I asked him how he knew the word *ratchet*, and he said, "I have teenage daughters." Obama then instructed an assistant to get him a glossy photograph, on which he wrote a personal note to the Obama Mama.

Months later I was invited to Obama's birthday party at the White House, and I knew I had to bring Mama. She was my first thought. She was eighty-six years old and could not move around without a wheelchair, but I was determined to bring her. My good friend Seth Byrd drove Mama and her personal care assistant to Washington, D.C., where I met them at the hotel, and Mama and I headed out into the August night. The most noticeable thing about going to the White House with Mama is that when you are an eighty-six-year-old Black woman at the White House, young white people automatically assume you are some civil rights leader they must show respect to. All night Mama was being thanked by young, well-intentioned white people for everything she had done for this country. Of course, y'all know she soaked it all up. Every bit of it. She turned to me while I was wheeling her around and said, "You didn't know I was more famous than you." When you bring an elderly Black woman to the White House, especially during the Obama administration, you become *her* guest.

Before arriving, we had been given two instructions. One: no gifts; two: no photos. The White House staff would be collecting everyone's camera phones so that the famous guests could party in peace without being asked for selfies every few minutes. None of this mattered to Mama. Not only was she determined to get a picture with Obama, but she also made a collage out of magazine articles of Obama's family. Mama got her arts and crafts on, and she brought her collage with her even though I warned her that we might never be able to get it to him. When we finally got inside, Mama was laser-focused. She spotted Obama's daughter Sasha across the room and said to me, "Hey, wheel me over there right now." I obliged. When Mama got in touching distance of Sasha she tugged on her dress and said, "Hi, I'm Beverly, it's a pleasure to meet you. Now, where's your mother?" Sasha, confused but amused, pointed to her mother, Michelle, who was surrounded by partygoers. Mama said to me, "Okay, now wheel me over there." I obliged.

While we were waiting for an opportunity to introduce ourselves to Michelle Obama, Barack Obama came strolling into the room. All eyes went to him and he warmly greeted everyone who came up to him. Before I was able to approach him, I caught his eye and he stopped his conversation short, walked right over, and said, "Is this the Obama Mama I've been hearing about?" Mama was on cloud nine when the president did this. She had been clutching her Obama collage the entire time, and now she was able to present it to him. He gushed over it and told her he would cherish it forever. At that moment, Obama declared to the room that he needed a picture with the Obama Mama. There were no cameras in the room, so he asked his assistant to go get her cell phone, which she used to snap what I believe to be the only picture taken of Obama from that night. It was wonderful of him to act just as excited to meet Mama as she was to meet him.

Mama was not an academic, but her life experience trumped the experience of most academics when it came to issues of race and politics. She spoke plainly and bluntly, but always had a firm grasp of the issues, and I am proud to say that I aligned with her on most things. She was certainly emotional about Obama, but she understood policy, she understood politics, and she understood the need for America to come together as a country so that we can better participate in the goal of making the world better for all of humanity, regardless of where you were born. Her approach to worldly issues was efficient and practical. She loved her country not out of a sense of patriotism, but because this is where her family was and she understood that the entire world can be better if we treat everyone like family.

Now she has left it up to us. The three daughters, Brenda, Jo

Ann, and Lori, are now the matriarchs of the family. The grand-kids now have to ensure that our mothers are respected and taken care of, and we now have to do the work of keeping the family together. We have to stay in touch. We have to plan family trips and cookouts. We have to check on one another's health and well-being. Beverly gave us the blueprint; we have to keep build-ing. We have to make the world a better place for Beverly's great-grandkids, our children. We have to fight for them. On that last day I spent with Mama, as she lay there with her eyes closed, she told me about several fights she had throughout her life, some physical, some mental, some spiritual. She said more than once, "Sometimes I was scared, but the fear never stopped me from fighting. I would fight thru the fear. We all get scared, but that doesn't mean we don't fight." Nobody in the world has had to fight like an elderly Black woman, nobody. Mama's fight gave me more life. I plan on using it to honor her forever. Mama Forever.

34

~~~

The Beginning

We artists are indestructible: even in a prison, or in a concentration
camp, I would be almighty in my own world of art,
even if I had to paint my pictures with my wet
tongue on the dusty floor of my cell.

—PABLO PICASSO

Of all the years I've been alive, my fortieth was
the most enlightening and liberating. While I was thirty-nine, I
could feel this newfound attitude approaching. I began to question myself less and others more. In most of the rooms I find
myself in, I am often the most experienced. I know exactly what I
like and what I don't, exactly what I need and what I don't, and I'm
not shy about going out and getting it. I speak not so much from a
place of knowledge but from a place of wisdom. And it feels good.
Damn good. When I was growing up, I was told Black men often
don't make it past twenty-one. I feel as if I've lived two lives, and
I have a lot more life left in me.

My father, Perry Greene, Ph.D., just retired from his job as vice president of diversity and inclusion at Adelphi University and continues to be my biggest influence and inspiration as a man. My mother, Brenda Greene, is still teaching at Medgar Evers College and curates its annual National Black Writers Conference. She is the executive director of the Center for Black Literature and is internationally known as a friend to writers who focus on issues of people of color. My firstborn, Amani Fela, is an ambitious young man who organizes movement-based events and has made quite a name for himself in New York City's independent music scene. My daughter, Diani Eshe, is a leader in her community and creates incredible music that I am looking to help support with Javotti Media. Cynthia "DJ Eque" Greene has become the matriarch of her family following the passing of her sister Gayle and her mother, Linda. Cynthia broke barriers for female DJs worldwide and remains one of Los Angeles's premier, in-demand party DJs.

My children, Amani and Diani, are my light. They are my inspiration and my reward all at once. If not for them, I would not be the man I am today, I may have given up. They remind me of not just who I am but of who I must be. Amani and Diani were not raised the way I was. My upbringing was far more traditional. My parents stayed together until my brother, Jamal, and I were old enough to deal with their split as adults would. My parents worked hard to provide stability by making sure they both came home every night for the vast majority of my childhood. Not only did Darcel and I split up relatively early in the lives of Amani and Diani, but I also carved out a life on the road for myself. I have lived as a bluesman, and bluesmen are hardly home. This nontraditional lifestyle spilled over into my children's lives. I wasn't home for them as much as I wanted to be, but they also often traveled the world with me and experienced things that many others their age have yet to see. I am proud of who they turned out to be, and

I pray that they remain proud of me for trying to provide them with the best life that I could.

Amani and Diani are adults now. There is no more raising of them; our relationship is now based on friendship. I am blessed that they both live close to me, and I am excited to see what kind of adults they will be. While my children must have been inspired by me to some degree, both of them developed their musical abilities without asking for my help. They are determined to make it on their own, and they are both hard workers. Even though they weren't raised traditionally, I am glad that they learned the lesson of hard work somewhere along their path.

America is going thru a transitional phase, one that I have never before seen. As a person of color, I was used to spotting the effects of systemic racism, both overt and covert. As a Black man with a traditionally Muslim name, I have always been able to easily spot the xenophobia and bigotry that are used to oppress communities of "others" who are not deemed American (white) enough to be respected as human beings. The Trump era has made me more aware of not just how misogynistic America is but also how marginalized white racists feel when they are forced to deal with diversity. As it's been said by folks smarter than me, when you are used to privilege, equality feels like oppression.

If anything gives me hope in this era of a Trump presidency, it is Amani and Diani. They are both compassionate, thoughtful, intelligent, and ambitious human beings. They both actively seek out goodness and pull the best out of bad situations. If they represent the future, I'm fine with living thru this era, because Amani and Diani represent the original promise of Nkiru: that the best is yet to come. It feels as if Darcel and I took the best parts of ourselves and gave them to our children, but even saying that is not giving our children enough credit for who they are. At times I have selfishly referred to Amani and Diani as me 2.0. In reality, they are the version 1 of themselves, and the world is so much better for it. My children led me to my best self. They help me vibrate higher.

When I wrote my first rap, it was because I wanted to be a famous rapper. I manifested that destiny and achieved that goal, but the cultural currency I picked up along the way is worth far more than fame. The lesson I received loud and clear was that the fame was never the prize. It was the love from the people that gave me the ability to feed my family. I am famous to some, but I only qualify as a celebrity in certain scenarios. I am revered by die-hard hip-hop heads, but like most rappers who don't have hits in constant rotation, I am considered largely irrelevant to people who judge human beings by their proximity to trends. Which for me is just fine, if not preferable. I am proud of being part of the fraternity of working-class MCs. When I travel the world, I see y'all out there, grinding, getting it in, defining and redefining what it means to be hip-hop, despite the trends.

When Jay-Z said, "If skills sold, truth be told / I'd probably be, lyrically Talib Kweli," it got me to thinking: What if I rapped about money more? Would I be richer or more successful? I certainly had the skill. Jay-Z had been rapping about money, well, since his first single, "Dead Presidents." His seemingly singular focus on money made him one of the richest musicians the world has ever seen. He manifested his destiny. Meanwhile, I'm over here patting myself on the back for being a working-class MC. There are days when I am up and days when I am down, and my next payday is not guaranteed. Couldn't I have taken a page out of Jay's book and dumbed down my heady lyrics in the name of the almighty dollar? I certainly had the skill to rap about anything I wanted, and it sure would've been nice to make some real money to support my family. Why did I constantly choose the least profitable subject matter? I used to have days where these kinds of questions would float thru my head.

But then I remember that I'm Talib Kweli. In the same way that Jay-Z's focus on money made him rich beyond his dreams, my focus on lyricism and culture has garnered me the type of respect money can't buy. My podcast, *People's Party*, is one of the best in the business. In 2017 I had the honor of doing a joint project with the hardest out, Styles P of the Lox. It was called *The Seven*, and it was two New York MCs with different perspectives going bar after bar for the culture. My last album, *Radio Silence*, has a song on it called "Write at Home," which features a poem from Datcha, a fan I met after he made a purchase on Kweliclub .com, that has lines that efficiently encapsulate my worldview:

> *Everything is one ocean of energy*
> *Everything is within you*
> *Everything IS you*

This is what makes sense to me. This is my religion.

My name means "student," and I have had many teachers. I have spoken my truth to power. Many of the people I had posters of as a teenager became my friends and, in some cases, my family. I carried crates for Funkmaster Flex. I toured with A Tribe Called Quest on their farewell tour. I watched J Dilla make beats. I did a record about graffiti with Rakim. From the front row of Carnegie Hall I watched Nina Simone perform "Mississippi Goddam." I sang "Brick House" by the Commodores with Prince on a Vegas stage. From Assata to Obama, I have had conversations with those who move and shape the paradigm. I have spent time in what Harry Belafonte once described as "the back rooms of history." It does the soul good when you count your blessings instead of your problems, and I have been blessed beyond my wildest imagination. I thank God for this, and it makes me want to work harder.

Nina Simone was my musical guardian angel. I learned breath

control from KRS-One. Rakim taught me how to travel thru space and time. Chuck D taught me how to use my platform. Yasiin Bey taught me how to know my worth. Sonia Sanchez taught me how to write in solidarity with all oppressed people. Dave Chappelle taught me how to live my truth. Q-Tip taught me how to love my voice. De La Soul taught me how to find inspiration from within. Common taught me that sincerity is king. The Roots taught me how to curate what I consume.

I am now a conscious consumer. A curator of my own destiny. An inner-city griot humbled by the love of the people. I am now in phase two of my career. I am enjoying making and exploring new relationships, and my family continues to grow. I have traveled from rookie to veteran of hip-hop and I feel as if I'm just getting started . . .

What's next?

A Note About the Author

Talib Kweli is one of the world's most talented and accomplished hip-hop artists. Whether working with Mos Def as one half of Black Star, partnering with the producer Hi-Tek for Reflection Eternal, releasing landmark solo material, or collaborating with Kanye West, Pharrell Williams, Just Blaze, J Dilla, or Madlib, Kweli commands attention by delivering top-tier lyricism, crafting captivating stories, and showing the ability to rhyme over virtually any type of instrumental. In 2011, Kweli founded Javotti Media, a record label and a platform for independent thinkers and doers, and in 2019, he launched the weekly podcast *People's Party with Talib Kweli*.